THE MASTER MUSICIANS

RACHMANINOFF

Series edited by Stanley Sadie

THE MASTER MUSICIANS

RACHMANINOFF

Geoffrey Norris

OXFORD
UNIVERSITY PRESS

OXFORD
UNIVERSITY PRESS

Great Clarendon Street, Oxford OX2 6DP

Oxford University Press is a department of the University of Oxford.
It furthers the University's objective of excellence in research, scholarship,
and education by publishing worldwide in

Oxford New York

Athens Auckland Bangkok Bogotá Buenos Aires Calcutta
Cape Town Chennai Dar es Salaam Delhi Florence Hong Kong Istanbul
Karachi Kuala Lumpur Madrid Melbourne Mexico City Mumbai
Nairobi Paris São Paulo Singapore Taipei Tokyo Toronto Warsaw

and associated companies in Berlin Ibadan

Oxford is a registered trade mark of Oxford University Press
in the UK and in certain other countries

Published in the United States
by Oxford University Press Inc., New York

© Geoffrey Norris 1976, 1993, 2001

First published 1976
First paperback edition 1977
Second edition 1993

First published by Oxford University Press in paperback 2001

British Library Cataloguing in Publication Data

Data available

Library of Congress Cataloging in Publication Data

Norris, Geoffrey.
Rachmaninoff / Geoffrey Norris.
p. cm.—(The Master musicians)
Includes bibliographical references (p.) and index.
1. Rachmaninoff, Sergei, 1873–1943. 2. Composers—Biography.
3. Pianists—Biography. I. Title. II. Master musicians series.
ML410.R12 N67 2000   780'.92—dc21   00–057115
ISBN 0–19–816488–2

1 3 5 7 9 10 8 6 4 2

Typeset by The Spartan Press
Lymington, Hants
Printed in Great Britain
on acid-free paper by
Butler & Tanner Ltd
Frome and London

Preface

Stravinsky famously referred to Rachmaninoff as a 'six-and-a-half-foot-tall scowl', though he acknowledged, too, that 'he was the only pianist I have ever seen who did not grimace'.[1] Journalists frequently remarked that Rachmaninoff seldom smiled in public. His platform manner was certainly reserved. And even socially he could emit an air of 'majestic indifference'.[2] But much of this was the result of natural shyness: among friends and family his personality was far sunnier and more relaxed. On the concert platform, he was, perhaps, quietly confident that he was giving audiences just what they wanted, and had no need to assert himself further. He was a remarkable artist: a composer, a pianist and a conductor, phenomenally gifted in all three professions. He may, as the Russian expression goes, have 'chased three hares', but he caught all of them in music which was privately emotional but expressed with an affecting openness and passion, in piano-playing which became legendary, and in conducting which was universally acclaimed.

Since the first publication of this book in 1976, Rachmaninoff's music has become more widely known. The concertos and symphonies have kept – maybe even strengthened – their place in the repertory, and at the same time the songs, the sacred works and the less familiar regions of the piano pieces have received more attention. There have been other developments too. First, the Rachmaninoff country estate at Ivanovka, deep in the south of Russia, has in part been restored. Destroyed after the 1917 Revolution, it was salvaged again in the 1970s, opened as a museum in 1982, and now offers a remarkable insight into the solitude and serene scenery from which Rachmaninoff took so much of his inspiration. Secondly, there have been new findings about dates and other facts relating to

[1] *Stravinsky in Conversation with Robert Craft* (Harmondsworth, 1962), pp. 55–6.
[2] T. Beaumont (ed.), *The Selective Ego: the Diaries of James Agate* (London, 1976), p. 116.

Rachmaninoff's works, by Russian scholars, and by Robert Threlfall and myself for our *Catalogue of the Compositions of S. Rachmaninoff* (London, 1982). This new edition draws on this information, and also incorporates work which I have done subsequently in Moscow, Ivanovka, London and Washington. In many cases the precise dating of Rachmaninoff's compositions is difficult, partly because he rarely mentions progress on them in his correspondence, partly because his own autographed datings probably do not take into account the periods of thought and gestation before he actually put pen to paper. Work on this aspect of Rachmaninoff scholarship is still going on in Russia and the USA; but, if the present book was ever to see the light of day, the line had to be drawn somewhere. Similarly, research continues in Novgorod on the identification of Rachmaninoff's birthplace. In the first edition, having read V. N. Bryantseva's article 'Gde rodilsya S. V. Rakhmaninov?' (Where was Rachmaninoff born?) in the journal *Muzykal'naya zhizn'* (1969), no. 19, p. 20, I fell in with the idea that Rachmaninoff was born at Semyonovo. Rachmaninoff himself thought he was born at Oneg, and christened at Semyonovo. There is also an eyewitness account – admittedly passed down through several genera-tions – of a maid who was present at Oneg when the baby was born. In this edition I have opted for Oneg as the birth-place, while acknowledg-ing that there is still a lobby of opinion which favours Semyonovo.

As before, I have tried to be consistent and systematic in trans-literating Cyrillic script. The soft- and hard-signs are omitted in all but bibliographical contexts, where they are both represented by an apostrophe. Well-known names pose a problem: there can be accusations of pedantry if one adheres rigidly to a system, of inconsistency if one favours other spellings. I have steered a course towards the former, adopting the rule that, if the subject was born in a country using a Cyrillic alphabet, the name should be transliterated according to the system: thus Shalyapin, Goldenveyzer, Kusevitsky, and so on. The case of Rachmaninoff himself is a special one, for he always spelled it and signed it that way when writing in Latin script during the 25 years of his life in Western Europe and the USA. In transliterating his name from Russian book titles, however, I have adhered to the system and used the spelling Rakhmaninov. I admit that courage about making names conform to a system failed in four cases: Cui, Tchaikovsky, Prokofiev and Medtner. These spellings, familiar to the eye, are the ones I have used in the text, but in bibliographical contexts they will be found as Kyui, Chaykovsky, Prokof'yev and Metner.

All Russian dates before the abolition of the Julian calendar on 1/14 February 1918 are given in their Russian, 'old style' form. To find the equivalent date in the Gregorian calendar used by Western countries, add 12 days in the nineteenth century and 13 days in the twentieth. All dates referring to events abroad, and any Russian dates from 15 February 1918 are given in the Gregorian, 'new style'. In this context it should be mentioned that Rachmaninoff's 'old style' date of birth (20 March 1873) yields the 'new style' date of 1 April, but that after leaving Russia in 1917 he habitually marked his birthday on 2 April, as is borne out by the inscription on his tombstone, 'Sergei Rachmaninoff. April 2, 1873 – March 28, 1943'. I have retained references to the 'Soviet Union' and to the historically accurate designations of places which have changed their names over the years: thus, St Petersburg, Petrograd, Leningrad and St Petersburg again are all mentioned at various stages in the book, without comment that they are one and the same place.

The following publishers have kindly given permission to reproduce extracts from their copyright scores: Anton J. Benjamin/Richard Schauer, London-Hamburg (ex. 1); Boosey & Hawkes, Music Publishers Ltd (exx. 2–4, 5 (second version), 12, 13, 17c, 18–21, 23, 25–7, 29, 30); and Belwin Mills Music Ltd (exx. 6, 14–16). Unless otherwise stated, all quotations from Rachmaninoff's letters are taken from the three-volume Russian collected edition, *S. Rakhmaninov: literaturnoye naslediye* (Moscow, 1978–80), edited by the late Zarui Apetian.

During my work on the first edition of this book in the early 1970s, I was indebted to the staffs of the British Library, the Biblioteka im. V.I. Lenina, Moscow, the Gosudartstvennyy tsentral'nyy muzey muzykal'noy kul'tury im. M.I. Glinki, Moscow, the Institut teatra, muzyki i kinematografii, Leningrad, and to the libraries of Liverpool and London. I also enjoyed the warm encouragement of the late Professor Gerald Abraham and benefited from many suggestions made by David Lloyd-Jones.

In preparing this edition, I should like specially to thank Irina Medvedeva, Alexey Naumov and Nina Graznova of the Glinka Museum, Moscow, for making material in the Rachmaninoff archive so freely available to me; Alexander Ermakov, curator of the Rachmaninoff Estate Museum at Ivanovka, for sharing with me his encyclopedic knowledge of the composer's life; Ms Kate Rivers of the Library of Congress, Washington, for her assistance; Sofiya

Vladimirovna Satina, Rachmaninoff's niece, for generous discussions about her uncle; Alexandre Rachmaninoff for talks about his grandfather; and my good friend Alexander Bazikov, Director of the Rachmaninoff Music College, Tambov, who opened up for me so many new research avenues in the southern part of Russia, which was so dear to Rachmaninoff's heart.

London, 1993   G.N.

Contents

Illustrations

(Unless otherwise stated, all photographs are reproduced by permission of the Glinka Museum, Moscow)

1

Early years

The marriage between Rachmaninoff's parents in the late 1860s appeared happily to bring together two families with long and distinguished Russian traditions and with comfortable financial assets. His mother, Lyubov Petrovna Butakova, was the daughter of a wealthy general, Pyotr Ivanovich Butakov; his father, Vasily Arkadyevich Rachmaninoff, also had military ancestors, though in recent times the running of the family estates had taken precedence over soldiering. Vasily had inherited not only the family fortune but also some of his own father's musical enthusiasm and ability, which, in the Rachmaninoff household, seem to have been above average and more than just a fashionable provincial pastime. However, Vasily lacked his father's application and tenacity, not merely in musical matters but in his business affairs as well. He squandered so much money that gradually the estates which Lyubov had brought with her as a dowry had to be sold. It was on one of the last remaining of them, Oneg, not far from Novgorod, that their second son, Sergey Vasilyevich, was born on 20 March 1873. At Oneg, on the banks of the River Volkhov and in the quiet countryside which Rachmaninoff was to cherish for the whole of his life, he spent his early childhood and showed first signs of his musical talent.

His mother encouraged him to play the piano, and, realizing that he needed a professional musician to supervise his studies, the family engaged a teacher from St Petersburg, Anna Ornatskaya, who had studied at the Conservatory with Gustav Kross, renowned as the pianist who had given the first Russian performance, in 1875, of Tchaikovsky's B flat minor Piano Concerto. For some years Sergey studied with her, and took great delight in performing for the family and playing duets with his grandfather. However, these pleasures were not to be enjoyed for long, for by the early 1880s, thanks to his father's profligacy, it became necessary to dispose of the estate at Oneg as well. In 1880 or 1881 the Rachmaninoffs moved to St Petersburg, where, while the family settled in to their small, crowded flat, Sergey spent a few weeks with Andrey and Mariya Trubnikov, his aunt and uncle, who were to prove invaluable at his marriage 20 years later. In the family's new state of penury Vasily was forced to abandon the idea of enrolling his two sons in the Corps des Pages: Vladimir, Sergey's elder brother, was sent at the public expense to a military academy, living away from home for most of the week and thus relieving the congestion; Sergey was awarded a scholarship to enter the St Petersburg Conservatory, where he was to study piano first with Vladimir Demyansky and then, provided that he achieved a high enough standard, with Kross himself. So it seemed that Rachmaninoff's career as a St Petersburg musician had begun, but soon the family was again in turmoil. Shortly after their arrival in St Petersburg the city was gripped by an epidemic of diphtheria. Vladimir, Sergey and their sister Sofiya all caught the disease. Vladimir and Sergey gradually recovered, both displaying the strength of constitution that was to help Sergey through several potentially serious illnesses during his lifetime, but Sofiya died. To make matters worse, relations between Vasily and his wife became so strained that they agreed to separate, and Lyubov was left to look after the children in St Petersburg.

In these difficult circumstances Sergey's only consolations were the visits of his grandmother Sofiya Butakova, who often travelled up to St Petersburg from her home in Novgorod. Of all her grandchildren Sergey was her special favourite, and primarily for his benefit she bought a small estate, Borisovo, near the river Volkhov. Here he spent many happy holidays, and the sound of the cathedral bells in Novgorod was to have a lasting effect on his compositions, just as Rimsky-Korsakov had been impressed in his formative years by the Russian Orthodox ceremonies at the monastery in Tikhvin. Through all the domestic difficulties Sergey continued as a pupil at the Conservatory, where, besides taking piano lessons, he studied harmony with Alexander Rubets and had to attend other classes in languages, geography, history, mathematics and Russian Orthodox doctrine. Because of the family separation and his mother's increased responsibilities in the running of the house, she was unable adequately to supervise Sergey's homework, which was more than necessary for a boy who was, like any young boy, more given to games than to study. At his end-of-term examinations in the spring of 1885 he failed all his general subjects, and, when the Conservatory hinted that the Kross scholarship might be withdrawn, Lyubov realized that something would have to be done to ensure that her son's obvious musical gifts were not wasted. She therefore approached Alexander Ziloti,[1] a highly successful pupil of Liszt, and sought his advice on how best to deal with her son's idle nature. He suggested that the only possible solution was to subject him to discipline and unavoidable hard work, both of which would be amply provided by Ziloti's own former teacher, Nikolay Zverev.

On Ziloti's recommendation Zverev accepted Sergey as a pupil, and it was agreed that he should begin lessons with him in Moscow in the autumn of 1885. Sergey faced with some apprehension the prospect of leaving the familiar surroundings of St Petersburg and his grand-mother's estate at Borisovo. He knew very few people in Moscow but was consoled by the thought that at least his elder sister, Elena, would also be there. Possessing a fine contralto voice, she had auditioned for and been accepted by the Bolshoy Theatre in Moscow, and the singer Ippolit Pryanishnikov had offered to coach her before she took up her appointment for the 1885–6 opera season. During the summer she was staying at the Pribytkovs'[2] estate in Voronezh, but just before she was due to leave for Moscow she died suddenly of pernicious anaemia. Sergey therefore embarked on the new phase of his education alone and completely cut off from the indulgent upbringing he had enjoyed with his mother and grandmother Butakova.

Nothing could have presented more of a contrast than his new life in Moscow. After three days at the Moscow home of his Aunt Yuliya, Sergey moved in to Zverev's apartment on Ruzheynyy pereulok, a street close to the Arbat, the artistic enclave of Moscow, within striking distance of the Conservatory. Here Zverev lived with his sister Anna Sergeyevna, and it was their practice to have some of Zverev's gifted young Conservatory pupils living in. In 1885 the other lodgers were the 15-year-old Matvey Presman, nicknamed Mo, and Leonid Maximov (Lyo), who was the same age as Rachmaninoff (Syo). Zverev himself was an exceptionally hard worker. He would begin private lessons at 8 o'clock in the morning, teach at the Conservatory from 9 o'clock until 2, then take more private pupils from 2 until 10 o'clock at night. The routine in the house was similarly strict. Practice had to begin at 6 o'clock in the morning and, after Zverev had left for

[1] Ziloti was the son of Vasily Rachmaninoff's sister Yuliya, and was therefore Sergey's cousin.
[2] Georgy and Anna Pribytkov were Vasily Rachmaninoff's brother-in-law and sister.

his classes at the Conservatory, the young pupils were diligently supervised by Anna Sergeyevna. This was just the treatment Rachmaninoff needed. His technique improved remarkably, and at the same time he acquired a sound general knowledge of music by playing through symphonies in four-hand piano arrangements and by attending concerts and operas in the city.

One of the many distinguished artists whom he heard at this time was Anton Rubinstein, composer, pianist and founder of the St Petersburg Conservatory. In January 1886 Rubinstein gave the first in his seven-week series of Historical Concerts, which were intended to trace the development of keyboard music from its earliest history to contemporary times. Rubinstein divided his time between Moscow and St Petersburg, giving a recital in the Hall of the Nobility in Moscow, repeating it for students the following day in the German Club, and giving in St Petersburg the same programme. Zverev and his pupils always attended both the Moscow performances, which implanted in Rachmaninoff a lifelong admiration of Rubinstein's playing and greatly increased his musical knowledge. Not only Rubinstein but many other famous names in Russian music visited the Zverev household, for on Sunday afternoons Zverev would keep open house for Moscow's musicians. He always called upon his pupils to perform before his distinguished guests, among whom were Ziloti, Vasily Safonov (soon to be director of the Conservatory), two of Rachmaninoff's future teachers, Sergey Taneyev and Anton Arensky, and the most influential composer of Rachmaninoff's formative years, Tchaikovsky.

Presman recalls that during the whole time he was living in Zverev's house he was never allowed to go for a holiday with his family, but that in the summer Zverev took them to his dacha near Moscow, always ensuring that a piano went with them so that practice would not suffer. He remembers also that they went to the Crimea, where Zverev gave lessons to the Tokmakov children on their wealthy father's estate at Simeiz. It was in the Crimea, possibly in the summer of 1886, that Rachmaninoff made his first attempts at composition:

I remember my stay at Simeiz chiefly because of Rachmaninoff. It was there that he first began to compose. As I remember, Rachmaninoff was very pensive, even gloomy. He wanted to be alone, and would walk about with his head lowered and his gaze fixed on some distant point; at the same time he would whistle something almost inaudibly and gesticulate as if conducting. This state lasted for a few days. Finally, waiting for a moment when nobody apart from myself was about, he beckoned me to the piano and began to play. When he had finished he asked me, 'Do you know what that was?' 'No,' I said, 'I don't know.' 'And how,' he asked, 'did you like this pedal point in the bass against the chromaticism in the upper parts?' Having received a satisfactory reply, he said complacently, 'I composed it myself and I dedicate this piece to you.'[3]

Exactly what this piece was is uncertain, for none of Rachmaninoff's early extant compositions fits Presman's scant description. About this time, however, Rachmaninoff did write a D minor *Song Without Words* for piano; and in 1887–8 he composed three nocturnes for piano, in F sharp minor, F major and C minor-E flat major. Four other short piano pieces – a Romance in F sharp minor, a Prélude in E flat minor, a Mélodie in E major and a Gavotte in D major – were also written during these student days and were originally intended to form Rachmaninoff's op. 1, but the pieces remained unpublished in his lifetime.

After a visit to his aunt Varvara[4] in the spring of 1888 Rachmaninoff returned to work at the Conservatory, where he now entered the senior department in the piano class of Alexander Ziloti, while still lodging at Zverev's. At the end of the academic year he passed his examinations in theory and composition with the highest possible mark, a 5+, and in the following autumn, resuming his piano studies with Ziloti, also joined Taneyev's class in counterpoint and Arensky's class in harmony. In Taneyev's class he was a fellow pupil of Skryabin. Both of them had known Taneyev before entering the class: Skryabin had already taken private lessons with him, and Rachmaninoff had seen him many times at the Sunday gatherings at Zverev's. Both appear also to have been equally reluctant to do the exercises that Taneyev set, and Skryabin's laziness was to some extent fostered by his living outside the rigorous regulations of the Zverev household. However, Taneyev partially surmounted the problem by an ingenious plan, as Rachmaninoff later told Alfred Swan:

Pelageya Ivanovna, his famous nurse, had a niece. All of a sudden this niece appeared in our kitchen with a sheet of manuscript paper. On it was written a theme and a request to make it into a fugue. 'All right,' I said. But she would not leave, because Sergey Ivanovich had instructed her to wait

[3] M.L. Presman, 'Ugolok muzykal'noy Moskvy vos'midesyatykh godov', *Vospominaniya o Rakhmaninove*, vol. i, ed. Z.A. Apetian (Moscow, 5/1988), p. 156.

[4] Varvara Arkadyevna Satina was the sister of Vasily Rachmaninoff and the wife of Alexander Alexandrovich Satin.

for the fugue and take it back with her. Once or twice I was caught, but the third time I gave orders to say that I was out, so she was obliged to leave the manuscript paper. In the same way she was sent to Skryabin.[5]

For all his disinclination to do Taneyev's exercises, Rachmaninoff's interests in composition were broadening. In February 1888 he wrote a D minor orchestral Scherzo – so Mendelssohnian that Rachmaninoff must have heard *A Midsummer Night's Dream* – and in October he sketched some ideas for an opera, *Esmeralda*, based on Victor Hugo's novel *Notre Dame de Paris*.

This awakening interest in writing music, as well as playing it, seems to have been the prime reason for a serious breach with Zverev in 1889. Zverev's concern was with nurturing Rachmaninoff as a pianist. With his approval, his young protégé continued lessons with Ziloti, and took part in student concerts at the Conservatory. But, as Matvey Presman reports, 'all day long the piano-playing in Zverev's flat never stopped. All three of us had to play, but it was obviously impossible for Rachmaninoff to compose when someone was playing in the next room.'[6] The atmosphere clearly became fraught. Rachmaninoff moved out of the flat. Zverev was furious, reacting 'over-sensitively', according to Presman. There was an 'astounding scene', forever engraved on Presman's memory. 'Zverev was so upset that he almost fainted. He considered that he had been deeply hurt, and none of Rachmaninoff's reasonings could change his mind. One needed the determined character of a Rachmaninoff to endure this whole scene.'[7]

For several years Zverev petulantly severed all links with his former pupil. Rachmaninoff's mother suggested that he should return to St Petersburg to study composition with Rimsky-Korsakov at the Conservatory there, but he decided to remain in Moscow, moving in temporarily with a fellow student, Mikhail Slonov, and then for the new academic year taking up more permanent residence with his Aunt Varvara and the rest of the Satin family in their Moscow house.

Here he was given not only the seclusion he needed for work, but also the friendship and companionship which had been denied him since the family's move from Oneg. His eagerness for composition was

[5] A. J. and K. Swan, 'Rachmaninoff: Personal Reminiscences', *The Musical Quarterly*, vol. xxx (1944), pp. 13–14.

[6] M. L. Presman, 'Ugolok muzykal'noy Moskvy vos'midesyatykh godov', *Vospominaniya o Rakhmaninove*, vol. i, ed. Z. A. Apetian (Moscow, 5/1988), p. 202.

[7] M. L. Presman, *ibid.*, p. 202.

fully encouraged and in November 1889 he sketched some ideas for a piano concerto in C minor; probably in the same year, he composed two movements for string quartet: a Romance in G minor and a Scherzo in D major, which he dedicated to Alexander Ziloti. In February 1890, as an examination exercise, he composed his six-part motet, *Deus meus*, and in the same spring wrote some of his earliest songs, *U vrat obiteli svyatoy* ('At the gate of the holy abode') (Lermontov), which he dedicated to Mikhail Slonov, and *Ya tebe nichevo ne skazhu* ('I shall tell you nothing') (Fet).

In the summer, the Satins, as usual, travelled to Ivanovka, their comfortably-sized estate deep in the Russian countryside about 600 kilometres to the south-east of Moscow, and about 100 kilometres from the nearest big town, Tambov. Rachmaninoff went with them for a holiday which was to have far-reaching consequences. In years to come, Ivanovka was to be the place where tranquillity and the companionship of family and friends combined to make it a prime source of his creative inspiration. Almost every year until his final visit in April 1917, Rachmaninoff and Ivanovka were to be synonymous with composition, be it the preliminary thinking, the actual writing, orchestration or proofreading. The vast majority of the works written in Russia owe something to Ivanovka and its peaceful surroundings. As Rachmaninoff once told a friend: 'I feel so good here that I have already begun to count with anguish the days before I leave.'[8]

Rachmaninoff would generally go to Ivanovka in the spring, in time to see the lilacs bloom, the trees bursting their buds, the surfaces of the lakes shimmering and serene after shedding the winter ice and snows. He would stay while the meadows and pastures ripened; he would see the estate's tree-lined alleys come into leaf; and he would often be there for the gathering of corn at harvest. It was another world from the noise and bustle of Moscow.

During this summer of 1890, he stayed with the Satins in the main house, built on two storeys and constructed of wood. Alongside it there was another, part-wood, part-brick house, which was where, on later visits, Rachmaninoff would do his work. It was eventually to become his own cherished home. Other Ivanovka guests this year included some distant relatives, Elizaveta Skalon and her three daughters Natalya, Lyudmila and Vera.[9] All were passionately fond of

---

[8] letter to Nikita Morozov, 6 July 1905.
[9] These three were Rachmaninoff's cousins by marriage.

music, and spent hours discussing and playing it with Rachmaninoff. He formed a special friendship with the youngest, Vera, who was two years younger than himself and for whom he had several nicknames: Brikushka (The Little Kicker), Psikhopatushka (The Little Psycho-path) and Belenka (The Little White Girl). Because of the too obvious affection which Rachmaninoff showed for her, her mother forbade him to write to her when he returned to Moscow after his holiday, but their communication continued in postscripts and subtle references in letters from Rachmaninoff to the eldest of the sisters, Natalya, who was to remain his closest confidante, the recipient of cheery, affection-ate letters right up until his marriage in 1902, to somebody else. While still at Ivanovka he dedicated to Vera his newly composed Romance for cello and piano, and also wrote a Waltz for six hands for the three sisters to perform.

The summer of 1890 was of particular interest for Rachmaninoff, because he had received, at the age of 17, his first commission from the publisher Jurgenson to make a piano reduction of Tchaikovsky's *The Sleeping Beauty*. In 1889 Tchaikovsky had asked Ziloti to make a two-hand transcription of the score, and the following year ap-proached him about doing a four-hand arrangement. Because of a minor injury to his hand, Ziloti was unable to write much and suggested that Rachmaninoff should be allowed to do it under his supervision for a fee of 100 rubles. Rachmaninoff had already had some experience at making transcriptions, for in the autumn of 1886, while still at Zverev's, he made a four-hand arrangement of Tchaikovsky's *Manfred* symphony. He worked at *The Sleeping Beauty* with enthusiasm, spurred on by his adulation of Tchaikovsky, and he was able to report to Natalya Skalon on 1 September 1890 that he had already completed the first act and was about to embark on the second. The finished product was not, however, a success. Rachmaninoff wrote on 11 July 1891: 'Tchaikovsky criticizes me terribly for the transcription, quite reasonably and justly. Of all transcriptions mine is undoubtedly the worst.' After seeing the proofs of the arrangement Tchaikovsky was enraged, complaining to Jurgenson and more vehemently to Ziloti about Rachmaninoff's unimaginative efforts. To placate him Ziloti undertook to correct the score, and after he had sent his revision of Act 1 Tchaikovsky's temper had obviously cooled when he wrote to Ziloti on 7 July: 'I am perfectly satisfied with your alterations and am confident now that the transcription will be fine . . .'

Returning to Moscow from his summer holiday at Ivanovka in 1890, Rachmaninoff began to teach in a class for prospective choral trainers, though his mind was occupied more with thoughts of Vera Skalon and with a new composition, *Manfred*, possibly inspired by the Tchaikovsky piece he had transcribed earlier. He told Natalya Skalon on 2 October 1890 that he had composed the first movement in two evenings, written it out during the next two days and played it through on the third day. However, apart from a passing reference to the second movement in another letter about a week later, no more is heard of *Manfred*, and the score has never been found. Towards the end of the year his love of Tchaikovsky's music took him to St Petersburg to hear *The Queen of Spades*. He had hoped to go to the première at the Mariinsky Theatre on 7 December, but had to content himself with a later performance, possibly that on 26 December 1890, which Natalya Skalon also attended. While in St Petersburg he stayed with his mother who was then living in an apartment in the agreeable part of the city near the Fontanka Canal, but he did not stay long; commenting that it was 'utterly useless to remain even one more day', he returned to Moscow and there set to work on a Russian Rhapsody for two pianos. He completed the piece quickly and was anxious to perform it with his friend Leonid Maximov at a Conservatory concert; but he had not reckoned with Zverev, who still felt vindictive towards him after their argument. Zverev refused to let Maximov play with him, and the piece was not heard until Rachmaninoff played it with Iosif Levin (later known internationally as Josef Lhévinne) at another student concert on 17 October the same year.

Throughout his life, Rachmaninoff rarely divulged much in his letters about his progress on compositions. Trawl the correspondence, and one is seldom rewarded with facts, even less (unlike Tchaikovsky's effusions) with any ideas about Rachmaninoff's thoughts on the music in question. Many autograph scores bear dates, but, even with those as a guide, one has to bear in mind that Rachmaninoff's usual method was to carry the music round in his head until it was fully formed, and only then commit it to paper. A letter he wrote to Natalya Skalon on 26 March 1891 is, therefore, not only manna from heaven to anyone documenting Rachmaninoff's life but also a clue to his working practices, and his distinction between 'composing' and 'writing'. Natalya had sent him a letter for his birthday on 20 March, and she had asked him what he was up to. Part of his reply revealed: 'I am now composing a piano concerto. Two movements are already written; the last movement is not written, but it is composed; I shall probably finish the whole concerto by the summer, and then in the summer orchestrate it.' Discarding his earlier, 1889 ideas for a concerto in C minor, this was to be his real First Piano Concerto, in F sharp minor, his op. 1. While thinking about how the last movement should go, he also composed two songs, one to a French text, *C'était en avril*, the other – *Smerkalos'* ('Twilight has fallen') – to a text by Count Alexey Konstantinovich Tolstoy, whose poetry Rachmaninoff was later to set in his mature groups of songs.

During the spring of 1891 some important changes occurred at the Moscow Conservatory. In 1889 Safonov had succeeded Taneyev as director, and relations between Safonov and Ziloti were tense from the start. Eventually the situation became so strained that in May 1891 Ziloti decided to resign, and his pupils were transferred to other teachers. Rachmaninoff was reluctant to be supervised by anybody else, for he had only one more year to study at the Conservatory and thought it unwise to be subjected to another teacher's methods at such a late stage. He asked Safonov if he could take his final examination in piano a year early, putting himself at considerable risk, for the examination was only about three weeks away. Safonov consented, and Rachmaninoff was told to prepare the first movements of Chopin's B flat minor Sonata and Beethoven's 'Appassionata'. Despite the acute shortage of time, Rachmaninoff graduated in piano with honours on 24 May, and passed his annual examinations in theory and composition on 27 May. Two days later, although he had been asked to spend some time with his family in St Petersburg, he and Ziloti travelled to Ivanovka, where the house was quieter than usual. The Skalon family was abroad for the benefit of Vera's health, and Rachmaninoff became increasingly bored. His periods of lethargy were interspersed with leisurely work, and on 18 June he told his Conservatory colleague Mikhail Slonov that he was working on the orchestration of his First Piano Concerto. He completed it on 6 July and wrote to Slonov on 20 July:

> I could have finished it much earlier, but after the first movement . . . I was idle for a long time and only began to write out the other movements on 3 July. I wrote down and orchestrated the last two movements in two-and-a-half days. You can imagine what a job that was! I wrote from 5 o'clock in the morning until 8 o'clock in the evening, so I was terribly tired when I finished work.

On the same day that he wrote this letter he completed another, much shorter work for piano, his Prélude in F.

In August Rachmaninoff stayed with his aunt Varvara on the Naryshkin estate, further to the south from Ivanovka, in the region of Saratov, where his uncle was the chief steward. From there he went on to Znamenskoye to visit his paternal grandmother Varvara Vasilyevna Rachmaninoff. It was a visit which almost ended in tragedy, for, displaying a characteristic reckless streak, he decided to take a swim in the river Matyr. Considering the rigours of the Russian autumnal climate, it is not surprising that, on returning to Ivanovka, he became ill and was forced to rest. His doctor diagnosed a fever which, according to Rachmaninoff, could have developed into a serious attack of typhoid had it not been for his strong constitution, already apparent from the earlier diphtheria epidemic. He had planned to move into a flat with Slonov for the new academic year. The illness postponed his return to Moscow for a few days, but, when he finally arrived, he was able to work quite satisfactorily. He wrote another piece, a Romance, for the six hands of the Skalon sisters on 20 September 1891, and some thoughts on a symphony manifested themselves a week later when he completed the first movement of a symphony in D minor. This latter – Tchaikovskian through and through – apparently earned little praise from Rachmaninoff's teacher, Arensky, and, like the majority of his student works, remained unpublished until the Soviet State Publishing House took them up in the late 1940s.

By this time the fever was recurring and Rachmaninoff's health deteriorated so drastically that Slonov arranged for him to be transferred to the house of one of his fellow students, Yury Sakhnovsky. By the end of October he was allowed out of bed, but he suffered from acute depression and longed to spend some time away from Russia. By December, however, he was speaking more happily of his recovery and of a new composition, *Knyaz' Rostislav* ('Prince Rostislav'), an orchestral piece based on A.K. Tolstoy's poem and dedicated to 'my dear professor Anton Stepanovich Arensky'. The doctors suggested that he should go abroad to recuperate thoroughly, but he decided that he was fit enough, and at the beginning of 1892 took part in six concerts in Moscow. One of these, on 30 January, he gave with the cellist Anatoly Brandukov and the violinist David Kreyn; besides many solo piano and cello pieces, the long programme contained two of Rachmaninoff's own new works, a *Trio élégiaque* in

G minor and the Prelude for cello and piano, one of his two pieces op. 2, recast from the earlier solo piano Prélude in F. Another important engagement that spring was to perform the first movement of his First Piano Concerto in F sharp minor, again at a student concert on 17 March, conducted by Safonov. One review commented that 'in the first movement . . . there was not yet of course any individuality, but there was taste, tension, youthful sincerity and obvious know-ledge; already there is much promise'.[10]

Rachmaninoff's confidence in his compositions had encouraged him to put a proposition to Arensky earlier in the year, as he later told Alfred Swan:

> When I was with Arensky in the free composition class, I asked him to let me graduate in one year. Skryabin, having heard about it, put in the same request. Arensky could not stand Skryabin and said, 'On no account will I let you do it.' Skryabin got offended, left the Conservatory, and never studied free composition again.[11]

Arensky was more amenable to Rachmaninoff's suggestion and so Rachmaninoff prepared himself to sit his finals in 1892. He wrote to Natalya Skalon on 18 February:

> At the Conservatory the day of the examination for the final year theory class has already been fixed. 15 April is the important day for me. On 15 March they will give us a subject for a one-act opera. As you see, I shall have to compose it, write it out and orchestrate it in one month. No mean task . . . All the best one-act operas will be performed at the end of May. If my opera is included among the best, I shall have only one task after 15 April, to attend the rehearsals of my forthcoming opera.

The opera was to be *Aleko*, based on Pushkin's poem *Tsygany* ('The Gypsies') in an adaptation by Vladimir Nemirovich-Danchenko, one of the foremost theatre directors of the day and a founder of the Moscow Art Theatre. The libretto was given to the three candidates, Nikita Morozov, Lev Konyus and Rachmaninoff, about a week late. Nevertheless, Rachmaninoff composed the two orchestral dances within a few days and had completed the whole opera by 13 April, despite the noise at his father's Moscow flat, where he was now living. Because of the late arrival of the libretto, the examination was postponed from 15 April to 7 May, when Rachmaninoff played his

[10] *Dnevnik 'Artista'* (1892), no. 1, p. 39.
[11] A.J. and K. Swan, 'Rachmaninoff: Personal Reminiscences', *The Musical Quarterly*, vol. xxx (1944), p. 14.

work before the Conservatory committee and was awarded another 5+. Immediately afterwards, Zverev, who had been sitting on the committee, followed him out into the corridor, warmly congratulated him and, to heal the ridiculous breach which had separated them, presented him with his gold watch as a memento. Ten days later the Conservatory announced the awards of gold medals. Three candidates received the small medal, but only one, Rachmaninoff, was granted the highly prized Great Gold Medal, previously awarded only to Taneyev and Arseny Koreshchenko, a pupil of Taneyev and Arensky. On 31 May 1892, after the graduation concert, Rachmaninoff left the Conservatory for the last time to begin his career as a 'free artist'.[12]

---

[12] Rachmaninoff's diploma from the Conservatory is dated 29 May 1892; his standard in all subjects is described as either 'very good' or 'excellent'.

2

Growing success

Immediately after graduating, Rachmaninoff sold his opera, two cello pieces and six songs to Karl Gutheil, who was to remain his loyal publisher until the firm was taken over by Kusevitsky in 1914.[1] During the summer he languished on the Konovalovs' estate in the Kostroma government to the north-east of Moscow, giving a daily music lesson to the son, Alexander, and also reading through the proofs of the cello pieces sent to him by Gutheil. The monotony of his existence was broken by a visit from his mother, and by thoughts of the public première of *Aleko*, as he told Natalya Skalon on 10 June:

> My opera *Aleko* has been accepted for the Bolshoy Theatre in Moscow. It is scheduled for performance after Lent. For me the performance of *Aleko* will be both pleasant and unpleasant. Pleasant, because it will be a good lesson to see my opera on stage and to witness my theatrical blunders. Unpleasant, because this opera is bound to fail. I say this quite candidly. It's just the way things are. All first operas by young composers fail, and for this reason: they always contain a multitude of mistakes which one cannot correct, because at first none of us fully understands the stage.

A few weeks later he became ill, suffering from insomnia and pains in the chest and back; he suspected cholera, and as a precaution ordered his rooms at the Konovalovs' house to be disinfected twice a day. Clearly a mild attack of fever, it passed quickly; by the beginning of August he was fit again and on 25 August returned to Moscow, where he moved into the Satins' apartment in the fashionable Arbat district. Here he composed a piano piece in C sharp minor which, when he played it for the first time at an Electrical Exposition concert on 26 September, attracted some attention. Later Rachmaninoff had cause both to thank and to regret this Prélude in C sharp minor. It was, on

---

[1] The Prelude and Oriental Dance for cello and piano were published by Gutheil as op. 2, and some of the six songs were eventually included in the set of 6 Songs op. 4. *Aleko* was published only in vocal and piano scores, and, although Gutheil expressed an interest in producing a full score, it did not appear until 1953, when it was published in Moscow by the Soviet State Publishing House.

the one hand, a powerful catalyst in the development of his worldwide reputation as a composer, though, because international copyright did not extend to Russia at that time, he received little financial benefit. On the other hand, the fame of the Prélude, so great that the piece could be referred to simply as 'Prelude' or 'It' with universal comprehension, also involved Rachmaninoff in playing it over and over again as a wearying encore at almost all of his concerts in Russia and abroad. In 1892, however, its success provided him with one of the few bright spots in a period of despondency: he was again complaining of ill-health, and was trying without success to get a permit to move to a new apartment; above all he was beset with financial problems, so severe that the Skalon sisters had to come to his rescue and buy him a very necessary overcoat for the winter. Some good news he received therefore acted as an effective tonic: he heard that *Aleko* was to be staged in the following March, that Safonov was to conduct the dances and other excerpts from *Aleko* at a concert, that Gutheil was to buy the First Concerto, and that the sale of *Aleko* (particularly the Old Gypsy's aria, Aleko's cavatina and the Young Gypsy's aria) was going well in Kiev. In fact none of the three promises was fulfilled completely: *Aleko* was not performed until April 1893, Safonov conducted only the dances at a Russian Musical Society concert on 19 February 1893 (with, however, enormous success),[2] and Gutheil apparently published the First Concerto only in a two-piano arrangement.[3]

At the end of the year Rachmaninoff was due to play a concert in Oryol, which seems not to have taken place, and also one in Kharkov. His friend Mikhail Slonov, a baritone, was also taking part in the Kharkov concert, and Rachmaninoff sent him the following sketch for a programme:

1 *a* Impromptu
    b Valse in G flat major
    c Berceuse   } Chopin
    d Valse in A flat major
    e Polonaise
2 Mishka Slonov will demonstrate the rotation of the earth

---

[2] *Moskovskiye vedomosti* (21 February 1893), p.5.
[3] The full score of this first version has since been published by the Soviet State Publishing House (Moscow, 1971).

Программа

1. a) Impromptu
   b) Valse (ges dur)
   c) Berceuse
   d) Valse (as dur)
   e) Polonaise
   } Шопенъ.

2. Мишка Слоновъ докажываетъ ...

3. a) Des Abends
   b) Aufschwung
   c) 12ᵃˢ rapsodie Листа
   } Шумана.

   Антрактъ.

4. a) Elegie
   b) Prelude
   c) Melodie
   d) Polichinelle
   e) Serenade
   } Рахманинова.

5. Мишка Слоновъ докажываетъ ...

6. a) Valse Impromptu — Листа
   b) ... — Рубинштейна
   c) ...

3 *a* Des Abends ⎫
   b Aufschwung ⎬ Schumann
   c Rhapsody no. 12   Liszt

Interval

4 *a* Elégie
   b Prélude
   c Mélodie   ⎬ Rachmaninoff[4]
   d Polichinelle
   e Sérénade

5 Mishka Slonov will demonstrate the complete groundlessness of Deroulède's arguments regarding the Panama Crisis

6 *a* Valse-Impromptu   Liszt
   b Barcarolle   Rubinstein
   c Fantasia on themes
        from *Eugene Onegin*   Tchaikovsky–Pabst

Rachmaninoff left Moscow on 25 December 1892 and gave the concert three days later. He played the programme as planned, but in place of his skittish suggestions Slonov sang arias and songs by Borodin, Tchaikovsky, Arensky, Rubinstein, Davydov and Mozart. After the concert Rachmaninoff returned to Moscow, though he was back in Kharkov for another concert on 27 January 1893, giving a repeat performance of the five *Morceaux de fantaisie* in a programme which also included Schumann's *Kreisleriana*, pieces by Arensky, Liszt, Chopin, Pabst and also the cavatina from *Aleko*, sung by Slonov.

In the spring Rachmaninoff became involved with firm preparations for the première of *Aleko*, which finally took place at the Bolshoy Theatre on 27 April 1893. The performance was conducted by Ippolit Altani, the Bolshoy's principal conductor, with a cast including Bogomir Korsov as Aleko, Mariya Deysha-Sionitskaya as Zemfira, Stepan Vlasov as the Old Gypsy and Lev Klementyev as the Young Gypsy. Tchaikovsky attended the final rehearsals and

---

(*Opposite*) Part of Rachmaninoff's letter (14 December 1892) to his friend, the baritone Mikhail Slonov, outlining the programme for their concert in Kharkov on 28 December 1892.

[4] This was the first performance of the five *Morceaux de fantaisie*, published by Gutheil as op. 3.

was present on the first night, reporting afterwards to Ziloti that the work was 'delightful'. Years later Rachmaninoff recalled how Tchaikovsky had encouraged him:

> I think success depended not so much on the quality of the opera as much as on Tchaikovsky's attitude towards it, for he liked it very much. By the way, at one of the rehearsals Tchaikovsky said to me, 'I have just finished a two-act [sic] opera *Iolanta*, which is not long enough to take up a whole evening. Would you object to its being performed with your opera?' He literally said that: 'Would you object . . . ?' He was 53, a famous composer, but I was a novice of 20! Tchaikovsky of course attended the première of *Aleko*, and at his insistence the director of the Imperial Theatres Vsevolozhsky came from St Petersburg. At the end of the opera Tchaikovsky, leaning out of the box, applauded with all his might, realizing how this would help a new composer.[5]

Shortly after the successful première Rachmaninoff went to see his maternal grandparents, the Butakovs, who still lived in Novgorod; he stayed there until 20 May before travelling on to visit Slonov on an estate owned by the Lysikov family at Lebedin in the Kharkov government. Here he was pampered by Madame Lysikova because, according to Slonov, he reminded her of her own son who had died six years before. In this ideal environment composition flourished. He produced the *Fantaisie-tableaux* (or Suite no. 1) for two pianos, op. 5, completed the op. 4 set of songs, a sacred choral piece *V molitvakh neusypayushchuyu bogoroditsu* ('O Mother of God vigilantly praying'), the Two Pieces for violin and piano, op. 6 and an orchestral fantasy *Utyos* ('The Rock'), op.7. This last work is headed by the first two lines from Lermontov's poem of the same name, but the true inspiration was Chekhov's short story *Na puti* ('On the Way'), published in the journal *Novoye vremya* in 1886 and bearing the same Lermontov quotation. Rachmaninoff freely acknowledged his use of the story in his inscription on a copy of the published score which he presented to Chekhov in 1898: 'To dear and highly respected Anton Pavlovich Chekhov, author of the story *On the Way*, the plot of which . . . served as a programme for this composition.' When the score was published by Jurgenson, Rachmaninoff dedicated the piece to Rimsky-Korsakov, in gratitude for his performance of the Gypsy Girls' Dance from *Aleko* at a Russian Symphony Concert in St

---

[5] 'Rakhmaninov o sebe', *Ogonyok* (20 March 1943), pp. 12–13.

Petersburg on 17 December 1894. Tchaikovsky heard a play-through of his young protégé's *The Rock*, and was so enamoured of it that he asked if he could perform it in St Petersburg the following season.

After the productive summer of 1893 in Kharkov Rachmaninoff returned to Moscow in August. At first he occupied a room in the Satins' new apartment on the Serebryanyy pereulok in the Arbat district, but soon moved to a block of furnished flats called America, not far away in the Vozdvizhenka. Again he settled down to steady composition, completing his Six Songs, op. 8 to Alexey Pleshcheyev's translations of Ukranian and German texts; he also considered writing an opera on the subject of *Undina*, but finally abandoned the idea in October (see pp. 129–30). During this autumn Rachmaninoff was deeply affected by the deaths of two of his most influential mentors. On 30 September Zverev, his former teacher, died at the age of 61, depriving Moscow of one of its central musical figures, and, for all that their relationship had been uneasy, robbed Rachmaninoff of the most powerful influence on his success as a pianist. The funeral was on 2 October. Twelve days later Rachmaninoff travelled to Kiev to conduct the first two performances of *Aleko* on 18 October and 21 October. It was just after his return to Moscow that he heard the news of the death of Tchaikovsky on 25 October 1893; as a direct result he immediately began work on a second *Trio élégiaque*, in D minor, which he dedicated to Tchaikovsky. On 30 November Rachmaninoff and Pabst performed the two-piano *Fantaisie-tableaux* also dedicated to Tchaikovsky; the new trio, completed on 15 December, was performed by Rachmaninoff, Konyus (violin) and Brandukov (cello) at a concert on 31 January 1894.

It was early in 1894 that, for financial reasons, Rachmaninoff undertook rather more teaching work than he usually liked. Apart from giving private piano lessons he began to teach music theory at the Mariinsky Academy for Girls, remaining there until 1901. Whether he actually enjoyed it is another matter. Certainly his methods were not those of a born teacher:

'He would come into the class', reports one of his pupils, 'with a soft, slow tread, sit down at the desk, quite often take out his handkerchief and wipe his face for a long time; then, dropping his head into the fingers of his hands, he would summon a pupil, sometimes not raising his head or looking at her, and ask for her homework. Rachmaninoff, like

Tchaikovsky, did not like teaching work, and did it because he needed the money'.[6]

For much the same reason he composed some undemanding lucrative piano duets (op. 11) and completed the seven *Morceaux de salon*, op. 10. On his birthday, 20 March, his fantasy *The Rock* was given its first performance in Moscow at a Russian Musical Society concert conducted by Safonov (the première had been postponed because of Tchaikovsky's death). He would have liked to spend the entire summer at the family estate at Ivanovka, but monetary considerations compelled him to go to the Konovalovs' Kostroma estate to give more lessons. Here he read through Jurgenson's proofs of *The Rock* and also began a subsequently abandoned work based on Byron's *Don Juan*, of which only the Chorus of Spirits and the Song of the Nightingale have survived in manuscript. The composition which occupied most of his time was his Capriccio on Gypsy Themes, the manuscript of which he took with him from the Konovalovs' estate to Ivanovka, where he spent the rest of the summer.

He had had this capriccio in mind since 1892, when he had written to Slonov on 2 August: 'I am now writing a capriccio for orchestra, not on Spanish themes, like Rimsky-Korsakov, nor Italian themes, like Tchaikovsky, but on gypsy themes. I shall finish it in four days. For the time being I think I shall write it for four hands and orchestrate it later.' The purpose of this was to allow him to make a thorough study of orchestration, and it appears that he kept the four-hand arrangement by him for two years before completing the scoring in September 1894. He dedicated the piece to Pyotr Lodyzhensky, the husband of the gypsy Anna Alexandrovna Lodyzhenskaya, to whom he dedicated the song *O net, molyu, ne ukhodi!* ('Oh no, I beg you, forsake me not', op. 4 no. 1) and was soon to dedicate his First Symphony.

Returning to Moscow in September Rachmaninoff again lodged with the Satins, who had now moved to a larger house, where he could be given more privacy and was able to put in order his first thoughts about his symphony. Again it was in D minor, though it bears no resemblance to his earlier D minor effort. Work on it took eight months, from the earliest ideas conceived in January 1895 to the completion of the score at Ivanovka on 30 August. After

[6] M. L. Chelishcheva, 'S. V. Rakhmaninov v Mariinskom uchilishche', *Vospominaniya o Rakhmaninove*, vol. i, ed. Z. A. Apetian (Moscow, 5/1988), p. 386.

correcting the score to his satisfaction he took a brief holiday in St Petersburg to hear the première of Taneyev's opera *Oresteya* ('The Oresteia') at the Mariinsky Theatre on 17 October 1895. In fact, he had a personal interest in the opera, for he had spent considerable time during the spring of 1893 checking through the vocal score for Taneyev. After the première he embarked almost immediately on a three-month concert tour of Russia which the Polish impresario Henryk Langiewicz had persuaded him to undertake with the Italian violinist Teresina Tua, a graduate of the Paris Conservatoire. He was showing signs of exasperation even after the first concert and wrote to Slonov just before the second concert in Belostok on 9 November 1895:

> In one hour ten minutes the concert begins, dear friend Mikhail Akimovich. I am not dressed yet, and therefore cannot write much. I have only just finished playing. Today I have played for six hours all but 15 minutes. Both hands ache as I am not used to it; yesterday I could not practise at all. At the first concert in Łódź [7 November] I played better than expected. I had a great success, but she, i.e. the Contessa Teresina Tua-Franchi-Verney della Valetti, had a greater success of course. Incidentally, her playing is nothing special; her technique is mediocre. To make up for it she plays wonderfully for the audience with her eyes and smiles. She is not a serious artist, though undoubtedly she has talent. But I cannot bear the sweet smiles she gives the public, her breaks on the high notes, or her fermate (like Mazzini). Incidentally, I have discovered one other trait in her. She is very mean. With me she is charming. She is very afraid I shall run away.

On 22 November he was in Moscow as part of the tour, and conducted the first performance of the Capriccio on Gypsy Themes. According to Sofiya Satina[7] he managed to extricate himself from the latter part of the tour, using the excuse that the impresario had failed to pay him his fee.

During 1896, largely through the influence of Taneyev and Glazunov, the Russian philanthropist and music publisher Mitrofan Belyayev agreed to include Rachmaninoff's First Symphony in a Russian Symphony Concert, having already arranged a performance of *The Rock* at a concert on 20 January 1896 under Glazunov. With the prospect of a performance of the symphony, his largest orchestral work so far, Rachmaninoff found it difficult to concentrate on any

[7] S. A. Satina, 'Zapiska o S. V. Rakhmaninove', *Vospominaniya o Rakhmaninove*, vol. i, ed. Z. A. Apetian (Moscow, 5/1988), p. 29.

other new compositions, though he did manage to complete his 12 Songs op. 14, his six *Moments musicaux* op. 16, and the Six Choruses for women's or children's voices op. 15, commenting that they were so difficult that no child would ever be able to sing them. In January 1897 Rachmaninoff wrote to Glazunov, who was to conduct the symphony, asking if he knew when the performance was to be, and finally it was arranged to take place in St Petersburg on 15 March, in the Hall of the Nobility, now the St Petersburg Philharmonic Hall.

It was a disaster. Rachmaninoff could not understand what was happening to his symphony when he heard the jarring, cacophonous noises being produced by the orchestra. The single consolation was that he was sitting backstage, so avoiding the personal humiliation of being surrounded by an uncomprehending audience and hostile critics. In the St Petersburg Philharmonic Hall of today, barely altered since the nineteenth century, there is, behind the curtains to the left of the platform, a spiral iron staircase. This, it is said, was Rachmaninoff's vantage point on this fateful evening. Certainly it is handily placed for making a quick, unnoticed getaway from the hall: immediately after his ordeal, without taking any bow, he rushed down into the street, frantic and tormented by the failure of this first important première which he had been anticipating with such high hopes for nearly two years. The more partisan critics of St Petersburg were swift to swoop on an unfortunate Moscow-based composer. César Cui, whose poison pen was legendary, began his lengthy notice of the Rachmaninoff symphony with a characteristically deadly jab:

> If there were a conservatory in Hell, if one of its talented students were instructed to write a programme symphony on the 'Seven Plagues of Egypt', and if he were to compose a symphony like Mr Rachmaninoff's, then he would have fulfilled his task brilliantly and would delight the inhabitants of Hell.[8]

Cui went on to tear the symphony to shreds, stemming the flow of venom only when he began to describe the other works in the programme: Tchaikovsky's overture *Fatum*, a Waltz-Fantasy by Nikolay Artsybushev, Glazunov's own Spanish Serenade for cello and orchestra, and a cello and piano Suite by Nikolay Sokolov (another first performance, but, unlike the Rachmaninoff symphony, given Cui's warm approval). In years to come, Cui's attitude towards

[8] Ts. Kyui, 'Tretiy russkiy simfonicheskiy kontsert', *Novosti i birzhevaya gazeta* (17 March 1897), p. 3.

Rachmaninoff was to mellow, but at this stage he could barely find a good word. Even conceding that Rachmaninoff was presumably striving for originality, this, said Cui, amounted to no more than a distorted mishmash of the music of Wagner, Tchaikovsky and Rimsky-Korsakov. Another critic, Nikolay Findeyzen, writing in the leading journal *Russkaya muzykal'naya gazeta*[9] (of which he was editor), acknowledged that, if the piece had its failings, so too did the performance. Years later, Rachmaninoff's wife was known to remark that Glazunov had been drunk on the podium, which, bearing in mind the reports of his alcohol consumption, could well have been the case. Rachmaninoff, if not going to these lengths, did make some significant comments on the quality of the interpretation to his friend, the composer Alexander Zatayevich:

> 6 May 1897
>
> I am amazed how such a highly talented man as Glazunov can conduct so badly. I am not speaking now of his conducting technique (one can't ask that of him) but about his musicianship. He feels nothing when he conducts. It's as if he understands nothing. When I was with Ant[on] Rubinstein one day, I asked him at supper how he liked the singer N, who had been singing the part of the Demon [in Rubinstein's opera], and Rubinstein, instead of replying, took a knife and stood it on end. I can say just the same thing. So I assume that the performance might have been the cause of the failure. (I do not say for certain; I am just assuming.) If the public had been familiar with the symphony, then they would have blamed the conductor (I continue to 'assume'); if a symphony is both unfamiliar and badly performed, then the public is inclined to blame the composer.

It crossed his mind to destroy the score, but this he did not do, for in 1908 he contemplated revising it, and in 1917 wrote to Asafyev, 'I won't show the symphony to anyone, and in my will I shall make sure nobody looks at it.' The symphony was never performed again during his lifetime, and the manuscript has never been found.[10]

Rachmaninoff had no money, but needed to get away from St Petersburg. With financial help from the Skalon sisters he hurriedly retreated from Moscow, travelling first to Novgorod to visit his grandparents. From there he went to stay for the rest of the summer

---

[9] N. Findeyzen, in *Russkaya muzykal'naya gazeta* (April 1897), no. 4, columns 650 and 651.

[10] In 1947 the Soviet State Publishing House produced a score compiled from Rachmaninoff's 1895 four-hand piano arrangement and from the original orchestral parts discovered in the Leningrad Conservatory. The first performance of this version was in Moscow on 17 October 1945.

with the Skalons on their estate at Ignatovo. Although he had told Zatayevich that the failure had not unduly affected him, he was unable to compose anything else of importance for two years. That summer he managed to sketch some ideas in C major for a new symphony: a mere 55 bars of piano score, which, far from consolidating the boldness of the pilloried D minor Symphony, retreat into the insipid manner of Glazunov himself, whose Sixth Symphony, in C minor, Rachmaninoff had just arranged for piano duet for publication by Belyayev. By 4 November 1897, Glazunov (writing to Mikhail Slonov) admitted that he had not 'had time to write and thank' Rachmaninoff for doing the arrangement. And Rachmaninoff's own symphony sketches looked like an equally thankless task. As he wrote at the top of the manuscript: 'Sketches from my new symphony, which, judging from them, will be of no significant interest. 5 April 1897'. He was right, and the material was never used.

With inspiration at such a low ebb, it was fortunate that, just then, Savva Mamontov, a wealthy Moscow industrialist, offered him a conducting post. In 1885 Mamontov had founded the Moskovskaya Chastnaya Russkaya Opera (The Moscow Private Russian Opera Company) and for the 1897–8 season he decided to engage Rachmaninoff as deputy to the principal conductor, the Italian Eugenio Esposito. Mamontov attracted many young and gifted performers, including the soprano Nadezhda Zabela-Vrubel, the tenor Anton Sekar-Rozhansky and above all the then virtually unknown Fyodor Shalyapin, with whom Rachmaninoff formed a deep and lasting friendship. Rachmaninoff's first engagement for the season was to be a performance of Glinka's *Zhizn' za tsarya* ('A Life for the Tsar'). Esposito, who had little talent, rightly feared for his position when Rachmaninoff was appointed, and he resolved to be utterly unhelpful to the comparatively inexperienced newcomer. For the Glinka he allowed only one rehearsal, during which Rachmaninoff failed to grasp why it was that everything went well when the orchestra was playing alone but that the singing was catastrophic. Esposito gleefully took over the performance at the eleventh hour, and Rachmaninoff, watching closely, learnt the vital fact that singers had to be cued in. This valuable lesson he put to good use in his next opera, Saint-Saëns's *Samson et Dalila*, which he conducted on 12 October and again three days later. Despite his unfortunate start, he found his new job quite congenial, as he told Natalya Skalon on 19 October: 'On Wednesday I conducted S[amson] et D[alila] for the second time.

It went as satisfactorily as the first time. My next opera is *Rogneda*. All the papers praise me. I do not trust them much! I get on well with everybody in the theatre, but I still swear quite violently. I'm on good terms with Mam[ontov], just as he is with me.' His next opera was not in fact Serov's *Rogneda* but Dargomyzhsky's *Rusalka* (19 October) in which Shalyapin sang the Miller, a role which was to become one of his favourites. Rachmaninoff followed this with *Carmen*, Gluck's *Orphée et Eurydice*, Serov's *Rogneda*, Verstovsky's *Askol'dova mogila* ('Askold's Tomb'), and early in 1898 Rimsky's *Mayskaya noch'* ('May Night'), again with Shalyapin, singing his subsequently famous role of the Headman, and Serov's *Vrazh'ya sila* ('The Power of Evil'). These opera performances were to stand Rachmaninoff in good stead. In years to come, he was to be invited to conduct both at the Bolshoy Theatre in Moscow and at the Mariinsky in St Petersburg. In 1912, the young Nikolay Malko, who had just embarked on his own conducting career, heard Rachmaninoff direct six performances of Tchaikovsky's *Pikovaya dama* ('The Queen of Spades') at the Mariinsky. 'Astonishingly fresh', he wrote later. 'All kinds of clichés were erased, and the opera came across to the listener in a new, lively way, as if it had just been "washed".'[11]

After such a highly successful conducting season in 1897–8 Rachmaninoff again settled down to a period of inactivity. He mulled over some ideas for a new piano concerto, and Goldenveyzer wrote to ask if he could play it at one of Belyayev's Russian Symphony concerts. His first choice had been Skryabin's recently-composed concerto, but Skryabin would not let Goldenveyzer play it as he was planning to perform it himself. Rachmaninoff postponed giving Goldenveyzer a firm answer, but by August had committed nothing to paper, and Goldenveyzer had to perform Arensky's concerto instead. During the summer Rachmaninoff went to stay at Putyatino, north of Moscow in the region of Yaroslav, in a dacha belonging to Tatyana Lyubatovich, a friend of Mamontov's. Fellow guests included many members of the Private Opera, among them Shalyapin and the young Italian ballerina Iola Tornaghi, whom Shalyapin married that same summer. It was also during this holiday that Shalyapin and Rachmaninoff worked together on the operas of Rimsky-Korsakov and Musorgsky, making a special study of *Boris Godunov*. This

---

[11] N. A. Mal'ko: 'Rakhmaninov – dirizhor', *Vospominaniya o Rakhmaninove'*, vol. ii, ed. Z. A. Apetian (Moscow, 5/1988), p. 229.

collaboration sparked a warm and lasting professional and personal friendship. According to Shalyapin, Rachmaninoff was a 'lively, cheerful, companionable person. An excellent artist, a splendid musician and a pupil [*sic*] of Tchaikovsky, he particularly encouraged me to study Musorgsky and Rimsky-Korsakov. He introduced me to the basic rules of music and even, to some extent, of harmony. Altogether he tried to educate me musically.'[12] For Rachmaninoff, his association with Shalyapin was 'one of the strongest, deepest and finest experiences of my life'.[13] It may, too, have reawakened his creative instincts, for he decided to approach Modest Tchaikovsky about a new opera libretto. Instead of Rachmaninoff's suggestion of a Shakespearian subject Tchaikovsky sent him some ideas for *Francesca da Rimini*. This project, too, lay fallow for several years before Rachmaninoff was sufficiently inspired to complete it (see pp. 132–7).

After his summer holiday Rachmaninoff was recommended to go to the Crimea for the benefit of his health; again he was accompanied by Shalyapin and artists from the Private Opera, and they gave a number of concerts with considerable success. Returning home, he decided to live in the countryside around Moscow, going in to the city once a week to give piano lessons and to see his relatives. A *Morceau de fantasie* in G minor and a Fughetta in F were the only products of these comparatively sterile days, but, as he told Zatayevich (3 March), he was far from idle: he was, in fact, 'extremely busy, because at the end of March I am going to London, to play and conduct'.

This was Rachmaninoff's first engagement abroad. He had been invited by the Philharmonic Society to appear at one of its Queen's Hall concerts. The Society anticipated that Rachmaninoff would be playing his Second Piano Concerto, but another 18 months were to pass before even two movements were ready for performance in Moscow. Declining to play the First Concerto (because he regarded it as a mere student work), Rachmaninoff offered to conduct one of his orchestral works instead. So, in a programme largely overseen by Sir Alexander Mackenzie (Beethoven's Fifth Symphony, the aria 'Medlenno den' ugasal' ['Slowly fades the day'] from Act 2 of Borodin's *Prince Igor*, and an *Idyll* by B. Luard Selby, a modest British talent of the time), Rachmaninoff was to conduct his own *Rock*

[12] F. I. Shalyapin, *Stranitsy iz moyey zhizni*; pubd in E. A. Grosheva (ed.), *Fyodor Ivanovich Shalyapin: literaturnoye nasledstvo*, vol. i (Moscow, 1957), p. 147.

[13] Z. A. Pribytkova, 'S. V. Rakhmaninov v Peterburge – Petrograde', *Vospominaniya o Rakhmaninove*, vol. ii, ed. Z. A. Apetian (Moscow, 5/1988), p. 87.

fantasy. He was also to play the Elégie and the Prélude in C sharp minor from op. 3.

The concert took place on the evening of Wednesday 19 April. 'Qualified Success' – the headline in next morning's *Daily Mail*[14] – summed up the general critical reaction, which, however, should be seen in the context of current establishment attitudes. Russian music was then new to British ears. Works which today are familiar repertory items were, with the exception of certain admired pieces by Tchaikovsky and Rimsky-Korsakov, virtually unknown at the turn of the century. Enthusiasts like the writer on music Rosa Newmarch – who had actually been to Russia – tried to get more works played in London, but it was a struggle. Even Henry Wood, who in due course was to do more for Russian composers (including Rachmaninoff) than any other British conductor of the time, felt constrained to reply to one of Mrs Newmarch's pleas just after her return from St Petersburg in 1897:

> . . . I don't care to do too much Russian music just yet, as I am afraid my audiences are not quite educated up to it, but give time and I shall do so, and I think if we are to have originality in music, I don't know where else to go for it, as I consider it very original and always splendidly scored and orchestrated.[15]

London critics, generally intent on promoting the cause of British composers, regarded music by Russians, if not with xenophobic dislike, then certainly with suspicion. Russian music was enjoying a 'vogue', moaned *The Daily Telegraph*; in different circumstances, it claimed, 'Mr Rachmaninoff would probably have gone without the invitation which made him last evening the honoured guest of the Philharmonic Society'.[16] 'We are all being seduced', said *The Times*, 'into the belief, willy-nilly perhaps, that nothing but good can come out of Russia. Yet it would not necessitate a journey far beyond the four-mile radius from Charing Cross to find a musical composition at least as nearly "great" as the orchestral fantaisie in E major.'[17] The received idea, put simply, was that Russians had a good grasp of orchestral colour but lacked backbone and substance. 'Small, ill-nourished' themes, which 'creep about in apologetic half-tones' (*The Musical Times*'s verdict on *The Rock*[18]) were not going to find much

[14] *Daily Mail* (20 April 1899), p. 5.
[15] unpublished letter, 2 February 1897, in British Library (MS 56421/1).
[16] *The Daily Telegraph* (20 April 1899), p. 10.
[17] *The Times* (21 April 1899), p. 15.
[18] *The Musical Times*, vol. xl (1899), p. 311.

favour with the British press, any more than a work based on the 'fantastic idea of a rock lamenting the departure of a cloud' (*Monthly Musical Record*[19]). 'This is carrying symbolism far enough, God wot', the *Daily Mail* exploded.[20] Altogether, *The Rock* was far too namby-pamby for the British, not a patch on Elgar's *Caractacus*, as *Musical Opinion*[21] was quick to remind its readers.

Predictably, however, Rachmaninoff was praised for 'superb and original' orchestral effects (*The Times*[22]), which were 'amazingly clever, some quite new, others charming or startling, occasionally impressive as mere combinations of *timbre*, and the whole dazzling like the flashes from a brilliant gem' (*The Musical Times*[23]). As a pianist, Rachmaninoff's playing of the Prélude – a piece already universally deemed 'hackneyed' – 'was doubtless an object lesson to the many amateurs who know it by heart' (*The Musical Standard*[24]); *The Daily Telegraph*[25] asserted that Rachmaninoff was 'not a pianist of colossal technique', while the *Monthly Musical Record* found him 'a highly cultivated player'.[26] *The Times*, judging that Rachmaninoff's playing was 'not so effective' as that of Mr Leonard Borwick,[27] nevertheless liked his conducting technique: 'His command was supreme; his method, quietness idealized.'[28] 'He succeeded in making the Philharmonic orchestra play as it has not played for many a long day', said *The Musical Standard*.[29]

For a London debut by a young Russian musician, famous only for one piano prelude, this reception was reasonably encouraging. Certainly the Philharmonic Society thought so, because it invited Rachmaninoff back the following year. However, he did not return to London until 1908. By then the Second Concerto, which the Philharmonic Society had hoped for, was complete and Rachmaninoff played it, but with the London Symphony Orchestra.

[19] *Monthly Musical Record*, vol. xxix (1899), p. 106.
[20] *Daily Mail* (20 April 1899), p. 5.
[21] *Musical Opinion*, vol. xxii (1899), p.521.
[22] *The Times* (21 April 1899), p.15.
[23] *The Musical Times*, vol. xl (1899), p. 311.
[24] *The Musical Standard* (22 April 1899), p. 244.
[25] *The Daily Telegraph* (20 April 1899), p. 10.
[26] *Monthly Musical Record*, vol. xxix (1899), p. 106.
[27] Leonard Borwick (1868–1925), English pianist, highly regarded as a match for even the most illustrious foreign names.
[28] *The Times* (21 April 1899), p. 15.
[29] *The Musical Standard* (22 April 1899), p. 244.

Returning to Russia after his first Queen's Hall concert, Rachmaninoff was faced with the St Petersburg première of *Aleko*. Arensky had decided to arrange a special concert on 27 May 1899 to celebrate the centenary of Pushkin's birth. The concert consisted entirely of works inspired by Pushkin's poetry, including several by Arensky himself and concluding with Rachmaninoff's opera. The part of Aleko was sung by Shalyapin, and after the performance Rachmaninoff remarked on his unique acting ability and sensitivity of interpretation, which were to be the source of much inspiration to him in the composition of his two later operas and of many songs: 'I can still hear how he sobbed at the end of the opera. Only a great dramatic artist or a man who had experienced such great sorrow as Aleko can sob like that', he told Slonov on 18 July 1899. Shortly before this première, Rachmaninoff had sent to 'Natasha', probably Natalya Satina (Natalya Skalon cannot be entirely ruled out as the dedicatee, though Rachmaninoff generally referred to her as 'Tatusha'), the manuscript of a song *Ikalos' li tebe* ('Were you hiccupping?'), with the inscription 'No! My Muse has not died, dear Natasha. I dedicate my new song to you.' At least his sense of humour was intact. He had set (and altered) a joke text by the poet and critic Pyotr Vyazemsky (1792–1878) lauding the merits of champagne, giving it an oompah piano accompaniment unlike anything else he ever wrote and cunningly tucking in a musical reference (in the piano part) to Lensky's declaration of love to Olga in Tchaikovsky's *Eugene Onegin* at the words, added by Rachmaninoff, 'loving Natasha'. On a more serious note, he wrote a choral anthem, *Panteley-tselitel'* ('Panteley the Healer'), dating it 18 October 1899, but all this was small fry. It was ironical, therefore, that the critic Yuly Engel should choose this time to ask for a short biographical sketch for inclusion in the Russian edition of Riemann's *Musik-Lexikon*. Rachmaninoff, rather than sending him anything new, merely enclosed with his letter (27 October 1899) a copy of a biography from a London newspaper. 'I can find nothing longer', he told Engel.

Early in 1900 Princess Alexandra Liven, concerned at Rachmaninoff's torpor, arranged for him to meet Tolstoy, saying, according to Rachmaninoff: 'Will you please see him, Lev Nikolayevich? The young man will go to ruin. He has lost faith in his powers; try to help him.' Tolstoy in fact made Rachmaninoff's condition even worse. Of his first visit Rachmaninoff later told Swan: 'He made me sit next to him and stroked my knees. He saw how nervous I was. And then, at table, he said to me, "You must work. Do you think that I am pleased with myself? Work. I work every day," and similar stereotyped phrases.'[30]

Their next meeting, at which Rachmaninoff was accompanied by Shalyapin, was yet more discouraging. Shalyapin recalled later:

> It was on 9 January 1900 in Moscow ... We climbed up the wooden staircase to the second floor of a very nice, comfortable, quite modest house, apparently half built of wood. We were met by Sofiya Andreyevna [Tolstoy's wife] and her sons, Mikhail, Andrey and Sergey. Of course they offered us tea, but I was in no mood for tea. I was very nervous. My only thought was that I was about to behold the face and eyes of the man whose words and thoughts excited the whole world. Until then I had seen Lev Nikolayevich only in portraits. And there he was in the flesh! He was standing by the chess table talking about something to the young Goldenveyzer (Goldenveyzer, father and son, were regular partners in the family chess tournaments) ... Seryozha Rachmaninoff was apparently more courageous than I was, but he was also nervous and his hands were cold. He whispered to me, 'If I'm asked to play, I don't know how – my hands are like ice.' And indeed Lev Nikolayevich did ask Rachmaninoff to play. What Rachmaninoff played I do not remember. I was nervous and was thinking all the time: I'll have to sing. I got even more cold feet when Lev Nikolayevich asked Rachmaninoff point-blank, 'Tell me, does anybody need music like that?'[31]

Rachmaninoff never returned to Tolstoy's Moscow house, nor did he ever accept the annual invitation to Yasnaya Polyana, Tolstoy's country estate. His disillusionment, his discovery that his 'god' was in fact a 'very disagreeable man' was the last straw in this period of extreme depression and lack of self-confidence, and finally the Satin family decided that it would be wise for him to seek medical help. They chose Dr Nikolay Dahl, who had for some years been specializing in treatment by hypnosis. It seems likely that actual hypnosis played a less important role in the treatment than the extended, confidence-building conversations which Dahl had with Rachmaninoff on a wide range of musical topics, for Dahl himself was an accomplished amateur musician.

During the early part of the year, besides giving a concert with Shalyapin and Goldenveyzer on 9 March 1900, Rachmaninoff went

---

[30] A. J. and K. Swan, 'Rachmaninoff: Personal Reminiscences', *The Musical Quarterly*, vol. xxx (1944), p. 185.

[31] F. I. Shalyapin, *Maska i dusha*; pubd in E. A. Grosheva (ed.), *Fyodor Ivanovich Shalyapin: literaturnoye nasledstvo*, vol. i (Moscow, 1957), pp. 321–2.

with Shalyapin to the warmer climate of Yalta, where they stayed in a house on Prince Liven's estate. The extreme south of the Crimea was a favourite venue for artists wishing to cure themselves of an illness or to recuperate from a season's hard work. This summer was no exception; many members of the Moscow Art Theatre were there, including the director himself, Konstantin Stanislavsky, and they all met frequently with Chekhov and Gorky; the composer Vasily Kalinnikov was also there, undergoing treatment for tuberculosis, and Rachmaninoff cheered him greatly by persuading Jurgenson to publish some of his works. Jurgenson even asked to be Kalinnikov's sole publisher, but within months Kalinnikov had died at the tragically early age of 34.

Whatever the nature of Dahl's treatment for Rachmaninoff's mental state, it had an almost immediate and startling effect, for by the summer his enthusiasm for composition was already being rekindled. While in the Crimea, Shalyapin received an invitation to sing in Boito's *Mefistofele* at La Scala, Milan, and invited Rachmaninoff to stay with him in the house he had rented at Varazze, near Genoa. Living there with Shalyapin in June and July, Rachmaninoff composed the love duet for *Francesca da Rimini*; he also began the long-postponed work on the Second Piano Concerto. These ideas were written down after his return to Russia in August, and the two completed movements, the second and third, were performed for the first time on 2 December 1900 despite a severe cold and much understandable nervousness. So successful were they that he was encouraged to complete the first movement, and also to begin work on his Suite no. 2 for two pianos. By the end of February 1901 he was able to show three of the four planned movements of the Suite to Goldenveyzer, and the piece was performed for the first time by Rachmaninoff and Ziloti at a Moscow Philharmonic Society Concert on 24 November 1901. A month earlier a much more significant event had taken place, for, having now added the first movement to his Second Concerto, he had played it at a Moscow Philharmonic Society concert on 27 October, conducted by Ziloti. Shortly before the première he had grave misgivings, largely because of his old friend Morozov's tactlessness. In response to Rachmaninoff's request for his opinion of the piece, he had given it in blunt terms. Rachmaninoff wrote him this despairing reply on 22 October:

You are right, Nikita Semyonovich!
   I have just played through the first movement of my concerto, and only now has it suddenly become clear to me that the transition from the first

theme to the second is no good at all; in this form the first theme is not a first theme, but an introduction. Not even a fool would believe, when I start to play the second theme, that that is what it is. Everyone will think that this is the beginning of the concerto. To my mind the whole movement is spoilt, and from this moment it is absolutely repulsive to me. I'm in despair! And why on earth did you have to bother me with your analysis five days before the performance?

Yet the concerto was an astounding and lasting success, and finally assured Rachmaninoff that his ability to compose had not faded. Even Cui was later to express his enthusiasm for the concerto. 'Tell Rachmaninoff', he wrote in a letter of 27 March 1903, 'that the other day I heard the last two movements of his Second Concerto, and that, with the exception of some longueurs, they made a thoroughly pleasant impression on me through their beauty, taste and elegance, undoubtedly testifying to the composer's talent.'[32] Rachmaninoff was going to have to put up with other Cuis as his career developed, but for the next 16 years music flowed from his pen with such fluency that by the time he left Russia in 1917 he had composed no less than 39 of his 45 opus numbers.

[32] M. O. Yankovsky (ed.), *Ts. A. Kyui: izbrannyye pis'ma* (Leningrad, 1955), p.295.

3

Conductor and composer

His confidence restored, Rachmaninoff completed almost at once a
new piece, the Sonata for cello and piano, in which the piano virtuosity
and sumptuous themes show it to be, like the Suite no. 2 for two pianos,
closely related to the Second Concerto. He dedicated the Sonata to his
friend, the cellist Anatoly Brandukov, and they performed it together in
Moscow at the end of 1901. Early the following year he composed his
first important choral work, the cantata *Vesna* ('Spring'), which has a
prominent solo part, almost certainly inspired by Shalyapin, who sang
it at the first St Petersburg performance on 8 January 1905.[1] Just after
completing the cantata, which tells how the mollifying effects of spring
cause a husband to abandon a plan to murder his unfaithful wife,
Rachmaninoff himself announced that he was shortly to be married to
his cousin, Natalya Alexandrovna Satina. From his earliest days at the
Moscow Conservatory he had been a frequent guest in the Satins' home,
and had lived and worked with them in Moscow and at Ivanovka. He
was treated as one of their immediate family and had formed a
particularly happy association with his second eldest cousin, Natalya.
Despite their obvious friendship, the news that they were to marry
startled all close relatives and acquaintances, not least, perhaps,
Natalya Skalon, Rachmaninoff's close confidante for more than a
decade. Right at the end of a chatty letter, scrawled in pencil at a
railway station, he sprang the news:

1 April 1902
. . . At the end of this month I am being incautious enough to get married. I
certainly expect from you some sort of superior, expensive present such as
is fitting for *you* to give *me*. I do not expect you to be there in person! For
God's sake don't come, I implore you. The fewer people there the better. I
say that in all seriousness. As regards the present, whatever you decide on,
maybe you can send it in time for the wedding day itself . . .
I am terribly tired, Tatusha! Not because of today's journey, nor because

[1] At the première in Moscow on 11 March 1902 the solo had been sung by
Alexander Smirnov and the performance conducted by Ziloti.

of this letter, but because of the whole winter, and I don't know when I shall be able to rest. When I get to Moscow, I shall have to spend a few days messing about with the priests, and then perhaps go to the country to write at least 12 songs before the wedding, so that there is something with which to pay the priests and to go abroad. And even then there will be no rest, because in the summer I shall have to write, write and write indefatigably if I am not to go bankrupt. And, as I've already said to you, I'm already terribly tired, worn out and weak. I really don't know what will happen!

Farewell, Tatusha! So, a résumé of my letter: forgive me and send me a present, and have pity on me.

It is not recorded what sort of present Natalya Skalon sent Rachmaninoff after this extraordinary note, but their correspondence seems to have ceased immediately.

The prime obstacle to the marriage between Rachmaninoff and Natalya Satina was that, under Orthodox Canon Law, first cousins were not permitted to marry; additional hazards were presented by the need for a certificate stating that Rachmaninoff worshipped and attended confession regularly, neither of which he did. Rachmaninoff's Aunt Mariya Trubnikova came to the rescue. She knew a priest at the Arkhangelsky Cathedral in the Moscow Kremlin, Fr Valentin Amfiteatrov,[2] and she arranged for Rachmaninoff to see him. Without doubt, considerable sums of money had to change hands before the doctrinal difficulties could be waived. Somebody advised Rachmaninoff that he stood a greater chance of arranging the ceremony in an army chapel, where the priests were answerable to the military authorities and not to the Orthodox Synod, and were therefore more likely to be willing to take risks. Thus on 29 April 1902 Rachmaninoff and Natalya Satina were married in the barracks of the 6th Tavrichesky Regiment on the outskirts of Moscow. As Natalya later recalled,

> I drove in a carriage and wore a wedding dress. It was bucketing with rain, and to get to the church we had to go through endless barracks. Soldiers were lying on bunks, and looked at us with amazement. Ziloti and Brandukov acted as best men. Ziloti . . . whispered to me in fun: 'You can still change your mind. It's not too late.' Sergey Vasilyevich was in tails, very serious, and I, of course, was terribly nervous. From the church we went straight to Ziloti's, where there were refreshments and champagne. After that we quickly changed and went straight to the station.[3]

[2] Father of the writer Alexander Valentinovich Amfiteatrov (1862–1938). See A. A. Trubnikova, 'Sergey Rakhmaninov', *Ogonyok* (27 January 1946), pp. 20–1.

[3] N. A. Rackmaninova, 'S. V. Rakhmaninov', *Vospominaniya o Rakhmaninove*, vol. ii, ed. Z. A. Apetian (Moscow, 5/1988), p. 292.

The bizarre wedding was followed by a fairly conventional, if lengthy, honeymoon; the couple visited Vienna and Venice, and then travelled to Switzerland, where Morozov stayed with them in their hotel near Lucerne, and where Rachmaninoff completed his set of 12 Songs op. 21. From there they went to Bayreuth to attend part of the Festival, and did not return to Russia until August. They went straight to Ivanovka, moving in to the smaller of the estate's two houses, which the Satins had given to them as a wedding present. The small study overlooking the garden, in which Rachmaninoff had already worked so successfully on the Second Concerto, was now his own, and he got down straightaway to preparing the score of *Spring* for publication by Gutheil the following year, having persuaded Morozov to write into the score Vladimir Chumikov's German translation of the Nekrasov text. He also began a new piano composition, the Variations on a Theme of Chopin.

After their long absence abroad and at Ivanovka the Rachmaninoffs returned to Moscow and in October moved into a flat in the America block on the Vozdvizhenka, where Rachmaninoff had spent some of his bachelor days. During the autumn Rachmaninoff accepted an undemanding appointment as music teacher at the St Ekaterina Ladies' College[4] and later at the Elizavetinsky Institute. As with his earlier job at the Mariinsky Academy, he faced neither with particular enthusiasm, but was only required to teach piano once or twice a week and to be present at examinations. His own professional life as composer and pianist had to take prime place, and, almost immediately after his arrival back in Moscow he found himself in the middle of the old conflict between Ziloti and Safonov. He had been invited to play his Second Concerto in Vienna and Prague, and he discovered that the performances were to be conducted by Safonov. While anxious to accept the engagement and the handsome fee, he was unwilling that this should seem to be a mark of ingratitude or disloyalty to his cousin Ziloti. He therefore sought advice of Taneyev, who assured him that he could accept the lucrative engagements without appearing to fawn on Safonov. For his advice Rachmaninoff presented Taneyev with a copy of the Cello Sonata, specially inscribed 'To dear Sergey Ivanovich Taneyev, who came to my aid yet again today. A deeply respectful and grateful S. Rachmaninoff, 28 November 1902'.

Shortly after his return from these foreign concerts in the spring of

---

[4] See M. M. Ellanskaya, 'S. V. Rakhmaninov v Uchilishche ordena sv. Ekateriny', *Vospominaniya o Rakhmaninove*, vol. i, ed. Z. A. Apetian (Moscow, 5/1988), pp. 390–96.

1903 his first daughter, Irina, was born on 14 May, but the happiness of this event was considerably marred by the illnesses of Irina, Natalya and Rachmaninoff himself. As a result, he was able to do little work during the early part of the summer holiday at Ivanovka, but by August they had all recovered sufficiently for him to begin work on a new opera, *Skupoy rytsar'* ('The Miserly Knight'), for which he set Pushkin's dramatic poem (1830) more or less word-for-word. This occupied him until the following spring, when he committed himself to two time-consuming engagements for the next season, one to conduct a series of operas at the Bolshoy Theatre and another to take on some orchestral concerts planned by the husband-and-wife organizers of the Moscow Music-Lovers' Circle, Arkady and Mariya Kerzin, he a lawyer by profession, she a pianist.

It was, therefore, a very busy Rachmaninoff who, in March, finally took up the threads of his other long-contemplated opera, *Francesca da Rimini*. Irina's illness again interrupted progress on the work, but an even greater obstacle was presented by Modest Tchaikovsky, who made very unsatisfactory attempts to write the libretto (see pp. 132–7). However, on 21 July 1904 Rachmaninoff was able to report to Nikita Morozov, who had just been checking through the German translation of *The Miserly Knight*:

> A week ago I sent off the prologue of *Francesca* to be translated.[5] One scene and the epilogue are left to do. As for the Bolshoy Theatre, I am still not prepared because I want to finish *Francesca* soon; this begins not merely to worry me but to torment me. If I begin to learn the operas, then I shall never finish *Francesca*.

He decided that *Francesca* should be finished at all costs, as he was anxious for it to be performed with *The Miserly Knight* in December, during his own season at the Bolshoy. He rushed to complete the piano score, and left himself with only a month to study the operas. Luckily, for his first night on 3 September 1904 he was to conduct Dargomyzhsky's *Rusalka*, well known from his experiences at Mamontov's Private Opera, and his performance was warmly acclaimed by the critics. Nikolay Kashkin, for example, commented that 'the first appearance of the young *Kapellmeister* this season justified the hopes placed upon him . . . Even in the first bars of the overture the audience began to feel a freshness and cheerfulness,

[5] Like *The Miserly Knight*, the score of *Francesca da Rimini* was published with a Russian and German text.

clearly revealing the rich and lively temperament of the conductor'.[6]

Rachmaninoff's other engagements for the season were *Eugene Onegin*, *Prince Igor*, *A Life for the Tsar*, *The Queen of Spades*, *Oprichnik*, Rubinstein's *Demon*, his own *Aleko* with Shalyapin in the name part, and finally *Boris Godunov* on 27 January 1905. Besides opera he conducted several programmes of Russian orchestral music for the Kerzins, and then retired to Ivanovka to work on the orchestration of *Francesca*, which he had been unable to complete in time for the 1904–5 Bolshoy season. Ironically, although his conducting engagements had precluded other creative work, he had been awarded a prize for one of his own compositions at the end of 1904. In that year Mitrofan Belyayev, who had already been instrumental in having Rachmaninoff's D minor Symphony performed in 1897, established a series of monetary prizes to encourage Russian composers. These 'Glinka Awards' were administered by a committee consisting of Lyadov, Glazunov and Rimsky-Korsakov, and, although Belyayev was primarily associated with the St Petersburg composers, the 1904 1000-ruble prize went to Taneyev, doyen of the Moscow circle, for his First Symphony. The other recipients of smaller prizes were Arensky, Lyapunov, Skryabin and Rachmaninoff, who was awarded 500 rubles for his Second Piano Concerto.

After completing the scoring of *Francesca* in the summer of 1905, Rachmaninoff had to prepare more operas for another season at the Bolshoy. His first engagement was to be an important one, the Moscow première of Rimsky-Korsakov's opera *Pan Voyevoda* on 27 September 1905. Rimsky travelled to Moscow to attend the rehearsals and performance, and was so impressed by Rachmaninoff that he also asked him to conduct his recently completed opera, *The Invisible City of Kitezh*, should it ever be produced at the Bolshoy. However, the increasing unease in the political situation in Russia convinced Rachmaninoff that it was unwise to remain employed in a State institution like the Bolshoy. The strikes and disturbances which had occurred throughout 1905 following the January massacre before the Winter Palace finally persuaded him that he needed to leave Russia for a while. The level of his concern about the state of life and the arts in Russia can be judged from an open letter which he and 28 other musicians wrote to the newspaper *Nashi dni*:

[6] N. D. Kashkin, in *Russkiy listok* (5 September 1904); quoted in Yu. V. Keldysh, *Rakhmaninov i evo vremya* (Moscow, 1973), p. 211.

'Only art that is free is vital, only creativity which is free is joyful.' We musicians associate ourselves entirely with these fine words by our artist colleagues. The freedom of art must not be limited by anything else in the world other than the inner self-determination of the artist and the fundamental requirements of society, if it wants to be truly powerful, truly sacred and able to respond to the deepest spiritual needs of the human soul. But when life is bound hand and foot, art cannot be free, for feeling is only part of life. When there is freedom neither of thought nor of conscience in the country, no freedom of speech or the press, when obstacles are raised against all the keen creative undertakings by the people, then artistic creativity withers. The title 'free artist' then sounds like a bitter joke. We are not free artists, but, like the rest of the Russian citizens, are victims without rights in today's abnormal socio-legal conditions. We are convinced that there is only one way out of these conditions: Russia must at last embark on the road to radical reforms . . .[7]

It was obviously time for Rachmaninoff to seek a change of surroundings. After seeing his two operas safely through their premières in January 1906, he resigned on 12 February and left almost at once for a holiday in Italy.

Staying at first in a hotel in Florence and then moving into a roomy villa called the Marina di Pisa, Rachmaninoff quickly settled down to work on a new opera project, *Salammbô*. He sketched a detailed scenario from Flaubert's novel, and sent it to Morozov with a request to approach the poet Mikhail Svobodin about writing a libretto. Svobodin was so dilatory that Morozov embarked on the project himself and eventually passed it on to another of Rachmaninoff's old Conservatory colleagues, Mikhail Slonov. By the end of May Slonov had still not produced a text which entirely satisfied Rachmaninoff, and he abandoned the whole idea without writing a single note. Although the inadequacies of the libretto were the prime cause, he was again troubled by his daughter's ill-health and was also deeply embroiled in administrative duties. He was called upon to advise Brandukov, recently appointed director of the Philharmonic Society's Academy of Music and Drama in Moscow, on whom he should employ as instrumental and singing teachers, and also had to decide for himself which engagements to accept for the following season. He had three offers: one to conduct at the Bolshoy Theatre for a fee of 8000 rubles, another to conduct ten concerts for the Russian Musical

[7] Letter, dated 2 February 1905, in *Nashi dni* (no. 37); quoted in A. V. Ossovsky (ed.), *Nikolay Andreyevich Rimsky-Korsakov: Vospominaniya V. V. Yastrebtseva*, vol. ii (Leningrad, 1960), p. 327.

Staying at first in a hotel in Florence and then moving into a roomy

Society for 4500 rubles and three Kerzin concerts for 900 rubles, together with a possible contract for an American tour. In July he decided to reject the operas and the tour, and to concentrate on the orchestral concerts. He was keen to perform Glazunov's new symphony, no. 8 in E flat, and also wrote to Rimsky-Korsakov expressing an interest in performing excerpts from *Kitezh* and his orchestral piece *Dubinushka* ('The Little Oak Stick'), an arrangement of the sardonic folksong which had achieved widespread popularity with the revolutionaries, if not with the authorities.

By the middle of July Rachmaninoff was so concerned about Irina's recurrent illness that he sent the family from Pisa to seek medical advice in Florence, and finally took them back to Russia to consult the more trusted doctors in Moscow. Irina recovered completely, but Rachmaninoff was still anxious and restless, so much so that during August and September at Ivanovka he managed to compose only his set of 15 Songs op. 26. These, however, included one of his most serene, lyrical and beautifully imagined creations, the song *U moyevo okna* ('Before my window'): with its image of a blossoming, perfumed cherry tree, it encapsulates perfectly the stillness and magic of Ivanovka itself which Rachmaninoff could see from his own study window. In August he heard from Boris Jurgenson, who, with his brother Grigory, had inherited his father's publishing business, that the Russian Musical Society was in a state of chaos. The political unrest in Russia increased his doubt as to whether any invitations to perform and conduct could be accepted with any certainty that the concerts would take place. He therefore cancelled his concerts, resigned from all his commitments in Russia, and in the autumn decided to leave with his family to live in Germany, where, unrecognized and undisturbed in their retreat at Dresden, he was able to devote himself entirely to composition.

His first thoughts turned once more to opera. In great secrecy he approached Slonov about preparing a libretto from Maeterlinck's play *Monna Vanna*, and work progressed so well that by 15 April 1907 he had completed the first act in piano score. In June he attempted to cut down to a reasonable size Slonov's 1000-line text for the second act, and he composed fragments of the music; by July, however, other work had intervened, and when he again took up the work in 1908 he discovered an insuperable hazard. Maeterlinck's contract with Heugel's, the music-publishers, prevented him from granting the international opera rights to any composer but Henri

Février (whose own *Monna Vanna* was eventually produced at the Paris Opéra in January 1909). Rachmaninoff could have limited the performance of his opera to Russia, not then a signatory to the copyright convention, but, disheartened, he decided not to pursue the idea, though he kept the completed parts of the score with him until the last days of his life.

The work which first interrupted *Monna Vanna* in the spring of 1907 was the orchestration of a new symphony, the Second in E minor, with which the surviving music of *Monna Vanna* shows a marked affinity. Displaying his characteristic reserve and love of surprise, he had worked on it without telling any of his acquaintances in Russia, but he was compelled to say something when Slonov read in a Russian newspaper that the symphony was complete. Rachmaninoff added a postscript to a letter from Dresden on 11 February 1907: 'I have composed a symphony. It's true! It's only ready in rough. I finished it a month ago, and immediately put it aside. It was a severe worry to me and I am not going to think about it any more. But I am mystified how the newspapers got onto it!' Despite his absence abroad he had certainly not been forgotten in Russia. In 1906 the Glinka Award Committee had again given him a prize, 500 rubles for *Spring*, and the Kerzins had arranged an all-Rachmaninoff programme for one of their Music Circle concerts on 12 February 1907. In the first half his op. 26 Songs were to be performed for the first time, and at Rachmaninoff's request Goldenveyzer played the taxing piano parts; in the second half Goldenveyzer, Brandukov and the violinist Karl Grigorovich performed the *Trio élégiaque* op. 9, specially revised by Rachmaninoff for the occasion.

With much of the Second Symphony (and also the First Piano Sonata) to show for his stay in Dresden, Rachmaninoff prepared to leave Germany to spend the summer in Russia. Natalya, who was expecting their second child, left for Moscow on 10 May, but Rachmaninoff had to travel first to Paris to take part in the Saison Russe organized by Dyagilev. Shortly after the concert there on 26 May, at which he played his Second Concerto and conducted *Spring* with Shalyapin singing the solo part, he joined his wife at Ivanovka to await the birth of what he was sure would be a son. On 21 June at 9.05 in the morning Natalya gave birth to their second daughter, whom they christened Tatyana. The newly augmented family rested throughout the summer in Russia, and after a few concerts abroad in the autumn they all returned to their winter retreat in Dresden. At

Christmas they entertained the Satins and Rachmaninoff's elder brother Vladimir. Glad as he was to be surrounded by his relatives, Rachmaninoff was equally pleased when the festivities were over and he could concentrate on the final corrections to the Second Symphony in preparation for its first performance in St Petersburg on 26 January 1908. He himself conducted, as he did also at the Moscow première on 2 February. After the Moscow performance he repeated the symphony in Warsaw before returning to Dresden, where he put the finishing touches to the scores of the symphony and the First Piano Sonata before sending them off to the publisher. He also contemplated revising the First Symphony, the Capriccio on Gypsy Themes and the First Concerto, but only the concerto was ever recast, and that some nine years later.

It was about this time that one of Rachmaninoff's admirers began to show her esteem by sending to each concert a bouquet of blossom, always white lilac, whatever the season. Not a concert or train journey would pass without an array of white lilac appearing on the platform or in the railway carriage; this happened not only in Russia, but at his concerts abroad, and it was not until many years later that the family discovered that this admirer was one Fekla Yakovlevna Rousseau, a former teacher now in middle-age who had developed a positive passion for Rachmaninoff's music and playing. For the first performance of *The Bells* she sent a particularly intricate display of lilac delicately woven into the shape of a bell, and in gratitude Rachmaninoff sent her his rough copy of the Poe poem, with the inscription 'B.S., S. Rachmaninoff, 1 January 1914'; B.S. was his abbreviation for 'Belaya siren' (White Lilac), the name by which the Rachmaninoffs always referred to the admirer, whom Rachmaninoff never met.

The family were to spend the summer of 1908 at Ivanovka as usual, though before that Rachmaninoff had to fulfil one more engagement, to play the Second Concerto in London at Queen's Hall on 26 May under Kusevitsky. The concert was well received, and it concluded a season which had been highly successful for Rachmaninoff both as composer and performer:

> The direct expression of the work, the extraordinary precision and exactitude of his playing, and even the strict economy of movement of arms and hands which M. Rachmaninoff exercises, all contributed to the impression of completeness of performance. The slow movement was played by soloist and orchestra with deep feeling, and the brilliant effect of

the finale could scarcely have been surpassed, and yet the freedom from extravagance of any kind was the most remarkable feature. We wished that all the amateur and other pianists, who delight in producing sensational effects with his prelude in C sharp minor, could have heard the composer playing it as his second encore. His crisp, almost rigid, treatment of it would be a revelation to many.[8]

Stopping off only at Brest station to collect some tobacco sent to him from Warsaw by Zatayevich, he travelled with all haste to join his family. He spent much of the summer reading through Gutheil's proofs of the Second Symphony, a time-consuming task which precluded all other work, save the composition of a musical letter of greeting to Stanislavsky on the tenth anniversary of the founding of the Moscow Art Theatre. Shalyapin sang the song in Moscow at a special celebration on 14 October, and a few days later Konstantin Igumnov gave the first performance of the First Piano Sonata. Igumnov had been intimately acquainted with the work since its conception, for he had been present on an evening late in the spring of 1907 when Rachmaninoff played it privately for some friends in the Moscow flat belonging to the pianist Vladimir Vilshau. He had also advised Rachmaninoff on certain changes, and when he compared the two versions of the manuscript Igumnov found that in the first movement much of the recapitulation had been rewritten and shortened by more than 50 bars; in the last movement about 60 bars had been cut, mainly from the recapitulation. Rachmaninoff could not attend Igumnov's concert, as he had already returned to Dresden. Nor could he hear the repeat performances in Leipzig and Berlin on 10 and 16 November, as he had by then embarked upon a typically energetic concert season. After conducting the Second Symphony in Antwerp, he had a brief rest in Dresden before performing the second *Trio élégiaque* in Berlin with members of the Czech Quartet. From there he went on to Holland to rehearse his Second Concerto for a series of concerts in Amsterdam and The Hague. The conductor for these performances was Willem Mengelberg, whose musicianship impressed Rachmaninoff so much that a few years later he dedicated to him, and the Concertgebouw Orchestra, his choral symphony *The Bells*.

Returning to live in Dresden, with only a brief trip away to play at a concert in Frankfurt-am-Main, Rachmaninoff learnt that the Glinka Awards committee had again decided to give him a prize, this time the

[8] *The Times* (28 May 1908), p. 12.

much coveted 1000 rubles for his Second Symphony, Skryabin taking second place with a 700-ruble prize for the *Poem of Ecstasy*. The award came as a particular surprise, as the symphony had been withdrawn by Nikisch from his two concerts in Berlin and Leipzig. Rachmaninoff suspected, however, that this was a purely personal sign of displeasure on Nikisch's part, because the symphony was dedicated to Taneyev, and not to him.

Early in 1909 more concerts in Russia encroached on his time, but back in Dresden in the spring he began work on another orchestral work, the symphonic poem *Ostrov myortvykh* ('The Isle of the Dead'), inspired by a black-and-white reproduction of Böcklin's painting, which Rachmaninoff had spotted in an exhibition. He completed the score by the middle of April and gave the première shortly afterwards at a Moscow Philharmonic Society concert. In the early days of the summer he began to contemplate with some apprehension his first extensive tour of the USA, though there were some doubts whether this would take place. Wolfsohn, his American agent, had died and the business had been taken over by his widow. Rachmaninoff returned his contract so that it could be endorsed by the new managers, and he supposed that they would be so delighted to rid themselves of an encumbrance that they would destroy it and cancel the tour. By July, however, arrangements had been finalized and he prepared himself for the ordeal, his sole consolation being that the tour would earn him sufficient money to buy a car. He found little to appeal to him in the USA, where, as he told Zoya Pribytkova, 'all around one there are Americans and the "business", "business" they are always doing.' His list of engagements was formidable, starting at Northampton in Massachusetts on 4 November 1909 and lasting until the end of January 1910. The most important concert was in New York on 28 November, when he played a new piano concerto, his Third in D minor, which he had worked on secretly during the previous summer at Ivanovka. He repeated the concerto a few days later and again on 16 January at Carnegie Hall, this time with Mahler conducting. The concert was attended by the largest audience the Philharmonic Society had had for a Sunday concert that season, and the notices next day were complimentary but not uncritical:

> The impression made at the earlier performances of the essential dignity and beauty of the music and of the composer's playing was deepened, and the audience was quite as enthusiastic in its expression of appreciation as at the performance at The New Theatre on 28 November last and at the Carnegie

Hall two days later. It is regrettable that the feeling to which expression
was given after the first production, that the composition, despite its many
beauties, suffers from over length, was also confirmed. There is remplis-
sage in the first and last movements which could be removed to the
advantage of the work. Judicious curtailment would help the concerto to a
deservedly long term of life.[9]

The work grows in impressiveness upon acquaintance and will doubtless take rank among the most interesting piano concertos of recent years,
although its great length and extreme difficulties bar it from performances
by any but pianists of exceptional technical powers.[10]

When the tour was over Rachmaninoff returned thankfully to
Russia, declining further offers of American contracts and even the
Russian Musical Society's invitation to conduct in St Petersburg
during the following season. After a few concerts in Moscow and St
Petersburg, including the Russian première of the Third Concerto, he
was content to retreat to Ivanovka. The relaxed atmosphere helped
him to complete several works, the 13 Preludes op. 32 and also his
most ambitious unaccompanied choral work up to that time, the
Liturgy of St John Chrysostom op. 31. He sought advice on various
liturgical points from Alexander Kastalsky, director of the Synodical
Academy where the Liturgy was first performed later in the year under
Nikolay Danilin. Rachmaninoff conducted it himself some months
later on 25 March 1911 in a performance by the Mariinsky Theatre
chorus in St Petersburg, his last concert in a busy season which had
included several performances of the Third Concerto, a number of
conducting engagements in Moscow, St Petersburg, Kiev, Odessa and
Warsaw, and a special memorial concert to the actress Vera Komissarzhevskaya on 10 February, at which he and Ziloti played the Suite
no. 2 for two pianos.

During the summer of 1911 there were changes at Ivanovka. The
Satin parents had made over the whole estate to two of their children,
Vladimir and Natalya, Rachmaninoff's wife. This effectively meant
that Rachmaninoff himself was in charge of the estate's affairs, buying
new machinery, improving the stock and crop yield and overseeing the
day-to-day business. 'What a job!',[11] he exclaimed in the spring of
1911, while evidently enjoying every minute of it. The village of
Ivanovka was not (nor is it now) large. During Rachmaninoff's time

[9] *New York Daily Tribune* (17 January 1910), p. 7.
[10] *New York Herald* (17 January 1910), p. 12.
[11] letter from Rachmaninoff to Maksimilian Kreytser (20 April 1911).

there, it consisted of only about a hundred peasant homes and farms. The estate itself, however, was comfortably sized, and was surrounded for as far as the eye could see by fields of rye, wheat and oats, flax, millet and sunflowers. The land was laid out according to the English plan, with parkland, ponds and summerhouses, gardens, orchards and copses. With all that and two houses (the Satins' and his own), there was plenty to keep Rachmaninoff occupied, and he divided his day between practising, composing, study, rest, socializing and business matters. Yet despite his new responsibilities, Ivanovka retained that special quality of peace and quiet which Rachmaninoff needed for composition. Lyudmila Skalon, the middle of the three sisters who had played such an important part in Rachmaninoff's earlier years, recalled: 'In moments of creative inspiration he would stand concentrated and pensive, as if far away. He would avoid everyone, lock himself in his room or go out to his favourite "red" alley' [one of the several tree-lined avenues branching out from the main house; this one, of elms, maples and poplars, was called 'red' because there were broken bricks in among the soil. The path has now been built up and renovated, but a square of the original surface has been preserved]. 'From a distance', continues Lyudmila Skalon, 'one could see his tall figure in a Russian shirt. He would walk, head bowed, drumming his fingers on his chest and sort of singing to himself.'[12] That was in the 1890s, but Rachmaninoff's way of working at Ivanovka did not change significantly through the years. Ivanovka, with its remote hideaways, was ideal for a composer seeking both inspiration and silence, and in the summer of 1911 he composed nine *Etudes-tableaux* for piano, op. 33, and in the autumn he began another active season with eight concerts in England, a tour of cities in the south of Russia, and several more performing and conducting engagements in St Petersburg. This included a concert on 10 December at which he conducted Skryabin's Piano Concerto with Skryabin himself as soloist, mystifying the musical circles in Russia who had always imagined Skryabin and Rachmaninoff to be the bitterest of enemies. In the spring of 1912 Rachmaninoff did become involved in a dispute, not with Skryabin but with the Russian Musical Society. Early in 1900 he had been invited by Princess Helene of Saxe-Altenburg, the newly elected President of the Society, to be her Vice-President. He accepted

[12] L. D. Rostovtsova (Skalon), 'Vospominaniya o S. V. Rakhmaninove', *Vospominaniya o Rakhmaninove*, vol. i, ed. Z. A. Apetian (Moscow, 5/1988), p. 236.

and immediately devoted himself to his duties with characteristic enthusiasm, inspecting the music schools attached to many outlying branches of the Society and also devising a plan to revise the regulations of the Moscow Conservatory. His old Conservatory colleague, Matvey Presman, had been responsible for founding and successfully running the Rostov-on-Don classes of the Russian Musical Society in 1896, and his work had been highly praised by the Society on his tenth anniversary in 1906. In 1911, however, Presman recommended that one of the teachers in the Nakhichevan branch of the Rostov Music Academy should be reprimanded for failing to carry out his duties. The rest of the committee in Rostov did not agree with Presman and in January 1912 passed a resolution relieving him of his post as director of the Rostov Academy. The central committee of the Society, sitting in Moscow, could not intervene, and in protest Rachmaninoff submitted his resignation to Princess Helene on 21 January, believing that the Society would so value his services that it would reverse its decision over Presman. This did not happen; Presman left Rostov and moved to Saratov, Rachmaninoff withdrew his resignation in March and for a few months continued to serve the Society. On 28 May, however, he resigned finally, and the Society never again appointed a Vice-President.

Earlier in the year, shortly after he had taken part in one of the Kerzin concerts, Rachmaninoff received a letter from a female admirer. This was not in itself unusual: he had his regular supply of white lilac as evidence of that. This particular letter, however, was signed simply 'Re', though Rachmaninoff discovered quite quickly that the sender was the poet Marietta Shaginian. Thus began a curiously distant but highly fruitful association which lasted until his final days in Russia. Shaginian sent him a number of books of poems, and early in 1913 dedicated to him an anthology of her own verse entitled *Orientalia*. At Rachmaninoff's request she suggested some poems for a set of songs (op. 34) he was contemplating in the spring of 1912, and, as he told her in a letter of 19 June, about half of them were composed to poems suggested by her. The first in the group, a setting of Pushkin's poem of 1828, *The Muse*, he dedicated appropriately to the muse herself, Shaginian.

Just before completing these songs Rachmaninoff had displayed almost childlike excitement at the acquisition of a motorcar (a Loreley), which had been delivered from Moscow and was then one of the few cars to be seen in the country districts of Russia. At first he found cause to complain vehemently to the suppliers, Krylov's, because the car had come without its hood, box of tools and spare wheel. Also he discovered during test runs that the acceleration was poor, and he told Krylov's that the Ford 20 h.p., a much less powerful car, had better acceleration and was nearly half the price of his own. The fitting of a new carburettor partially overcame the problem, and by the following year he was telling Marietta Shaginian that whenever work became too much for him he would get into his car and drive away to the open country. Indeed, work was particularly pressing during the 1912–13 season, for he had undertaken to appear at so many concerts that composition was likely to be impossible. After his opening concert on 6 October, a conducting engagement with the Moscow Philharmonic Society, he began to suffer stiffness in his hands and was compelled to write to St Petersburg withdrawing from a concert at which he was to have played Tchaikovsky's First Concerto under Emil Cooper. However, he continued his taxing schedule in Moscow, conducting four more concerts for the Philharmonic Society in addition to a special Grieg concert, a memorial evening to the composer Ilya Satz who had died on 11 October, and two more concerts at which he had to accompany the singers Antonina Nezhdanova and Leonid Sobinov. He had been booked to conduct six concerts for the Philharmonic Society, but after the fifth of them on 1 December he was so tired that he cancelled his final appearance and left almost at once for a holiday.

Taking his family with him, he travelled first to Switzerland and then on to Rome, where they lived in a flat on the Piazza di Spagna, once occupied by the Tchaikovsky brothers. Here his inspiration to compose, frustrated for so long by conducting and playing commitments, was allowed to come to the fore, and he immediately began to write his largest choral work, *Kolokola* ('The Bells'). During the previous summer he had been able to do no more than sketch ideas for a new symphony, but, while he was doing so, a young cellist named Danilova sent him anonymously a typescript copy of Edgar Allan Poe's poem in a Russian adaptation by the symbolist poet Konstantin Balmont. The musical potential of Poe's verses immediately appealed to him. While in Rome he was able to complete much of the score, but work was interrupted abruptly when his two daughters contracted typhoid fever. The family rushed to Berlin to consult doctors, and for some time Tatyana lay desperately ill in hospital. Both recovered sufficiently to travel, and the family decided to return to Ivanovka to allow them to convalesce. There Rachmaninoff again settled down to work, completing not only the orchestration of *The Bells* but also the Second Piano Sonata in B flat minor, which he had been contemplating since January. Later in the year he conducted the first performance of this choral symphony, and a few days afterwards gave the première of his new sonata at a recital on 3 December.

During the early days of 1914 Rachmaninoff was on a concert tour of England, and while there he agreed that *The Bells* should have its British première at the Sheffield Festival in the autumn. However, because of the outbreak of the First World War, the concert had to be cancelled, and it was not until 1921 that Sir Henry Wood gave the first performance with the Liverpool Philharmonic Society. The Sheffield performance did not take place until 1936:

> Rachmaninoff came to England to supervise the performance of *The Bells* which I had originally introduced to England with the Liverpool Philhar-monic Society in 1921, and had repeated at the Norwich Festival of 1927. For the Sheffield performance Rachmaninoff remodelled the choral parts of the third movement, as it was found in previous performances that there were too many notes and words to be chorally effective. I was most grateful to him for going to the trouble and expense of having the movement re-engraved specially for Sheffield. Isobel Baillie, Parry Jones and Harold Williams were the soloists; they excelled themselves (as did the chorus) no doubt inspired by the presence of Rachmaninoff. I hope I may hear again, one day, Harold Williams's beautiful quality intoning 'Hear the tolling of the Bells, mournful Bells.'[13]

The spring and summer of 1914 were again spent at Ivanovka, where Rachmaninoff received an invitation to set to music a scene from *King Lear* in connection with the 350th anniversary of Shake-speare's birth. Marietta Shaginian sent him a Russian translation of the play, but the music was never completed and the manuscript is lost. In fact he composed nothing of importance during 1914 and throughout the summer concerned himself mainly with *The Bells*, which was being transcribed for piano by Goldenveyzer. In September the family went to stay with Natalya's brother Vladimir on his estate, Pokrovskoye, in the Ryazan district, and while there Rachmaninoff agreed to conduct a special concert in the autumn dedicated to the memory of Lyadov, who had died in August. The concert took place in Moscow on 25 October, and, apart from Rachmaninoff's own Second

---

[13] H. J. Wood, *My Life of Music* (London, 1938), p. 336.

Symphony, the programme consisted entirely of works by Lyadov: *Baba-Yaga* op. 56, Eight Russian Folksongs op. 58, *Volshebnoye ozero* ('The Enchanted Lake') op. 62, *Kikimora* op. 63, and *Iz Apokalipsisa* ('From the Book of Revelation') op. 66. Shortly afterwards he toured some south Russian cities with Kusevitsky, playing his Second and Third Concertos in concerts for the war effort.

Returning to Moscow he considered breaking his year's abstention from composition by writing a ballet called *Skify* ('The Scythians'). The libretto was by the choreographers Alexander Gorsky and Kasyan Goleyzovsky, on whose evidence Rachmaninoff is said to have written part of the music and later incorporated it into his last orchestral work, the Symphonic Dances. However, the score of the completed portion of the ballet has not survived, so it is not possible to verify the fact. A composition which has survived from the period is the *Vsenoshchnoye bdeniye* ('All-night Vigil'), written at extraordinary speed during January and February 1915: at least, the score is said to have been written in 1915, but, bearing in mind Rachmaninoff's long gestatory thought-processes and the work's intensity, it had probably been in his mind for some while before he actually set it down on paper. Certainly his finest sacred work, it was dedicated to the memory of Stepan Smolensky, the former director of the Court Chapel Choir, and it was first performed at another fundraising concert for the war on 10 March.

In May the Rachmaninoffs went to stay with Ziloti in Finland, and it was there that they all heard of the sudden death of Taneyev on 6 June. In April Skryabin had died, and while attending the funeral Taneyev had caught a severe chill, to which he finally succumbed. Rachmaninoff had always had great admiration for Taneyev, whom he had known ever since his days at Zverev's house 25 years before. In the warm tribute which he wrote for the *Russkiye vedomosti* he revealed just how great Taneyev's influence had been:

> For all of us who knew him and sought him out, he was the finest judge, possessing wisdom, a sense of justice, affability and simplicity. He was a model in everything, in his every act, for everything he did he only did well. Through his personal example he taught us how to live, how to think, how to work, even how to speak, for he spoke in a particularly Taneyev way: concisely, clearly and to the point.[14]

By this time the war was taking its toll. Rachmaninoff grew more and more depressed and composed nothing for over 18 months after the

[14] S. Rakhmaninov, 'S. I. Taneyev', *Russkiye vedomosti* (16 June 1915), p. 4.

All-night Vigil. In August 1915 he had to go to Tambov to be assessed for his suitability for war work. The tribunal took place in the town's music school (now the Rachmaninoff Music College), with which he had had a friendly association, having inspected it (favourably) as long ago as 1909 on behalf of the Russian Musical Society. But the concert hall was now given over to military interviews. 'If I am called up', he wrote to Alexander Goldenveyzer (9 August 1915), 'I shall almost certainly be given the post as precentor to an episcopal choir or conductor in the municipal park at Tambov. And that won't be bad . . .' In the event, Rachmaninoff was excused active service on health grounds, and on 26 September he began a fairly normal, exhausting season of concerts with a performance of Skryabin's Piano Concerto. This was part of a plan, made shortly after Skryabin's death, to perform a number of his piano works, and it was a plan which misfired, for his recitals of Skryabin's music were received by the press with the utmost hostility. In his autobiography Prokofiev, admittedly no friend of Rachmaninoff, said that when Skryabin had played the Fifth Piano Sonata the music somehow took wing; when Rachmaninoff played it, all the notes were extraordinarily clear but remained firmly on the ground. After the recital Prokofiev, realizing that the music was open to more than one interpretation, remarked to Rachmaninoff, 'After all, Sergey Vasilyevich, you played very well!' Rachmaninoff retorted, 'And I suppose you thought I would play badly.'[15] Prokofiev rarely spoke to Rachmaninoff again. Other critics, both in Moscow and Petrograd, were yet more bitter in their condemnation of Rachmaninoff's interpretation of Skyrabin, praising the technical facility but suggesting that he had failed to grasp the unique emotional power of Skryabin's music.

Upset but undaunted, Rachmaninoff continued his season, and on 30 November performed his Third Concerto with Kusevitsky, who had arranged an all-Rachmaninoff programme containing also *Spring* and *The Bells.* Shortly after a concert with Nezhdanova in the New Year, Rachmaninoff met again another old friend, Nina Koshits, the soprano. She asked Rachmaninoff if they could do some concerts together, and Rachmaninoff wrote to arrange it with Ziloti. The first concert took place in Moscow in October, when Koshits

---

[15] S. I. Shlifshteyn (ed.), *S. S. Prokof'yev: materialy, dokumenty, vospominaniya* (Moscow, 1956), pp. 35–6.

sang the aria 'O ne riday moy Paolo' from Rachmaninoff's *Francesca da Rimini*. To her Rachmaninoff dedicated his recently completed Six Songs, op. 38, of which she gave the first performance on 24 October 1916.

A few months earlier, on returning from a summer holiday in the southern resorts of Essentuki and Kislovodsk, Rachmaninoff learnt of the death of his father, who had gone to spend part of the summer at Ivanovka. Despite the fact that Vasily Arkadyevich had deserted the family, Rachmaninoff had always retained a special affection for him. For years he had sent him regular gifts of money, and he had maintained, too, that of all his close relatives only his father had any real concern for him. The uneasy and unsettling political situation in Russia served only to augment Rachmaninoff's grief. By November 1916 it seemed as grave as it could possibly be. Successive governments appointed by Nicholas II failed to make it any better, and there were strikes throughout the country. On 15 March 1917 the Tsar abdicated in favour of his brother, the Grand Duke Michael, but as he was unwilling to accept the crown the 300-year-old Romanov dynasty came to an end. That this had a deep effect on Rachmaninoff cannot be doubted, but for the time being he continued with his concerts. In fact, after playing Tchaikovsky's First Concerto with Kusevitsky on 13 March 1917, in a concert in aid of the army, he had offered his fee to the revolutionary effort, enclosing it in a letter of 14 March: 'Free artist S. Rachmaninoff donates to the needs of the free army the fee for his first concert in his free country.' This letter[16] is often seen as Rachmaninoff's acceptance of the new regime, yet this view does not take into account his letter to Ziloti of 1 June, in which he said that he was quite unable to work in the restless, threatening atmosphere prevailing in Russia:

> My dear Sasha, . . . I'm turning to you with a problem, which I ask you to deal with as quickly as possible and send me a reply . . . I will be brief . . . To begin with, just a few words of explanation. I have spent almost everything I have earned in my life on my estate at Ivanovka. At the moment about 120,000 [rubles] are tied up in Ivanovka. I can kiss goodbye to that and I think that ruin is in the offing so far as that goes. Aside from which, the conditions of life there are such that after spending three weeks there I have decided to return there no more. I still have about 30,000 in cash. Of course, that's 'something', particularly if I can work and earn . . .

[16] The original has never been found, but the text was published in *Russkiye vedomosti* on 15 March 1917.

But now I am frightened of another sort of ruin: everything around me makes it impossible for me to work and I am frightened of becoming completely apathetic. Everybody around me advises me to leave Russia for a while. But where to, and how? And is it possible?

My question to you is this: can you find a free moment with M.I. T[ereshchenko, an official at the Imperial Theatres] and ask his advice? Can I count on getting a passport to leave the country with my family, even if only to Norway, Denmark, Sweden . . . It doesn't matter where! Just somewhere! . . .

Is it possible to get permission by July? Can I take with me my remaining money? Or part of it? How much?

Ziloti could do nothing, and, after giving a concert in Yalta on 5 September 1917, Rachmaninoff returned to Moscow, resigning himself to remaining in Russia. In their flat on the Strastnoy Bulevard, which he and the family had occupied since 1905, and which – now part of the Ministry of Press and Information – is the only Moscow building to bear a commemorative Rachmaninoff plaque, he set to work on the revisions to the First Concerto, and completed the new, substantially altered score on 10 November. By this time the whole future of Russia had been changed by the October Revolution on 24/ 25 October, and Rachmaninoff found himself part of a collective, required to attend house committee meetings and to take his duty on guard at night. It was just then that he received an invitation to take part in some concerts in Stockholm; he saw this as the opportunity he had longed for, and immediately accepted. He left his family in Moscow and hurried to Petrograd to obtain the necessary visas for them all. Natalya and the two girls followed a few days later, and just before Christmas 1917 the whole family boarded the train for Scandinavia, ironically enough at the same station which had been the scene of Lenin's dramatic arrival only a few months earlier. They never returned to Russia.

4

Life in the New World

The discomfort of the journey only increased the family's anguish at having to leave behind them their homeland, their relations and their property at Ivanovka, confiscated by the Communist authorities. Eventually, the large wooden house would be razed to the ground, the smaller one, in which Rachmaninoff had done so much of his work, allowed to become derelict. Shalyapin had sent to the station some caviar and home-made bread, which doubtless was put to good use during their cold night journey across Finland to Sweden, which had to be made in a sledge. At the Swedish border they took a train for Stockholm, occupying sleeping compartments for part of the way, though they were woken up at 6 a.m. and moved to other carriages. Wearied and utterly miserable, they arrived in Stockholm on Christmas Eve, and for the first time spent Christmas many hundreds of miles away from their friends. So distressing did they find their isolation in this foreign country that, early in January, they moved to Denmark to join Nikolay Struve, a composer and member of the editorial board of Kusevitsky's Editions Russes de Musique, whom they had first met in Dresden and who had himself recently emigrated from Russia.

Rachmaninoff had to begin to think seriously about his own and his family's future. He was in debt and could scarcely hope to make a comfortable living from composition. As far as he could see, his only means of support was piano-playing and it was therefore from a desperate need for money rather than from any sense of ambition that at the age of 44 he embarked upon a new full-time career as a performer. Until this critical moment he had not needed to play for a living; his technique was rusty and his repertory was small by the standards set by contemporary virtuosos, centred as it was upon his own compositions, with only a few solo pieces by Chopin, Liszt, Tchaikovsky and a handful of concertos. He therefore had to practise. With Struve's help the family managed to rent the ground floor of a house in Copenhagen, and, despite the bitter cold and the lack of adequate heating, Rachmaninoff set to work. His new programmes were not ready for his first concert in Copenhagen in 15 February 1918, at which he performed his own Second Concerto with the Copenhagen Symphony under Georg Hoberg. On 22 February he gave a recital of his own works and then went on to Stockholm to give the concerts which had provided the original reason for leaving Russia. On 12 March he played his Second Concerto and Liszt's First, performing Tchaikovsky's First two days later. These three concertos and programmes of his own compositions were the staple ingredients of his concerts for the rest of the season in Malmö, Oslo and Copenhagen, and it was not until the end of the season that he could begin to think about developing his technique and broadening the scope of his repertory. By September he was ready to give two recitals, at Lund and Malmö, of Mozart, Schubert, Beethoven, Chopin and Tchaikovsky; during the month between 18 September and 18 October he gave 14 concerts, and on 2 October completed his commitments in Scandinavia with a performance of his Second and Third Concertos.

It was around this time that he received three offers from the USA, even though the concert season had already begun. He was asked to conduct the Cincinnati Symphony Orchestra for two years, to give 25 piano recitals, and also to conduct 110 concerts in 30 weeks for the Boston Symphony Orchestra. All three offers promised lavish fees and he considered them carefully; but he resolved to decline them all because he was reluctant to commit himself to any long-term contracts in a country he scarcely knew. The three offers did, however, convince him that the USA might be the answer to his financial problems, although he had loathed his first tour there in 1909. The sole hazard was that he did not have enough money for the fares for himself and his family. However, a Russian banker called Alexander Kamenka, a fellow émigré, offered to advance him the money for the journey and also a guarantee against loss of earnings when he got there. Gratefully the Rachmaninoffs accepted, packed their meagre belongings and on 1 November set sail from Oslo on the *Bergensfjord* for their new life in the New World. The crossing took ten days, and they arrived in New York harbour on 10 November. It was the day before the Armistice was signed, and on 11 November the family sat in their hotel and listened with bewilderment to the noisy celebrations outside. As soon as it became known that Rachmaninoff was staying at the Sherry Netherland Hotel on Central Park, hosts of people, fellow musicians, artists and ordinary visitors arrived to wish him well. One particularly useful visitor was a young lady called Dagmar Rybner. 'For a long time', she later recalled,

> I had loved [Rachmaninoff's] compositions and had played many of them. Hearing that he and his family had safely arrived in America and although I didn't know him, I wrote him a letter of greeting out of some impulse, adding that I would be glad to help him in some way ... Imagine my astonishment when next morning Mrs Rachmaninoff telephoned me and asked if it would be possible for me to go to the hotel, because Rachmaninoff very much needed advice. Needless to say, I abandoned all my work, and, snatching a bunch of roses on the way, hurried round.
>
> Mrs Rachmaninoff greeted me, but after a few minutes the curtains over the door leading to the bedroom twitched slightly, and out of the corner of my eye I saw Rachmaninoff himself, scrutinizing me. Soon he came shyly into the room, accompanied by his no less shy younger daughter, Tatyana. I realized that he did not like meeting people he did not know. When we had exchanged a few words, I suddenly felt that I was probably the right person for him and that he trusted me. He showed me his piano, piled high with letters, telegrams and all sorts of messages, and he asked me to help him 'with all these'. I got down to sorting out all his correspondence and dealing with telephone calls, and subsequently helped him generally in familiarizing himself with his new circumstances and looking into all sorts of problems which he could not solve himself, because he did not know the language and was unfamiliar with American ways.'[1]

Miss Rybner (later Mrs Barclay) was eminently suited to the post. She was the daughter of the Professor of Music at Columbia University and she herself had had a musical education. For several years she remained his secretary, invaluable aide and interpreter.

Among the visitors during these first few days in the USA was Josef Hofmann, who, having prepared the way by telling several American concert managers that they would be foolish not to add Rachmaninoff to their books, gave him much helpful advice on professional matters. Rachmaninoff decided to put the management of his concert affairs in the hands of Charles Ellis, who had already dealt with him over the Boston Symphony Orchestra's offer of concerts. During his American tours either Charles Ellis himself or one of his representatives would travel with Rachmaninoff; on some occasions this was Charles Foley, who, on Ellis's retirement, was to take over Rachmaninoff's manage-

---

[1] D. Barklay [Barclay], untitled article, *Vospominaniya o Rakhmaninove*, vol. ii, ed. Z. A. Apetian (Moscow, 5/1988), pp. 179–80.

ment entirely and who was to become his American publisher towards the end of his life. This problem disposed of, Rachmaninoff then had to decide which piano he would use. Various firms saw in him a possible advertising investment and offered him large sums to play their instruments. Yet he chose the piano given to him by the one firm which did not offer him money, Steinway's, and he formed a lasting friendship with the then managing director, Frederick Steinway. The problems of practising in a hotel room were alleviated when an American lady offered him the use of her studio, and, even before he had fully recovered from an attack of Spanish flu, he began to prepare for his first full American season, which he opened on 8 December 1918 with a recital in Providence.

If he had had doubts in Copenhagen that he would be able to make a living in the USA, these were swiftly dispelled during these first months, for he was engaged to play in 36 concerts, concluding with three charity evenings. After his final concert on 27 April, which he had opened with his own piano arrangement of the *Star-spangled Banner*, he decided to take his family to the West Coast. Here they occupied a house near San Francisco, where he had time to recuperate from his last season and prepare for the next. Opening on 10 October, his solo recitals included, besides his own works, the music of Mendelssohn, Chopin and Liszt; but his concerto performances still centred on his old favourites, the Tchaikovsky and Liszt concertos and his own First, Second and Third. The number of engagements was almost double that of the previous season, and for several years his life was to follow the same pattern: a hectic programme of concerts followed by relaxation and practice during the summer. By today's standards, when swift travel eases the passage between one concert venue and another, Rachmaninoff's schedules were punishing. It was also at the end of the 1919–20 season that he signed a recording contract with the Victor Talking Machine Company and began a long association with RCA, during which he produced historic recordings of most of his repertory, including all his own concertos.

For their summer holiday in 1920 the Rachmaninoffs took a house at Goshen, near New York, where they received the news that Nikolay Struve had been killed in Paris in a lift accident. Almost as if to counteract this further break in his links with Russia, Rachmaninoff managed in the autumn to contact his relatives to inform them that he was safe and well in the USA. Having established this line of communication he proceeded to arrange with his bank to send sums of money to the Satins, to his mother and to many colleagues including his old Conservatory friend Nikita Morozov. This was the start of a stream of parcels and monetary gifts which he sent from the USA to all sorts of people in Russia, particularly to the needy students of the conservatories and other musical institutions. Early in 1921 he made an application to visit Russia, and at the end of the 1920–1 season received the necessary papers, but by then he was ill in hospital. He had been troubled again by severe pains in his right temple. In Russia he had always attributed this to eyestrain and the continual bending over manuscript while he was composing. But he had composed nothing for three years, and the stabbing pains recurred with worrying frequency; only when he was on stage performing was there any relief. One American doctor diagnosed some disturbance in a facial nerve, others thought the root of the trouble was an infection, perhaps in the jaws or teeth. Finally he agreed to undergo surgery, and the news that he was in hospital and could not visit Russia started a rumour there that he had died. The operation had no effect, and it was not until the end of the 1920s, when he was treated in Paris by the Russian dentist Kostritsky, that he was finally relieved of the pain.

After leaving hospital Rachmaninoff decided to make his permanent home in an apartment at 33 Riverside Drive, in that desirable part of New York facing the Hudson River, where he planned to spend the autumns. For the summer the family rented a house at Locust Point in New Jersey, where they were visited by many Russian friends, including some from the Moscow Art Theatre. They consciously set about creating for themselves a small Russian community, where Russian was spoken and Russian customs were observed. After Dagmar Rybner resigned as secretary in 1922 to get married, Rachmaninoff engaged a Russian secretary, Evgeny Somov. He also employed a Russian chauffeur, a particularly necessary acquisition in the summer of 1921, for he had failed his test for a New Jersey driving licence. Whenever possible he consulted Russian doctors, and when his French cook left he replaced her with a Russian one.

In the autumn Rachmaninoff had to return to the realities of making money. He opened the new season on 10 November 1921, adding Debussy's *Children's Corner* to his programmes of Chopin, Liszt, Grieg and Beethoven. He continued his work for Russian sufferers with two benefit concerts, one on 2 April 1922 for the American Relief Administration and the other on 21 April for the relief of Russian students in the USA. A few days later he sailed to England to give two recitals on 6 and 20 May: Mozart now found a place in his Queen's Hall programmes (the A major Sonata K 331), together with Beethoven's E minor Sonata op. 90, Mendelssohn's Andante Cantabile and Rondo Capriccioso, a Chopin group and a selection of Rachmaninoff's own pieces. Natalya for once broke her custom of accompanying her husband to all his concerts by staying in the USA to look after Irina and Tatyana, who were in the throes of school examinations. It was prearranged that after their various commitments the whole family should meet in Dresden, where the Satin family had also recently settled. Sofiya Satina gives a description of the pleasant, relaxed atmosphere of this summer, which the Rachmaninoffs spent in a rented villa on the Emser Allee:

> After a short walk in the morning Rachmaninoff would drink coffee and, when he had glanced at the papers, he would work until breakfast. During the afternoon he would usually lie down for a short while; then he would sit down at the piano and after an hour or an hour and a half of work he would go for another walk. After dinner at 7 or 8 o'clock he would go with his whole family to spend the whole evening with the Satins, or else the Satins would visit the Rachmaninoffs.[2]

In the autumn Rachmaninoff returned to New York and embarked on his most crowded concert season yet, with 71 concerts between 10 November and 31 March. So formidable was the travelling, including visits to Cuba and Canada, that he decided to hire a railway carriage, which he equipped with an upright piano and personal belongings, thus creating a temporary home and obviating the need for packing and unpacking at different hotels. But soon he grew sick of the sight of the train and resumed the suitcase existence of a concert performer. In the summer the family returned to their Russian haven in New Jersey, where they were visited by Shalyapin, the theatre director Vasily Luzhsky and other members of the Moscow Art Theatre. It was just like the days when Rachmaninoff used to go with Shalyapin to the Crimea; they performed songs together until the small hours, despite his need to practise systematically each day.

From 1924 onwards Rachmaninoff decided to alter his annual routine so that he could spend some time in Europe. As a result he cut his programme for the American 1923–4 season by half, playing only 35 concerts between 13 November and 10 March. A fortnight later the

[2] S. Satina, 'Zapiska o S. V. Rakhmaninove', *Vospominaniya o Rakhmaninove*, vol. i, ed. Z. A. Apetian (Moscow, 5/1988), p. 65.

family set sail for Italy, where he rested for several weeks in Florence. From there they travelled on to Dresden and occupied the same villa on the Emser Allee which had been their home in 1922. It was while they were there that their elder daughter, Irina, announced her engagement to a Russian aristocrat, Prince Pyotr Volkonsky, and the family remained in Dresden for the wedding on 24 Septemner 1924. It was a marriage which was to end in tragedy, for less than a year later Volkonsky died suddenly, leaving Irina a widow at 22. Shortly afterwards she gave birth to a child, Rachmaninoff's first granddaughter, Sofiya. He was utterly devoted to her and always introduced her to visitors with pride and pleasure.

After the wedding Rachmaninoff, Natalya and their younger daughter left for England, Irina and her husband remaining in Dresden for the winter. Rachmaninoff was in England to give concerts during October: concerto engagements in London and Manchester, and recitals in London, Liverpool, Leeds, Bournemouth and Eastbourne. After playing the Second Concerto in Manchester, he sailed to the USA for his season there. He was soon back in Europe, however, for his summer break. Natalya, Irina and Pyotr Volkonsky sailed directly to France from the USA; Rachmaninoff and Tatyana went on to Holland and then to Dresden, where he rested for five weeks in a sanatorium while Tatyana stayed with the Satins. The family was reunited in Paris, and spent the summer in a villa 40 kilometres from Paris, the Château de Corbeville à Orsay.

During this summer holiday Rachmaninoff made several important resolutions. With the sudden death of his son-in-law he decided to found his own publishing house to help occupy the minds of his two daughters, particularly the widowed Irina. Based in Paris, the firm was called Tair, a name derived from the names *Ta*tyana and *I*rina. Its prime purpose was to publish the works of Russian émigré composers, and for many years Rachmaninoff's own works appeared under the Tair imprint. His other decision was to dispose of his property in the USA. After several exhausting seasons it seemed sensible to limit his number of engagements in the USA to no more than 25 in any one year; for the remainder of the year he would rest either in the USA or Europe, and make gramophone records. A permanent home in the USA was therefore an unnecessary extravagance, and they sold their apartment on Riverside Drive. The decision to limit his number of appearances came into effect immediately, for he undertook only 22 engagements in the USA between 29 October and 11 December. This gave him a nine months' break before the start of the next season, and at once his mind turned from performing to composition. He had long felt the need to add another concerto to his repertory. In fact, 12 years earlier, on 12 April 1914, the weekly magazine *Muzyka* had reported that he was working on a new concerto, his fourth, but the war severely affected his concentration and he was unable to complete it. He occasionally referred in letters to 'a large work begun while I was still in Russia' and it seems more than likely that he kept sketches and ideas for the concerto with him until he needed a new piece for his American audiences in 1926.

In the New York flat which the Rachmaninoffs were now occupying at 505 West End Avenue, he took out the sketches and began to put the concerto into shape. He worked at it throughout the spring and took it with him to Europe, where he completed the score in the villa Suchaistrasse in the Weisser Hirsch district of Dresden. He sent the score to be copied and, when it arrived back, his first reaction was that it was too long, so long in fact that, as he joked to Medtner,[3] it would have to be performed on consecutive nights, like *The Ring*. He put the score in his case and took the whole family off to Cannes, where they rented a villa belonging to the Rothschilds. Here he studied his new concerto and made certain cuts before returning to New York. He gave the first performance himself on 18 March 1927 in Philadelphia, during a concert which also included the première of another recently completed work, the Three Russian Songs for chorus and orchestra, op. 41. The poor, at times caustic, reviews of the concerto encouraged him to take yet another critical look at the score. In July he wrote to his friend, the composer and violinist Yuly Konyus in Paris, asking if he would undertake the tedious task of transferring to the orchestral parts all the corrections which he was noting in the full score. Konyus agreed, and Rachmaninoff, anxious to see the work in print, wrote to him again from Dresden on 28 July 1927: 'After one and a half months' solid work I have finished the corrections to my concerto. I am sending all the material to Paris and hope that, as you promised, you will enter all these corrections in the parts ... The first 12 bars are rewritten, and also the whole of the coda.' These pre-publication revisions were even more drastic than

[3] In a letter from Cannes of 9 September 1926; see Z. A. Apetian (ed.), *N. K. Metner: pis'ma* (Moscow, 1973), p. 548.

this last sentence suggests. As Robert Threlfall has pointed out,[4] he cut 21 bars from the first movement, 2 from the second, 91 from the finale, and made many alterations to the orchestration and piano writing. The score was published by Tair in 1928 but it was still greeted with indifference. After a few more performances in 1929 Rachmaninoff decided to withdraw the piece from his concerts until he had more time to examine its faults more closely.

He had begun his American concert season on 15 January 1928, and gave 31 recitals in the USA and one in London on 19 May, consisting mostly of Chopin, but also with Liszt's 'Dante' Sonata, some Busoni transcriptions of Bach and, of course, some Rachmaninoff. His final concert of the American season was on 22 April, another charity concert arranged for the benefit of Russian wounded in the war, for which he raised $4635. For the summer the family decided to return to France, but this time rented a villa, 'Les Pelouses', at Villers-sur-Mer, four to five hours' drive from Paris and not far from where their friend Medtner was living. Here, as was their custom, the family created a small Russian community and were visited by many of their Russian acquaintances, including the artist Konstantin Somov, who had painted Rachmaninoff's portrait during the summer at Corbeville in 1925. From France they went to Dresden, where Rachmaninoff planned to establish a base for a European concert tour. He gave 26 concerts in the autumn, visiting Scandinavian countries, Holland, Germany, Italy, Hungary and France. In the summer of 1929 the family was back in France, after 31 concerts in the USA, and rented another villa, at Clairefontaine about 35 miles from Paris and not far from the French President's summer residence, Rambouillet. The family spent several happy summers there: the very Russian atmosphere, completely cut off from the outside world, is best described by the Swans who visited them there in 1930:

> The château-like house, Le Pavillon, protected from the street by a solid wrought-iron fence, lent itself well to this Russian life on a large scale, which rolled on comfortably in the cheerful rooms, just big enough to remain livable. The wide steps of the open veranda led into the park. The view was lovely: an unpretentious green in front of the house, a tennis-court tucked away among shrubs, sandy avenues flanked with tall, old trees, leading into the depth of the park, where there was a large pond. The

---

[4] See R. Threlfall, 'Rachmaninoff's Revisions and an Unknown Version of his Fourth Concerto', *Musical Opinion*, vol. xcvi (1972–3), p. 236.

whole arrangement was very much like that of an old Russian estate. The park of the Pavillon adjoined the summer residence of the President of France. A small gate opened into the vast hunting grounds: pine-woods with innumerable rabbits. Rachmaninoff loved to sit under the pine-trees and watch the games and pranks of the rabbits. In the morning the big table in the dining-room was set for breakfast. As in the country in Russia, tea was served and with it cream, ham, cheese, hard-boiled eggs. Everybody strolled in leisurely. There were no rigid rules or schedules to disturb the morning sleep. Pasha, the maid who had come with the Rachmaninoffs from Russia, was always at hand. She considered herself part of the family, with a broad smile she wished everybody good morning, and kept saying, 'Please help yourself'.[5]

Rachmaninoff spent the whole summer there, walking, driving, playing tennis and chatting with friends. He made occasional visits to Paris to consult his doctor and Kostritsky the dentist. It was on his return from one of these visits that he heard of the death of his mother on 19 September. Lyubov Petrovna had been living in Novgorod during the last years of her life and Rachmaninoff had continued to send her gifts of money. He had, however, always been more devoted to his father, and commented once in his youth that his mother did not really like him and only asked him to the house to keep up appearances. It was too late for him to attend the funeral, even if he had been allowed to, but he sent a letter to Mariya Litvinova, a relative who had written to tell him of his mother's death, asking whether there was any letter for him. But he swiftly had to brush the matter aside to begin a new European concert season which lasted for two months from 19 October, taking him to Germany, England, Holland, Hungary, France and Austria, before returning to America to complete the season with 24 concerts between 21 January and 5 April. It was there in Philadelphia that Swan observed Rachmaninoff's generosity, already apparent from the vast sums of money he had given to friends and donated to charitable causes:

> We walked back to the hotel with Rachmaninoff. He was leaving alone at midnight for Boston, where he was to play the following day. The slummy streets were dirty and crowded. Rachmaninoff walked quietly and rather slowly. He looked at the squalid world with that peculiar gaze of his – somewhat aloof, quiet, wise and at the same time sharp, noticing everything about him. 'Look, look here!' he said suddenly, stopping in

[5] A. J. and K. Swan, 'Rachmaninoff: Personal Reminiscences', *The Musical Quarterly*, vol. xxx (1944), p. 4.

front of a smelly fish stand. 'Look, this dealer is cheating this old man. He is not giving him the full weight. The scoundrel! Look!' At the next corner we saw the weird shape of an old negress. Wrapped in dirty rags, she sat on the box, stretching out her trembling hand and looking somewhere into space with her blind eyes. Her eye-lids were red and swollen. 'Oh, what is this? Look,' said Rachmaninoff with a shudder, and pulled out his wallet.[6]

In April 1930 the family left again for Paris and spent the summer at Clairefontaine. At about this time two of Rachmaninoff's acquaintances, Richard Holt and Oscar von Riesemann, asked him if they could each write his biography and if he would help them. Rachmaninoff agreed, provided that it would not take up too much of his time and also that Sofiya Satina, his sister-in-law and constant companion at all his concerts, would check details of dates which he could not remember. He and Sofiya gathered together some photographs and reminiscences and sent them off in an English translation to Richard Holt in London and in Russian to Riesemann, who was then living in Switzerland. Holt died suddenly without completing his project, but Riesemann pursued the idea and asked if he could visit Rachmaninoff in France. They walked and talked at Clairefontaine and Riesemann went off to finish his biography. When it appeared Rachmaninoff was horrified: in its title, *Rachmaninoff's Recollections told to Oscar von Riesemann*, it clearly implied that Rachmaninoff had dictated the reminiscences. There were long passages in quotation marks, yet much of it, apparently, was pure fiction. Sofiya Satina did not find this surprising, for she said that Riesemann did not have so much as a pencil with him at Clairefontaine. There was, however, one profitable result of this unfortunate encounter with Riesemann. Rachmaninoff and Natalya had long felt the need for a more permanent European home. They had considered Germany, France and Czechoslovakia, but when they were visiting Riesemann at his home in Switzerland they decided that Switzerland was the ideal country. They bought a site near Lucerne, at Hertenstein on the Vierwaldstätter See, and there began to build a villa which they called Senar, derived from their own names: *Se*rgey and *Na*talya *R*achmaninoff. Throughout the next season, besides giving 22 concerts in Europe and 24 in the USA, Rachmaninoff was involved in discussions with architects, builders and lawyers about the new house, and in the following summer they were able to occupy part of it. Senar, like Ivanovka before it, was to be a welcome place of seclusion.

[6] ibid., pp. 17–18.

The acquisition of this house served in some small way to take the family's minds off a shattering blow dealt by the Soviet musical authorities. As a Russian national living in a foreign country, Rachmaninoff had usually avoided political comment about the regime in the Soviet Union. Nevertheless, on 12 January 1931 the scholar and chemist Ivan Ostromyslensky, Count Ilya Tolstoy and he wrote a letter to *The New York Times* condemning the Soviet Union's attitude to education and other social questions, which had recently been praised by Rabindranath Tagore. Couched in phrases like 'the horrors perpetrated by the Soviet Government', 'the Communist oppressors of Russia' and 'the indescribable torture to which the Soviets have been subjecting the Russian people for a period of over 13 years', the letter concluded:

> At no time, and in no country, has there ever existed a government responsible for so many cruelties, wholesale murders and common law crimes in general as those perpetrated by the Bolsheviki . . . By his evasive attitude toward the Communist grave-diggers of Russia, by the quasi-cordial stand which he has taken toward them, [Tagore] has lent strong and unjust support to a group of professional murderers. By concealing from the world the truth about Russia he has inflicted, perhaps unwittingly, great harm upon the whole population of Russia, and possibly the world at large.[7]

The Moscow press was not slow to react, and in March the evening paper *Vechernyaya Moskva* published a bitter attack on Rachmaninoff's *The Bells*, which had just been performed at the Moscow Conservatory. That this was motivated politically rather than aesthetically is amply revealed in this passage:

> Who is the author of this text, who is the composer of this mystical music? The music is by an *émigré*, a violent enemy of Soviet Russia, Rachmaninoff. The words (after Edgar Allan Poe) are also by an *émigré*, the mystic Balmont; the concert was conducted by the former conductor of the Mariinsky Theatre, Albert Coates, who deserted Russia in 1917 and now returns with a foreign passport.[8]

The Soviet Union's final word on the subject came at the end of March, when the Leningrad and Moscow Conservatories, promptly followed by other music institutions, forbade the study and performance of all

[7] *The New York Times* (15 January 1931), p. 22.
[8] D. G., 'Kolokola zvonyat: ob odnom kontserte v konservatorii', *Vechernyaya Moskva* (9 March 1931), p. 3.

64

Rachmaninoff's works. However, with one of those strange ironies which were frequently to dog Soviet officialdom's attitudes towards music it did not like, the State Music Publishing House chose, at this very same time, to launch a new series of Rachmaninoff's piano music, as surviving editions of the op. 3 pieces – published in 1931, year of the savage *Bells* review – categorically prove. Even if, in musico-political manoeuvres, the Soviet Union's right hand did not know what the left was doing, Rachmaninoff sensed that his links with Russia under the Communist regime had finally been severed. Little had he known that the final sentence of an interview he gave to *The Musical Times* in June 1930 was to be quite so forcefully emphasized less than a year later: 'Only one place is closed to me, and that is my own country – Russia.'[9]

---

[9] S. Rachmaninoff, 'Some Critical Moments in My Career', *The Musical Times*, vol. lxxi (1930), p. 558.

5

The end of a career

In fact very little seemed to be going right for Rachmaninoff. His American concerts in the spring were coolly received, as were his Paris appearances early in the summer. It was, therefore, with some relief that he relaxed for a while in Lucerne and spent the summer at Clairefontaine, where as usual he was visited by Russian friends, including Shalyapin. Here he was able to compose a new solo piano piece, the Variations on a Theme of Corelli, which he dedicated to Kreisler, and also to revise completely the Second Piano Sonata. It was also around this time that he became concerned about his performances. After playing the new Variations to Swan he commented:

> The blood-vessels on my fingertips have begun to burst, bruises are forming. I don't say much about it at home. But it can happen at any moment. Then I can't play with that spot for about two minutes; I have to strum some chords. It is probably old age. And yet take away from me these concerts and it will be the end of me.[1]

The Variations were not immediately understood by the public and did not enjoy success. In December 1931 Rachmaninoff sent a copy to Medtner from New York with a letter:

> I have played them here 15 times, but only one of these 15 performances was good ... I have not played them in full once. I was guided by the coughing of the public. When the coughing increased, I would leave out the next variation. When there was no coughing, I would play them in order. In one concert (I don't remember where – a small town) the coughing was such that I played only 10 variations (out of 20). My record was 18 variations (in New York). However, I hope that you will play them all and that you will not 'cough'.[2]

---

[1] A. J. and K. Swan, 'Rachmaninoff: Personal Reminiscences', *The Musical Quarterly*, vol. xxx (1944), p. 9.
[2] Letter of 21 December 1931; see Z. A. Apetian (ed.), *N. K. Metner: pis'ma* (Moscow, 1973), p. 556.

He had played the Variations for the first time in Montreal in October 1931, and after several more concerts in the USA, including performances of the *Etudes-tableaux* recently orchestrated by Respighi, he sailed back to Europe. In London in March he played his Third Concerto with Sir Henry Wood, and after the concert was presented by the Duchess of Atholl with the Royal Philharmonic Society's gold medal. Ernest Newman, a great admirer of Rachmaninoff, recorded the event in *The Sunday Times* with the cynical comment: 'I hope this intrusion of his into the sacred circle will not be resented by some of the other initiates – the gifted singer of *Abide with me*, for example.'[3] Newman was presumably referring to Dame Clara Butt, awarded the medal in 1903, but Rachmaninoff also joined the ranks of Sir Henry Wood, Sir Thomas Beecham, Elgar, Vaughan Williams and Bax, Paderewski, Anton Rubinstein and Kreisler. From England the family travelled to Paris, and then at the end of March on to their villa at Hertenstein, where Rachmaninoff immersed himself with characteristic enthusiasm in the running of the estate, attempting to create in Senar a second Ivanovka. A further diversion was provided by the marriage of his younger daughter, Tatyana, to Boris Konyus. Composition was impossible, and in this respect it was a despondent Rachmaninoff who returned to the USA in October to begin a particularly demanding season of 50 concerts. Nor was it a successful season: the financial crisis in the USA meant that the concert halls were seldom full, and Rachmaninoff himself had lost a considerable amount of money through the depreciation of his investments in stocks and shares. During this season, in which he included a recital programme of piano fantasies by Skryabin, Haydn, Schumann, Chopin, Beethoven and Liszt, he celebrated the fortieth anniversary of his debut as a pianist in 1892. Despite his wish that there should be no celebration of his advancing years (he had already had a sharp reminder of that in an acute attack of lumbago, so painful in San Antonio that he had to be assisted to and from the piano), his Russian friends in America resolved to mark the occasion, and in New York on 22 December they presented him with a scroll and a wreath.

In London at the end of April 1933 he not only played the Corelli Variations for the first time in England but also introduced his transcription of the Scherzo from Mendelssohn's *A Midsummer*

3 *The Sunday Times* (13 March 1932), p. 7.

Night's Dream (which he recorded two years later) and of the prelude from Bach's E major violin partita. Returning to Paris in May he was greeted with a double celebration of his sixtieth birthday and his fortieth anniversary: many musicians delivered addresses at the Salle Pleyel on 5 May, and Alfred Cortot spoke on behalf of the Paris Conservatoire. This ordeal over, Rachmaninoff retreated once more to Senar, where this summer he bought a motorboat. As with his first car and any sort of machinery, he displayed enormous excitement over this most recent purchase: the Swans recall his characteristically boyish concern that he might be forbidden to use the boat after an incident in 1936:

> About an hour before dinner [Rachmaninoff] said, 'I think I shall go for a spin on the lake.' He got up quietly . . . It was a lovely afternoon, one of those rare and bright afternoons in the Swiss mountains in May. We joined him. At the last minute Mr Ibbs, Rachmaninoff's agent in England, asked permission to come along also . . . The lake was as still as a fish pond. Rachmaninoff took the wheel, and we glided smoothly out of the boat-house on to the lake. We were well out of sight of the house when Mr Ibbs asked if he could try his hand at the steering-wheel. Rachmaninoff handed it over to him and joined us on the back bench. No sooner had he sat down than something very strange happened. Evidently Mr Ibbs had decided to make a sharp turn. But, instead of turning, the boat began to spin and bend over to one side. We slid on the back seat and watched Mr Ibbs in dead silence. But when his face had turned as red as a beetroot, Rachmaninoff got up quietly, as if he had merely given Mr Ibbs time to correct his mistake, reached the wheel with a few big strides, and pushed Mr Ibbs aside. The screw was already thumping loudly in the air, and the left rim of the boat was touching the water. Just as the heavy boat was about to capsize and bury us under it, Rachmaninoff set it right and we glided back to the embankment of the Villa Senar. Nobody said a word. Silently we got out of the boat. On the way up to the house Rachmaninoff touched his left side several times and frowned. When we were quite near the veranda, he said, 'Don't say anything to Natasha. She won't let me go boating any more.'[4]

During his 1934 season in the USA Rachmaninoff learnt that the Soviet ban on his music had been lifted, and at Senar he heard from his friend Vilshau about the warm reception given in Moscow to the Corelli Variations, the Three Russian Songs and the Fourth Concerto.

[4] A. J. and K. Swan, 'Rachmaninoff: Personal Reminiscences', *The Musical Quarterly*, vol. xxx (1944), pp. 189–90.

In May he had to undergo a minor operation, but after a short holiday returned to Senar early in July and immediately set to work on his Rhapsody on a Theme of Paganini. He had completed it by August, and asked Sofiya Satina (in a letter of 19 August) to tell nobody except Evgeny Somov. In September he also told Vilshau about the new piece – then called 'Fantasy for piano and orchestra in the form of variations on a theme of Paganini' – in a letter outlining his plans for the coming season:

> 8 September 1934
>
> I leave [Senar] for Paris on 15 September and on 27 September go to America. I begin playing on 12 October. This time my season in America is only until Christmas. I return to Europe in January, and on 22 January begin to slack up in Europe until 10 May. For the past three years I have not allowed them to arrange more than 40 to 45 concerts for me. Well, for the coming season they persuaded me to give more. In America 29, in Europe 40. Will I survive?

The new Rhapsody was played in November in Baltimore, with the Philadelphia Orchestra conducted by Leopold Stokowski, and re-peated with great success both in America and in Europe. He continued to make corrections to the score throughout the tour in preparation for publication by Foley in 1934, and then introduced it to London on 21 March 1935, after its British première in Manchester. The tour through Europe was a particularly wearing one, and included some unfortunate incidents with talkative Spanish audiences which made the family resolve never to go to Spain again.

After his return to Switzerland Rachmaninoff's mind turned once more to composition, and from June until August 1935 he worked on a new symphony, his Third in A minor. He had time to complete only two movements before the necessity to practise for the next season intervened. The family left the villa for Paris on 30 September; about a week later they sailed for the USA to begin a season extending from 25 October to 2 April, which was to include more performances of the Rhapsody, notably one conducted by Cortot in Paris, and which was to take him as far East as Warsaw. He was back in Switzerland in April 1936, and in May resumed work on the symphony, completing·the third movement and revising the first. With this work out of the way and the promise of a performance by Stokowski in the autumn, the family moved to Aix-les-Bains for the benefit of Rachmaninoff's health (he had recently been suffering from arthritis); but, as he told

Vilshau in a letter of 18 July 1936, he was very happy to be leaving the spa on 25 July and to be able to resume intensive practice on 1 August. In October he was in London and Sheffield (to advise Sir Henry Wood on the performance of *The Bells* for which he had specially revised the choral parts of the third movement), giving concerts also of the Second and Third Concertos and the Paganini Rhapsody in London, Liverpool, Manchester and Sheffield, and undertaking a whistle-stop recital tour of Oxford, London, Birmingham, Brighton, Sheffield, Bristol, Leeds, Newcastle and Hastings, but he returned to America for the first performance of the Third Symphony on 6 November, again with Stokowski and the Philadelphia Orchestra. The symphony was received, as he later told Vilshau on 7 June 1937, 'sourly' both by the audience and by the critics, being criticized for, among other things, its length. Rachmaninoff made a few alterations to the score, sent it off to Foley and corrected the proofs during a tour of the USA with Ormandy and the Philadelphia Orchestra. After some successful London appearances, he was able to return to Paris and then to Senar for the summer. It was during this summer of 1937 that the choreographer Mikhail Fokin visited him and first discussed the possibility of a ballet based on the Paganini legend and using Rachmaninoff's Rhapsody. Both artists thought much about the idea; by February 1939 Fokin was able to inform Rachmaninoff from New Zealand that he was preparing the ballet, and the first performance was given at Covent Garden under Antal Dorati on 30 June, attended by Rachmaninoff's two daughters.

In September 1937 he was due to be in London to record the Third Symphony and the First Concerto, but all the sessions were postponed: anxious though he had been to see the symphony in print (it was published by Foley in May 1937), he may have felt that the score still needed further revision, and he was reluctant to commit his first version to record; he did not in fact record it until December 1939, after he had revised the score, and the First Concerto was not recorded until 1939–40. In October 1937 he was back in the USA for 32 concerts crammed into a short season from 17 October until 20 December. During January he rested, and then embarked upon a European tour. However, he was not to get very far; the tour was cut short in Vienna, where a performance of *The Bells* had to be cancelled because of the worsening political situation in Europe. Concerts in Britain, however, were able to go ahead, and Sir Henry Wood gave a performance of the Third Symphony:

I have recently had the pleasure of studying with [Rachmaninoff] his third symphony in A minor, and have since directed it at the Liverpool Philharmonic Society's concert (22 March 1938) and at a studio broadcast with the BBC Symphony Orchestra (3 April). Rachmaninoff attended the morning rehearsal of the latter and expressed his unbounded satisfaction both with the playing and reading of his work, making a charming little speech to the orchestra ... The work impresses me as being of the true Russian romantic school; one cannot get away from the beauty and melodic line of the themes and their logical development. As did Tchaikovsky, Rachmaninoff uses the instruments of the orchestra to their fullest effect. Those lovely little phrases for solo violin, echoed on the four solo woodwind instruments, have a magical effect in the slow movement. I am convinced that Rachmaninoff's children will see their father's third symphony take its rightful place in the affection of that section of the public which loves melody. In fact, I go so far as to predict that it will prove as popular as Tchaikovsky's fifth.[5]

Despite these favourable comments Rachmaninoff set about revising the symphony at Senar during the summer of 1938, which was clouded by Shalyapin's death in Paris on 11 April. The revisions were complete by the end of July, and the new score was again published by Foley. At the same time Rachmaninoff also expressed a wish to revise the Fourth Concerto, but this he did not do until 1941. Before leaving Europe for his American season, he took part in a special jubilee concert for Sir Henry Wood. So high was Wood's regard for Rachmaninoff that he wanted him as the one and only soloist in this concert, a charity affair to provide hospital beds for musicians. So high was Rachmaninoff's standing that the date was shifted back from 22 November 1938 (it had been planned to coincide with St Cecilia's Day) to 5 October, to accommodate Rachmaninoff's forthcoming American concert season. This even meant that there could be no royal presence at the concert, because the royal family was still on holiday. And Rachmaninoff was able to stipulate, too, that his performance was not broadcast over the wireless. He had an absolute aversion to broadcasting, and, in the USA, when a concert in which he was participating was being transmitted, Rachmaninoff's 'live' performance was always replaced by a gramophone record of the same piece. The BBC was much sniffier about doing this, which meant that only half of the Wood jubilee concert could in fact be broadcast: the half in which Rachmaninoff was not playing. But for the audience in the hall

[5] H. J. Wood, *My Life of Music* (London, 1938), pp. 451–2.

he gave his Second Concerto, in the context of a long orchestral and choral programme which included music by Sullivan, Beethoven, Bach, Bax, Wagner, Handel, Elgar and Vaughan Williams. Next morning, from his customary room at the Piccadilly Hotel, Rachmaninoff sent a handwritten note to Wood (in English):

Dear Sir Henry,
Before leaving London I would like to again offer you my congratulations hearty and sincere, on the wonderful tribute paid you by every one, artists and audience alike, at the great Concert last night. It gave me the greatest pleasure to be able to join in it.

I was much impressed with Dr Vaughan Williams 'Serenade [to Music]' and if you have the opportunity, will you tell him I enjoyed hearing his work.

With kindest remembrances to Lady Wood and yourself.
S. Rachmaninoff.[6]

His American tour finished in the middle of January 1939, but Rachmaninoff was back in England by the middle of February to play the Second Concerto in Manchester (9 March) and to give a series of recitals in Birmingham, London, Liverpool, Sheffield, Middlesbrough, Glasgow, Edinburgh, Oxford and Cardiff. Still widening his repertory, his programmes included Rameau, Bach, Schubert, Schumann and two different Beethoven sonatas (op. 81a and op. 111) alongside his staple Liszt, Chopin and, needless to say, Rachmaninoff. These were to be his final appearances in England.

By early April the family were back in Paris and then at Senar, both severely overcast with the oppression of war. He had to decline Fokin's invitation to attend the première of *Paganini* in London, because he had fallen on the polished floor at the villa and was badly lame and shaken. He was fit enough to take part in the Lucerne Festival on 11 August, playing Beethoven's First Concerto and his own Rhapsody, and two days later travelled to Paris. The heavy atmosphere throughout Europe had convinced the family that they should return to the USA. Tatyana could not leave, because of her husband's work in France; she remained behind with her 6-year-old son Alexandre on the estate just outside Paris which Rachmaninoff had bought for her. The close-knit family thus separated for the last time. Leaving a caretaker at Senar, Natalya, Irina and Rachmaninoff sailed from Cherbourg on 23 August.

[6] unpublished letter of 6 October 1938, in British Library (MS 56421/117).

During this season in the USA the Philadelphia Orchestra had arranged a special Rachmaninoff series to celebrate the thirtieth anniversary of his American debut in 1909. It included the first three concertos and the Paganini Rhapsody, *The Isle of the Dead*, the Second and Third symphonies and *The Bells*; Rachmaninoff was soloist in the concerted works, and himself conducted *The Bells* and the Third Symphony at the final concert on 10 December. It was an exhausting season comprising 41 concerts, but after another small operation in May 1940 he was able to enjoy a very welcome period of convalescence during the summer at an estate called Orchard Point, near Huntington, Long Island. Nearby he had Russian friends, including Fokin and Somov, who had had to resign as Rachmaninoff's personal secretary in 1938 but had remained a close friend. In this restful, congenial atmosphere Rachmaninoff began to compose again, and succeeded in completing his last work, the Symphonic Dances. (He thought the dances might work in another Fokin ballet, but Fokin died in 1942 before any progress could be made on the project.) He had to prepare for a concert tour starting on 14 October 1940, but during practice and even during the tour itself he worked at the orchestration of the Symphonic Dances in anticipation of the first performance in January the following year. He attended the rehearsal, and the première took place on 3 January 1941 at Philadelphia, with Eugene Ormandy conducting. Generally the piece was received without enthusiasm, though time has shown that the Symphonic Dances are among his finest orchestral works. His American tour continued through Texas, Hollywood and Chicago, where he conducted the Second Symphony and *The Bells*. Returning to Orchard Point he was able to revise the Fourth Concerto, which he played, still with little public acclaim, on 17 October and recorded in December.

For the following summer the family decided to make a change from Orchard Point and spend some time in California instead, and in May they moved into a house in Tower Road, Beverly Hills. It was not far from the Horowitz house: Vladimir Horowitz and Rachmaninoff, who had for one another a deep personal and professional respect, met often to play duets. So pleasing did the family find the area that Rachmaninoff bought a house on Elm Drive in June, though they continued to occupy Tower Road for a while longer. In July he played at the Hollywood Bowl, suffering afterwards from lumbago and complaining of fatigue. He told his doctor, Alexander Golitsyn, that he had decided his next season – 1942–3 – would be his last. Little did he know that that decision would in fact be taken out of his hands. The relentless schedules of performing and travelling, coupled with frantic efforts to finish such works as the Third Symphony and the Symphonic Dances, had begun to take their toll: he was, literally, working himself to death.

However, the season opened, as planned, in Detroit on 12 October 1942, the proceeds from many of the concerts being donated to war relief. If Rachmaninoff was secretly planning to retire, the ecstatic American notices this season might have given him pause for thought. 'Rachmaninoff Recital Here Great Event', trumpeted the headline in the *Detroit Evening Times*, the paper's critic, Charles Gentry, going on to find innovative qualities in Rachmaninoff's playing:

> As he is a personality, so Rachmaninoff is technically an enigma. In an interpretative sense, the marvel only increases. While he may select a conventional programme, his interpretation grows more unorthodox at each hearing. He is more of a pioneer, a musical explorer, today than when we first heard him 20 years ago.[7]

Russell McLauchlin in *The Detroit News* noticed, however, that the unbending platform manner had not changed. After the encores, 'the wise old owl that he is, he firmly and politely closed the piano as he arose and, save for a single bow, was seen no more.'[8] But the press's encomia continued as the tour progressed. 'Rachmaninoff, Playing Magnificently, Warms Hearts of Pittsburg Audience', announced *The Pittsburgh Press* (17 October); 'Overflow Audience Hails Rachmaninoff', reported the *Philadelphia Record* (23 October). And so it went on: 'Rachmaninoff in Grand Form in Ottawa Concert' (*The Evening Citizen*, 29 October); 'Audience Thrills at Recital by Rachmaninoff' (*Rochester Democrat and Chronicle*, 31 October); 'Throngs Hear Rachmaninoff in Superlative Performance' (*The Washington Post*, 16 November); 'Rachmaninoff Makes Piano Speak its Soul' (*Chicago Daily Tribune*, 23 November).

At the turn of the year, Rachmaninoff rested for six weeks, but by the middle of January he was clearly unwell, abnormally tired and with pains in his left side. He also had a nagging cough and was losing weight. But the tour continued with a concert in Pennsylvania on 3 February ('Capacity Audience Applauds to Music of Famous Russian

[7] *Detroit Evening Times* (13 October 1942).
[8] *The Detroit News* (13 October 1942).

Conductor-Composer', *The Daily Collegian*, 4 February). On 5 February he was in Columbus, Ohio, and on the 11th and 12th again in Chicago, where he played Beethoven's First Concerto and his own Paganini Rhapsody.

The pains in his side increased, and the doctor diagnosed pleurisy, but Rachmaninoff insisted that he should carry on. He played in Louisville on 15 February. Underneath another headline of unequivocal praise – 'Rachmaninoff's Art Compelling, Beautiful' – the critic of the local *Courier-Journal* noted: 'The applause was tumultuous and several encores were added. It was an evening of beautiful music masterfully played.'[9] Two days later, on 17 February 1943 Rachmaninoff played in Knoxville, Tennessee. In the programme was a work which was to be sadly appropriate, Chopin's B flat minor – 'Funeral March' – Sonata. This was to be his last concert. En route for Florida he became so ill on the train that the family had to leave at Atlanta and cancel the Florida concert. They went straight to New Orleans, hoping that in the warm climate his health would improve sufficiently for him to play there. It did not. Planned concerts in Texas were cancelled, and the family returned on a slow train to Los Angeles, where Rachmaninoff was taken right away to the Hospital of the Good Samaritan. From there he wrote to Evgeny Somov on 27 February:

> . . . In New Orleans I definitely noticed that my cough was getting worse, the pain in my side likewise, and that I would soon be in a state of not being able to get up, sit or lie down. Emergency measures were taken, and three concerts in Texas were cancelled, and we took a ghastly train (60 hours) and came straight to Los Angeles. When I got on the train, I got undressed immediately and went to bed, intending to spend all 60 hours there. I kept on spitting phlegm (like Chekhov) into paper bags. And that turned out to be the surprise. All the phlegm was tinged with blood. I will make no secret of it: I was very frightened, and then telegrams were sent to all the ends of America. The consequences were these: Irinochka [Rachmaninoff's daughter, Irina] yesterday travelled out to us here. Dr Russel arranged with a doctor friend, who telegraphed to us on the train that he would meet us at the station with an ambulance. So then, yesterday evening we arrived here, two men took me under their arms and brought me here. It was 9 o'clock in the evening. A specialist was waiting and immediately they began to tap me and sound me. And this morning an X-ray. Now all has become clear. Here is the report for you. There are only two small, not terribly inflamed

[9] *Courier-Journal* (16 February 1943).

spots on the lungs. The blood in the phlegm disappeared as suddenly as it had appeared. But on the other hand my side has become so painful that I could cry out with pain when I cough, move or turn over. As you see, it was all much ado about nothing . . .

But Rachmaninoff's optimism was ill-founded. This was to be his last documented letter, ending with the achingly poignant words '. . . So I feel embarrassed and guilty . . .' Somebody in the hospital wrote on it: 'Mr R did not finish this letter'. They sent him home to Elm Drive, under the care of a Russian nurse, but soon small swellings began to appear and it became apparent that he was not suffering, as he had thought, from some nervous disorder, nor from the 'pneumonia, pleurisy and complications' which were handed out to the press as reasons for his confinement, but from a virulent, rare, rapid cancer. Within a month he was in a coma, and early on the morning of Sunday, 28 March 1943 he died peacefully, only a few days before his seventieth birthday and only weeks after becoming a naturalized American citizen.

Requiem Mass was celebrated that night at the Los Angeles Russian Orthodox Church. There was another the next day, and a Funeral Mass took place on 30 March. The body was taken back to New York for burial in the Kensico Cemetary, close by a village aptly called Valhalla. There, his grave, marked by a simple Russian cross, stands on a quiet hillside: the composer was now, in death, in those surroundings of tranquillity which he had craved in life.

Rachmaninoff was a truly professional, master musician, yet he confessed that he was never able to concentrate on more than one of his three careers as conductor, composer and pianist at any one time. This fact is borne out particularly by his years away from Russia, when the rigours of his life as a performer precluded nearly all composition other than that which he could do in the summer months when it was not so necessary to practise intensively. He often repeated that composition was the career he felt drawn to most strongly – he is described on his death certificate as a 'composer' – yet in his latter years his loss was in some respects our gain, for he was without doubt one of the finest pianists of his generation. Even when he had become established in the West as a performer, his concerto repertory was not large, nor indeed very adventurous. It included Beethoven's C major, Liszt's E flat, Tchaikovsky's B flat minor, his own four concertos and the Paganini Rhapsody; only very late in life did he add such a standard repertory piece as the Schumann. In his recital programmes he strayed slightly further afield, including (apart from Tchaikovsky, Liszt and

Schumann) pieces by Mendelssohn, Schubert, Grieg, Borodin, Debussy, his own transcriptions of Bach, Bizet, Musorgsky, Kreisler and Rimsky-Korsakov, Mozart and Beethoven sonatas and such nineteenth-century virtuoso pieces as Henselt's sparkling *Si oiseau j'étais*, Dohnányi's Etude in F minor and Moszkowski's *La Jongleuse*. Above all, however, he excelled in Chopin, with whose B flat minor sonata his name will always be inextricably linked.

For those of us born too late to hear him perform on the concert platform, there is the heritage of well over 100 recordings which he made, once he had overcome his initial dislike of being confined to a recording studio without an audience, whose reaction was usually so vital to him. Most of his records were made for the Victor Talking Machine Company (taken over by RCA in 1929), apart from some early records for the Edison Company and one private recording (the *Polka italienne*), which he made with his wife in about 1938. They include performances of a large number of his solo recital pieces, all his own works for piano and orchestra, as well as the Grieg Violin Sonata in C minor op. 45, the Schubert A major Sonata D 574 and the Beethoven Violin Sonata in G op. 30 no. 3, all of which he recorded with Kreisler in 1928. As a conductor he recorded *The Isle of the Dead* and his own orchestral version of the *Vocalise* op. 34 no. 14, both with the Philadelphia Orchestra in 1929, and the Third Symphony ten years later. In this last, particularly, he is scrupulously attentive to the details of expression in his own score, and produces a clarity and vigour of orchestral playing which have seldom been surpassed.

Rachmaninoff possessed a formidable technique and enormous hands: according to Cyril Smith[10] his left hand could play a chord comprising C-E♭-G-C-G while the right hand could accomplish C (second finger)-E-G-C-E (thumb under). It has been suggested by Dr David Young, formerly principal scientist of the Wellcome Foundation, that this 'arachnodactyly' could be a sign that Rachmaninoff had Marfan's syndrome, an hereditary disarrangement of connective tissue. This is a condition which, equally, could account for certain physical characteristics – Rachmaninoff's long limbs, slender figure, narrow head, thin nose and prominent ears – and might also be responsible for the various minor ailments – eye-strain, headaches, back pain, stiffness of the hands, arthritis and bruising of the

[10] C. Smith, *Duet for Three Hands* (London, 1958), p. 82.

77

fingertips – from which Rachmaninoff suffered at various times throughout his life. But, as Dr Young is the first to acknowledge, 'it was artistic genius, not large hands, that made his performance so memorable'[11]. Rachmaninoff's technical abilities, however they were derived, were always at the service of an intelligent, logical mind: he prepared his performances with infinite care, never entrusting the smallest detail to chance inspiration on the night. His theory of performance centred on the idea that every piece has a culminating 'point' (*tochka*), as he explained to Marietta Shaginian:

This culmination, depending on the actual piece, may be at the end or in the middle, it may be loud or soft; but the performer must know how to approach it with absolute calculation, absolute precision, because if it slips by, then the whole construction crumbles, the piece becomes disjointed and scrappy and does not convey to the listener what must be conveyed.[12]

Coupled with this studied, intellectual approach, Rachmaninoff's performances are characterized by rhythmic drive, a refined legato, accuracy of notes, and above all an absolute clarity in his execution of complex textures and swiftly moving passage work.

[11] D. A. B. Young, 'Rachmaninov and Marfan's syndrome', *British Medical Journal*, vol. 293 (20–27 December 1986), pp. 1624–6.
[12] M. Shaginian, 'Vospominaniya o S. V. Rakhmaninove', *Vospominaniya o Rakhmaninove*, vol. ii, ed. Z. A. Apetian (Moscow, 5/1988), p. 156.

6

The piano works

In his mature piano works Rachmaninoff made use of his own skills not to compose music of unreasonable virtuosity but rather to explore fully the expressive and technical possibilities of the instrument. The demands he makes are not for the faint-hearted, but there is an ineluctable feel that they are essentially pianistic. Even his earliest works, composed while he was still a student in the 1880s and treading ground that had already been well worn by Tchaikovsky, Schumann and Chopin, the essential tastefulness – and often the drama – of Rachmaninoff's style is revealed in embryo. The three youthful Nocturnes and the four pieces – a Romance, a Prélude, a Mélodie and a Gavotte – are not great works. Nonetheless, you find here those lovely left-hand melodies which peak through the textures, the nervous motifs, the busy activity in the piano-writing and the gorgeous harmonies which were to be brought under control and to much more subtle effect in his later works.

The two pieces – a Romance and a Valse – which he wrote in the 1890s for the six hands of his close friends, the three Skalon sisters, to play at one piano, are again not of lasting quality, though they are fun to perform, and, if your neighbours do not mind being nudged now and again, are an early testament to Rachmaninoff's knowledge of what could be achieved at the keyboard. Neither piece was ever published in Rachmaninoff's lifetime, but he must have kept them in his head, because he reused the slow, cross-rhythm, triplet introduction of the A major Romance when he came to write the E major central movement of his Second Concerto. The Russian Rhapsody for two pianos, another 1890s piece, is a *tour de force* of colour – a foretaste of his later two-piano suites in its sumptuousness – but insistent (even for only ten minutes or so) in its worrying over and embellishment of the basic folktune.

In his first published solo piano works, the five *Morceaux de fantaisie* op. 3 (1892), Rachmaninoff began to strike a more individual tone. Indeed one piece alone from the set, the Prélude in C sharp minor, became for millions the epitome of what they considered his style to be, couched as it is in dark melancholic terms with a more impassioned central section and a grandiose climax. This piece was published countless times, both in its original and in many bowdlerized forms: it was also arranged for organ, piano accordion, banjo, military band, guitar and even trombone quartet, and furnished accompaniments to a large number of sentimental songs. Only in 1938, in the USA, did Rachmaninoff make his own definitive arrangement of it for two pianos. Two years later he revised two more of the op. 3 pieces, the simple Mélodie in E major (no. 3), with its left-hand melody echoed chordally in the right, and the Sérénade in B flat minor (no. 5) with its slight Spanish inflections; he also revised the Humoresque in G major, no. 5 in the set of seven *Morceaux de salon* op. 10, composed in 1893–4. This Humoresque is notable both for its principal theme (presaging the First Symphony) and also for its brand of wit, which rarely entered Rachmaninoff's music but was to reappear in the Paganini Rhapsody and just one or two solo pieces and in the odd laconic song.

Between the two sets of solo pieces, ops. 3 and 10, Rachmaninoff composed his two-piano *Fantaisie-tableaux* (or Suite no. 1), musical images of four poetic texts. The one movement based on a non-Russian poem is the most effective; this is the second, headed with a quotation from Byron:

> It is the hour when from the boughs
> The nightingale's high note is heard;
> It is the hour when lovers' vows
> Seem sweet in every whisper'd word;
> And gentle winds, and waters near,
> Make music to the lonely ear.

An air of tranquillity pervades the movement; only the nightingale's song (heard first on the second piano), and the slightly more agitated 'gentle winds and waters' disturb the silence. In the first movement, a lyrical Barcarolle in G minor, bearing a quotation from Lermontov, Rachmaninoff relies on repetitions of the same melody, but, far more than in the Russian Rhapsody, he explores a variety of sonorities obtainable from the two instruments. The third movement is based on Fyodor Tyutchev's poem *Slyozy* ('Tears'), and consists almost entirely of pianistic decorations around a four-note motif (derived from the notes of the bells at St Sophia's Cathedral in Novgorod), which

Rachmaninoff always associated with sadness and was to use again in his depiction of the old woman in the central monologue of *The Miserly Knight*. The last movement is a rousing piece based on Alexey Khomyakov's poem *Svetlyy prazdnik* ('Easter festival') and contains the same Easter chant which Rimsky-Korsakov used in his Easter Festival Overture. In fact it was Rimsky who advised Rachmaninoff to revise the movement:

> Once [Mitrofan] Belyayev invited me and I was asked to play. I had just written my Fantasy for two pianos. They put Felix [Blumenfeld] at the second piano. He alone could [sight-] read music to perfection. I played from memory at the first piano. They were all there – Lyadov, Rimsky-Korsakov – and they listened very attentively and seemed to like it. Rimsky smiled all the time. Then they praised me, and Rimsky said, 'All is fine, only at the end, when the melody *Christ is risen* is sounded, it would be better to state it first alone, and only the second time with the bells.' . . . I was silly and stuck-up in those days – I was only 21 – so I shrugged my shoulders and said, 'And why? In real life it always comes together with the bells,' and never changed a note.[1]

Later Rachmaninoff came to realize the truth of Rimsky's criticism: the bell-like figuration does occur throughout the piece with wearying monotony.

The six duets of op. 11 (1894) are poor pieces, distinguished not so much by their inventiveness as by a thoroughly reliable technique. In the six *Moments musicaux*, op. 16, composed in 1896, however, Rachmaninoff's piano style began to show a marked development in both technique and expression: the figuration is more elaborate, the texture less homophonic than in some earlier pieces. In a sense they can be seen to be preparations for more mature pieces: no. 4 in E minor, for example, looks forward to the B flat major prelude (op. 23 no. 2) in its bravura left-hand writing and in its tightly controlled structure, while no. 3 in B minor has the more introspective character of the prelude in B minor (op. 32 no. 10). It is, however, no. 2 in E flat minor which is the most striking, with its yearning right-hand theme, intricate passage work and the characteristic rise and fall of dynamics (ex. 1).

During the barren period caused by the failure of his First Symphony, Rachmaninoff apparently composed only two piano pieces – a Fughetta in F (1899) which possesses a strange, concentrated wistfulness in among its academic workings, and a *Morceau de fantaisie* in G

[1] A. J. and K. Swan, 'Rachmaninoff: Personal Reminiscences', *The Musical Quarterly*, vol. xxx (1944), p. 177.

Ex. 1

minor (also 1899), little more than a minute long but attractive in its liquid right-hand figuration set against a quietly supportive bass line. The Suite no. 2 for two pianos op. 17 (1900–1) is made of more robust, more commandingly melodic stuff, instantly testifying to the restoration of Rachmaninoff's confidence after the success of the Second Concerto in 1901. In the way the two instruments are ingeniously integrated, this Second Suite displays an advance over the First Suite (*Fantaisie-tableaux*) comparable to that which the First Suite had over the Russian Rhapsody. Its lyricism is ripe and fertile (again placing it alongside the Second Concerto, and also the Cello Sonata); the form of the four movements is neatly balanced; its contrasts of mood and rhythm are sharply drawn.

A year after completing the Second Suite, Rachmaninoff began his most substantial piece so far for solo piano, the Variations on a Theme of Chopin op. 22 (1902–3). Taking as his theme Chopin's prelude op. 28 no. 20, he created 22 variations with a wide diversity of mood and texture, in which the piano is rather more richly colourful than in his later and far superior variations on a theme of Corelli. In the Chopin Variations there is much of the sort of piano figuration in which Rachmaninoff himself excelled as a performer, evident particularly in variation no. 6 with its cross-rhythms, nos. 8 and 18, in which the complexity of rhythm is enhanced by more elaborate activity in the right hand, and nos. 19 and 22 with their large, Schumannesque chords. Yet, by contrast, much of the music is conceived in sparser textures. The first three variations, for example, are extensions of a simple semiquaver idea (suggesting the C minor prelude, op. 23 no. 7) first expounded in the first variation: in no. 2 the continuous line is divided between the hands, and in no. 3 both hands play in counterpoint. Rachmaninoff's mode of expression in the Chopin Variations is more direct than in the later Corelli set (1931), a characteristic which also imbues his set of preludes op. 23.

Like Chopin, Rachmaninoff wrote preludes in all the major and minor keys. The first was the C sharp minor (op. 3 no. 2), to which he added the ten preludes of op. 23 and the 13 of op. 32. Like much of his music of the turn of the century, the op. 23 preludes (the first composed in 1901, the remainder in 1903) owe much to the Second Concerto for their style: no. 6 in E flat major and no. 10 in G flat major contain a number of melodic ideas which recall the concerto and the Suite no. 2. The whole set is marked by a greater economy of thematic material than is evident in his earlier solo piano music: no. 9 in E flat minor, for example, is based entirely on the two ideas mooted in the first bar, a gently rising melodic fragment in the bass, and the swiftly moving chromatic semiquavers in the right hand. But perhaps it is the most popular, the G minor (no. 5), which best illustrates the direction of Rachmaninoff's style in the set: the opening and closing sections, tautly constructed, are derived from the simple *alla marcia* idea of the first bar, while the central section consists of a broad lyrical melody typical of the Rachmaninoff of the early 1900s, sumptuously accompanied by sweeping left-hand arpeggios.

His technique of building a piece from tiny melodic or rhythmic fragments was developed further in his final set of preludes, the 13 of op. 32 (1910). Many of them derive from a simple dotted-note figure: the D flat major (no. 13), the B flat minor (no. 2), the B major (no. 11) and above all the B minor (no. 10). This last is by far the finest in the set, perhaps the finest of all the 24 preludes, with its close-knit structure (based entirely on the opening figure), its imaginative piano writing, and its intensity of emotion, towards which the more introspective of the *Moments musicaux* and the op. 23 preludes had been progressing. The purely technical aspects of the op. 32 preludes are possibly less taxing than op. 23, but the interpretational difficulties of a profound piece like the B minor prelude or the rather more texturally complex D flat major (with its hidden references to the earliest prelude in C sharp minor) are infinitely more demanding. Several in the set, the G major (no. 5) and the G sharp minor (no. 12) for example, have that ambiguous, hazy quality which was to characterize his last set of songs (op. 38) and his A minor *étude-tableau*, op. 39 no. 2.

They are in effect miniature tone poems, just as his two sets of *Etudes-tableaux*, composed in 1911 and 1916–17, are musical evocations of external visual stimuli, the exact nature of which Rachmaninoff usually concealed from the public. The études are in general longer pieces than any of the preludes, but like the preludes they achieve the effect of crystallizing a particular mood within the smallest possible structure. For the earlier set of *Etudes-tableaux*, op. 33, Rachmaninoff composed nine pieces, but he withdrew three before publication in 1914. Of these, no. 4 in A minor was altered slightly and included later as no. 6 of the op. 39 set; no. 5 in D minor, with its opening reference to the First Sonata and subsequent foretaste of the song *Krysolov* (op. 38 no. 4), was published posthumously; parts of no. 3 in C minor, with its atmospheric harmonic progressions on the opening page, were used later in the Fourth Concerto.

It is worth mentioning that, although Rachmaninoff never gave titles to any of these *études-tableaux*, he had no objection to Respighi doing so when he made orchestral arrangements of some of them in 1930. In fact there exists a letter (2 January 1930) in which Rachmaninoff actually tells Respighi what the inspiration for the pieces was. Thus, the E flat major (published as no. 4 in the op. 33 set) is 'a scene at a fair', and, to hear its fanfare opening and its

1 Rachmaninoff as a pupil at the St Petersburg Conservatory, early 1880s

2 (l. to r.) Matvey Presman, Rachmaninoff and Leonid Maximov with their Moscow teacher, Nikolay Zverev, 1886

3 Hay-making at Ivanovka, mid 1890s.
(l. to r., standing) Sofiya Satina,
Rachmaninoff, Alexander Satin, Father
Nikolay, Yuly Kreytser and Mikhail Bakunin
(nephew of Mikhail Bakunin, the
revolutionary); (l. to r., seated) Varvara
Satina, Natalya Satina, Elena Kreytser

4 On the veranda at Ignatovo, 1897. Rachmaninoff with the three Skalon sisters

5 The opening bars of Rachmaninoff's Second Piano Concerto, autograph score, 1901

6 With his daughter Irina on the steps of their house at Ivanovka, 1912

7 The house on the Ivanovka estate where the Rachmaninoff family lived

8 Rachmaninoff driving his car, the 'Loreley', near
Ivanovka, with (l. to r.) his cousins Anna Trubnikova and
Natalya Lanting, 1912

9 With his wife, Natalya, 1922

10 With his daughters, Irina and Tatyana, Locust Point, 1923

11 The composer in his study at Senar, late 1930s

12 The villa Senar, 1930s

13   At the piano, 1936

14   In his New York
apartment, early 1940s

subsequent bubble and bustle, there is no reason to doubt that Rachmaninoff was being anything but honest.

All the *études-tableaux* explore, in their various ways, the palette of keyboard colours and technique which, by this time in Rachmaninoff's career, was broad and rich. In a piece like the C minor *étude-tableau*, op. 39 no. 1 the virtuosity – expressive and technical – is exultant (see ex. 2). The set as a whole explores fully the pianist's and the instrument's capabilities, from the toccata-like textures of the B minor (no. 4) and the nerviness of the A minor (no. 6) – 'Little Red Riding Hood and the

Ex. 2   op. 39 no. 1

Wolf', according to Rachmaninoff – to the weighty chords of the D major (no. 9), an 'eastern march'. Yet, as with some of his songs, it is the pieces less concerned with elaborate figuration which live longest in the memory, and the least assertive of the set, no. 2 in A minor – 'the sea and the seagulls' –, is one of the finest of Rachmaninoff's miniatures, derived as it is from the simple triplet idea in the left hand and the cross-rhythm falling motif in the right hand (ex. 3). In these nine studies there is a wide diversity of mood, from the quiet lyricism of the A minor and the aura of tragedy in no. 7 in C minor – 'funeral march' – to the fiery E flat minor (no. 5).

It was in the miniatures like the later preludes and the op. 39 études that Rachmaninoff found the vehicle for the expression of his most intimate emotions. His two sonatas, on the other hand, display passion on a much broader scale. In the First Piano Sonata, which he completed in Dresden in 1907, Rachmaninoff manages to combine the thematic economy of the miniatures with a power of expression unprecedented in his solo piano works. It is a long piece, and, although the original idea for it to be a programme sonata based on Faust was abandoned, it is tempting to link the three movements with Faust, Gretchen and Mephistopheles. Like the First Symphony the sonata has

Ex. 3

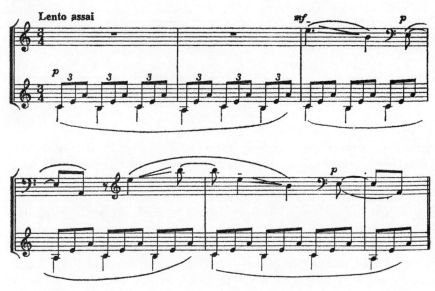

the appearance of a taut structure: the opening figure (ex. 4a) recurs throughout the piece, and the chant-like second subject (ex. 4b) is restated as a unifying idea in the long last movement.

Ex. 4a

In this fiendish finale Rachmaninoff manages brilliantly to maintain the momentum, despite reminiscences of motifs from the slower first and second movements, and even in the second movement the emotional intensity is rarely relaxed. Yet perhaps here lies the fault of the piece, for in the long process of building the climax (bars 65–80)

Ex. 4b

the complex piano part-writing defeats its own objects: the crescendo leads to what Rachmaninoff intended to be the 'culminating point' but which is in fact a scattered, cadenza-like anticlimax.

In his Second Sonata in B flat minor (1913) moments such as these are better judged, and, even though the work is again long, the structure is more tightly controlled, particularly in the fundamentally revised version of 1931: he reduced the sonata in length by some 120 bars, cutting long passages of purely virtuoso writing; but, more important, he completely rewrote much of the piece, not only to simplify the texture, as in ex. 5:

Ex. 5

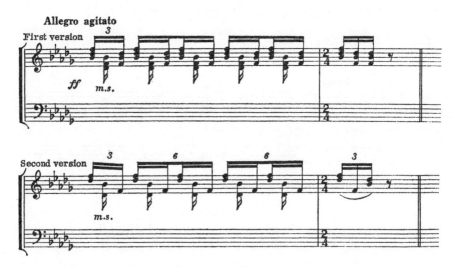

but also to make points more clearly and concisely in those passages where, as he said to Alfred Swan, 'so many voices are moving simultaneously'.[2] Although these revisions reveal much about the change in Rachmaninoff's piano style from the 1910s to the 1930s (just as the two versions of the First Concerto show how he developed between the 1890s and 1917), the Sonata is still very much a product of Rachmaninoff's mature Russian years in its lyricism and in its impassioned expression, very different from his other work of 1931, the Variations on a Theme of Corelli op. 42. Based not on a theme of Corelli but on the Portuguese tune *La folia* (see ex. 6a):

Ex. 6a

which Corelli had used in his Sonata no. 12, these 20 variations display a much more imaginative treatment of the theme than in the earlier Chopin Variations. Variation no. 16, for example (ex. 6b), has that greater rhythmic and harmonic freedom, and also the clarity of texture, which characterize the orchestral works composed during Rachmaninoff's Indian Summer of the 1930s and 1940s. It was with the Corelli Variations that he rediscovered his powers of composition after the comparative lack of success of the Fourth Concerto, and in some respects they can be seen to be preparatory exercises for the Paganini Rhapsody, composed three years later: for one, the variations are organized into an entirely logical structure, with a series of swift variations (16–20) reaching a dramatic climax before the pensive coda; for another, the rhythms are more vital than in his mature Russian

[2] A. J. and K. Swan, 'Rachmaninoff: Personal Reminiscences', *The Musical Quarterly*, vol. xxx (1944), p. 8.

Rachmaninoff

Ex. 6b

Allegro vivace

works (apparent, for example, in the incisive variation no. 5, with its frequently changing time signature) and the harmonies are more adventurous, more pungent, particularly in the slower nos. 3, 8 and 9 and in the masterly shift of key from D minor to D flat major in variation 14 after the mild turbulence of the Intermezzo. All of these characteristics constitute a new, more subtle mode of expression, and Vladimir Vilshau, in a letter which he sent to Rachmaninoff on 8 May 1934, rightly commented on the difference – the 'new sparkle' – that had overcome his style since the more extrovert *Etudes-tableaux* (during a performance of which Rachmaninoff had broken a string on the piano). Rather like his last set of songs, the Corelli Variations leave a feeling of regret that Rachmaninoff never again wrote a solo piano piece and allowed the new features of his later style to develop fully.

However, Rachmaninoff did continue to compose 'new' pieces in the form of transcriptions, which have a time-honoured place in the art of any pianist-composer. Rachmaninoff did not in fact make all that many of them, but throughout the last 20 years or so of his life – when his emphasis lay chiefly on performing – he from time to time added a transcription of his own to his gradually widening repertory. At the same Queen's Hall concert (29 April 1933) at which he gave the first London performance of the Corelli Variations he also included in his recital his transcription of the Scherzo from Mendelssohn's *A Midsummer Night's Dream* and the Prélude from Bach's E major Violin Partita BWV 1006, which he had made earlier in the year and had played during his American tour in February. He played the Prélude again (but this time with the Gavotte and Gigue as well) later in 1933 during his next American tour.

Tchaikovsky's *Lullaby* (from the set of Six Songs op. 16) was to follow – as Rachmaninoff's last transcription – in 1941, but in previous years he had introduced in the USA or played on international tours his Minuet from Bizet's *L'Arlésienne*, Kreisler's *Liebesleid* and *Liebesfreud*, the Hopak from Musorgsky's *Sorochintsy Fair*, Rimsky-Korsakov's *Flight of the Bumble Bee*, Schubert's *Wohin?*, and arrangements of his own songs *Siren'* ('Lilacs') op. 21 no. 5 and *Margaritki* ('Daisies') op. 38 no. 3. The piece published as the *Polka de V.R.*, heard in London in 1922 but written much earlier, is in fact a transcription of a polka – *La rieuse*, or *Lachtäubchen* – (op. 303) by Franz Behr, which, it must be assumed, was one of the pieces which Rachmaninoff's father –

V[asily] R[achmaninoff] of the title – entertained them with at home. Rachmaninoff even presented his visiting card to the USA when he emigrated there in 1918 by playing a transcription of *The Star-Spangled Banner*.

At various times he recorded them all. *The Star-Spangled Banner* is certainly, in its use of piano figuration and colour, more than just a dutiful arrangement, but there is much more invention in the other pieces. The transcriptions may only be an apostrophe to Rachmaninoff's output of piano music, but they combine a graceful, sometimes spectacular flourish with the individuality of imagination and tasteful interpretation and respect for music which marked his own piano-playing.

7

Orchestral works

For the most part, Rachmaninoff's earliest orchestral works reveal influences from three major Russian composers of his formative years: Rimsky-Korsakov, Borodin and above all Tchaikovsky. One notable exception is his first known work, the Scherzo in D minor (not F major as is often stated). He composed it in 1888, when he was 14 and just embarking on formal composition lessons. Despite this inexperience (which possibly explains his description of the piece as a 'scerzo' on the autograph score) it seems likely that he had the idea of composing a full-length symphony, for the manuscript is headed 'third movement'. The project was probably never realized (no other movements have survived), and there is no evidence to suggest that he intended to combine the Scherzo with his other abandoned D minor symphonic movement, composed in 1891. His model for the Scherzo was clearly Mendelssohn, for the piece abounds in Mendelssohnian harmonic progressions and opens with a passage markedly similar to the Scherzo from *A Midsummer Night's Dream*. Perhaps not surprisingly there is scarcely a hint of the mature Rachmaninoff, yet the piece does display some sensitivity in the orchestration, with attractive use of the woodwind in the plaintive solos of the central section.

The benefits which Rachmaninoff derived from his lessons with Arensky and Taneyev at the Moscow Conservatory are immediately apparent from his next orchestral work, the symphonic poem *Knyaz' Rostislav* ('Prince Rostislav', 1891). Although it was composed only four years after the Scherzo, *Prince Rostislav* contains many more of the traits which were to gain prominence in his later works. There are the characteristic melodic elements, which had been seen already in the First Piano Concerto (1890–1), and also the first signs of that ability for evocative tone-painting which was to reach its peak in *The Isle of the Dead* and some of the mature songs and piano miniatures. From the purely technical point of view, his studies at the Conservatory had taught him more about orchestration, about musical form and the organization of moments of tension and relaxation, and about harmony and the use of modulation techniques. *Prince Rostislav* is based on a poem by A.K. Tolstoy, telling of a prince who, after being killed in battle, lies forgotten on the Dnieper river bed. The motif associated with him throughout the piece is heard on the lower strings in the opening bars (ex. 7a).

Ex. 7a

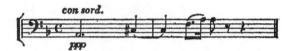

This fragment dominates the long first section, usually on the brass and in the form shown in ex. 7b.

Ex. 7b

In this opening section, too, the Dnieper's waters are suggested by the quietly surging strings, similar in effect to Tchaikovsky's *The Tempest* and to Balakirev's representation of the Terek in his symphonic poem *Tamara*. It is in the central episode that Rachmaninoff's lyrical talents come to the fore, though there is still much more than a hint of Tchaikovsky's *Romeo and Juliet* in the theme associated with the water nymphs, who caress the prince and comb his golden hair. The peace is shattered by the prince's three cries of despair, harsh declamatory motifs on trombones and tuba (ex. 8). He calls first to his young wife, then to his brother and finally to the priests of Kiev; but his wife is now betrothed to another, everyone else has long forgotten about him, and in any case his voice is too feeble to be heard. The music then reflects the prince's desperation, but subsides again as he resigns himself to oblivion, comforted only by the nymphs.

    Prince Rostislav was never performed in the composer's lifetime, and in fact remained unpublished until 1947; yet in many respects it has more to offer than his next orchestral piece, *Utyos* ('The Rock',

Ex. 8

1893), which was published as op. 7 by Jurgenson. It is another
descriptive piece, based on Chekhov's *Na puti* ('On the road') though
the score is headed by a quotation from Lermontov's poem *The Rock*:
'A little cloud slept on the breast of the giant rock', itself an allegory of
the more down-to-earth sentiments of Chekhov's story: a young girl
and an older man have a brief encounter at a wayside inn; the man
relates to the girl the tragedies of his disastrous life, and they part again
as abruptly as they had come together. Despite some skilful orchestration, *The Rock* is a work of fragmentary thematic ideas which are not
among Rachmaninoff's finest, and some occur with monotonous
frequency. Still less substantial is his *Kaprichchio na tsyganskiye temy*
('Capriccio on gypsy themes') or *Caprice bohémien* op. 12.
Rachmaninoff began composing the Capriccio in the summer of 1892,
shortly after completing his gypsy opera *Aleko*; in fact the Capriccio
contains occasional fleeting reminiscences of the opera: ex. 22b
(p. 127) is quoted more than once, as is the *Andante cantabile* passage
from the final bars of the opera. The orchestration, which again owes
much to Tchaikovsky and Rimsky-Korsakov, was done in 1894. The
Capriccio, set firmly in E minor and E major for much of the time, is
divided into three thematically linked sections. The first of these, an
allegro vivace, introduces a simple three-note motif (ex. 9a), one of the
germs of the piece, developing into ex. 9b and eventually into the
impassioned theme of the slow central section (ex. 9c).

Ex. 9a

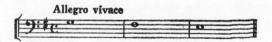

Ex. 9b

Ex. 9c

In the quick final section, too, a modified version of it is found to combine quite satisfactorily and ingeniously with the dance theme on the woodwind (ex. 9d).

Ex. 9d

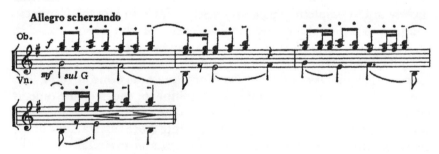

These and other thematic reminiscences lend a degree of unity to the Capriccio, but nevertheless it suffers from a lack of balance, like its contemporary *Aleko*. The vigour of the opening is all too swiftly dispelled by the long *Lento lugubre*, based entirely on an E minor pedal point. For another, shorter episode, attractively scored for flute, harp and strings, the pedal point shifts from E minor to C sharp minor, but it is not until a rapturous *Andante molto sostenuto*, thickly scored for unison strings and full orchestra, that any more fluid harmonic movement takes place. The final section relies too heavily on repetitions of the dance motif in ex. 9d, in an attempt to reproduce the wild character of a gypsy dance; the effect, while occasionally rousing, is tedious and banal, and not nearly so effective as the brief glimpse of inspiration in the cumulative excitement of the short opening. Rachmaninoff himself later realized the faults in the piece. It was one of the three which 'frightened' him in 1908, when he wrote to his old Conservatory colleague Nikita Morozov that he would like to see the Capriccio, the First Symphony and the First Concerto in a 'corrected, decent form'. But the Capriccio was never revised; indeed it would have needed far more drastic treatment than even the First Concerto to place it amongst Rachmaninoff's significant compositions.

Nor was the First Symphony revised, although Rachmaninoff admitted to the composer and critic Boris Asafyev in 1917 that there was much in it that was 'weak, childish, strained and bombastic'. Cui had stressed these aspects in his review of the première; after his opening reference to the conservatory in Hell (see p. 22) he went on to say:

> To us this music leaves an evil impression with its broken rhythms, obscurity and vagueness of form, meaningless repetition of the same short tricks, the nasal sound of the orchestra, the strained crash of the brass, and above all its sickly perverse harmonization and quasi-melodic outlines, the complete absence of simplicity and naturalness, the complete absence of themes.[1]

In fact there is more than a grain of truth in what both Rachmaninoff and Cui said, but it is worth considering the positive aspects first. One feature that points the way to Rachmaninoff's more mature compositions is the compact, cyclic form. He uses remarkably little material, combining all four movements with many thematic metamorphoses and more overt reminiscences. The first movement grows out of motifs first mooted in the slow introduction (see ex. 10):

Ex. 10

[1] Ts. Kyui, 'Tretiy russkiy simfonicheskiy kontsert', *Novosti i birzhevaya gazeta* (17 March 1897), p.3.

The theme marked (*b*), which forms the first subject in the main body of the movement, and the fragment (*a*) are the dominating features, though the semiquaver pattern in an answering phrase, marked (*c*), also plays an important contrapuntal role. The second subject (ex. 11) calls for a slower tempo; it is contemplative, almost like a recitative in its speech-like changes of time and shifts of stress, and it introduces an important rhythmic figure (*a*).

Ex. 11

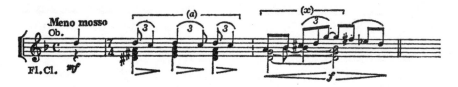

After a more rapturous statement of the second subject, a violent crash on the full orchestra heralds the development, in which Rachmaninoff makes extensive use of a fugato treatment of the motifs in ex. 10.

These are the seeds from which the entire symphony grows. The second movement, a scherzo, opens with a reference to ex. 10(*a*) on muted violas and then to the rhythmic fragment (*a*) in ex. 11; the principal theme of the movement is derived from ex. 10(*b*), and the central section comprises a blend of all these motifs. The slow movement begins in much the same way (with references to ex. 10(*a*) and ex. 11(*a*)), and the plaintive solo is derived from the first movement's second subject, without the augmented intervals. Ex. 10(*a*) also opens the finale, though this time the motif is extended with a dotted-note figure which is to play an important role in the rest of the movement. In a martial fanfare of brass ex. 10(*b*) returns, accompanied by *marcato* strings and wind with a prominent part for the side drum. Ex. 10(*a*) interrupts with its new dotted extension, and, despite the fanfare's attempts to return on muted horns, dominates the music and leads eventually into the yearning second subject, reminiscent of ex. 11 with a conspicuous reference to the figure marked (*x*). The relentless drive of the movement is slackened in the central episode, contemplative like the second subject of the first movement and containing the same motif (*x*); the rhythm from ex. 11(*a*) is also readily discernible. This section is long, perhaps too long to maintain the momentum of the movement, but eventually the dotted motif recurs with ex. 10 (*a* and *b*), and the music resumes its former breakneck speed, building to a magnificent and tightly controlled climax on the second subject. Ex. 10(*a*) is the dominating feature of the final, fearsomely insistent pages.

Formally the symphony would seem to be taut. Yet both the Scherzo and the slow movement suffer from serious longueurs. In the slow movement this is caused by a static central episode with growling references to ex. 10(*a*) in the lower strings; in the Scherzo's central section, too, the rambling repetitions of motifs from ex. 10 deprive the movement of much of its rhythmic drive and it is significant that somebody, presumably Glazunov (in rehearsals for the first perform-ance) or Rachmaninoff himself, indicated a cut of 36 bars on the orchestral parts. There is, at times, a brashness in the orchestration, which can sound clogged and make the piece seem too earnestly portentous; but a sensitive performance can contain all that and in fact elucidate it, and make it into the forceful, rapturous, dark and (in the finale) triumphant statement which Rachmaninoff must have intended. After all, Rachmaninoff is said (by his sister-in-law Sofiya Satina)[2] to have headed the score with the biblical quotation 'Vengeance is mine, I will repay', explaining, maybe, the music's fiery, brooding, reflective quality. The manuscript full score is still missing (see p. 23). However, in the preface to a 1977 Soviet edition (based, as was the 1947 first publication, on the surviving orchestral parts and Rachmaninoff's arrangement for one piano, four hands), the editors, Irina Iordan and Georgy Kirkor, say that the same quotation appears at the end of one of the orchestral parts. (Though I have seen the manuscript of the keyboard arrangement and the sketches – none of which carry the epigraph – I cannot confirm Iordan and Kirkor's assertion, but Sofiya Satina, who apparently had the score in her keeping until she herself left Russia in 1921, is a generally reliable and faithful witness.) There is much in the symphony which was ahead of its time and unlike anything Russia had heard. Even with its occasional gaucheries, it has a power, youthfully expressed, and, as in some of the very early piano pieces which looked forward to greater things in the future, contains much that already revealed a thoroughly personal way of thinking.

[2] S. A. Satina, 'Zapiska o S. V. Rakhmaninove', *Vospominaniya o Rakhmaninove*, vol. i, ed. Z. A. Apetian (Moscow, 5/1988), p. 29.

In 1908, when Rachmaninoff first expressed doubts about the First Symphony, he was enjoying a particularly intensive and fruitful period of work. In the seclusion of his Dresden home he had already produced the First Piano Sonata, some sketches for the never completed opera *Monna Vanna*, and also one of his finest orchestral works, the Second Symphony. The Second Symphony in E minor, op. 27, completed in 1906–7, has often been criticized for almost exactly opposite reasons to the First: few could deny its spontaneity or emotional sincerity, but the flow of inspiration did lead Rachmaninoff to compose a very long, and to some overlong, symphony in the late Romantic epic tradition. It is, however, a work packed with inventive ideas, expounded with that appeal and directness of expression which characterize his mature Russian works. Its musical balance is ruined by the savage cuts sometimes made in performance, for Rachmaninoff's lengthy melodic ideas need time and space to grow naturally. As in the First and Third Symphonies, he opens the Second with a motto theme (ex. 12):

Ex. 12

though here he allows it to develop freely rather than openly repeating it as in the First. There is, in fact, only one overt repetition of a theme throughout the symphony (the recurrence in the finale of the opening of the Adagio third movement), yet the almost consistently stepwise shape of the themes and frequent references to the fragment marked (*x*) in ex. 12 serve to bind the structure subtly. The Second Symphony is a prime example not only of Rachmaninoff's mature melodic style (evident above all in the Adagio, one of his most lyrical, long-breathed ideas) and his architectural skill, but also of his orchestration. The overall effect is one of opulence, but this does not imply that there are not varied colours and textures. Occasionally he lapses into heavy instrumentation (notably at the climax to the last movement, with full strings in unison and the rest of the orchestra playing block chords), but these instances are rare. In the second movement, for example (which, next to the Scherzo of *The Bells*, is the most vigorous orchestral piece he composed), the orchestration is vivid and sharply contrasted. He makes particularly effective use of the brass at the statements of the quasi-*Dies irae* theme heard first at the beginning, and also of the woodwind in the rocking figure which introduces the central, more sumptuously scored section. But he leaves the masterstroke until almost the end, where, in a mysterious half-lights passage, strings and woodwind combine to weave a counterpoint in simple scales ([35]–[36]).

The effectiveness in programmatic music of these elements of orchestral contrast and of Rachmaninoff's increasing ability to create large but logical structures is nowhere better illustrated than in *The Isle of the Dead*, op. 29, composed in 1909. Inspired by Böcklin's painting, a reproduction of which he had seen in Paris in May 1907, *The Isle of the Dead* is one of his most atmospheric pieces. It is also a highly dramatic, and in a sense free and expanded, interpretation of the painting. As Grigory Prokofiev commented in the *Russkiye vedomosti*, 'we find in the piece none of Böcklin's deathly stillness'.[3] But this is not entirely true of the quiet opening, which portrays, in the regular repetition of a motif of five quavers (ex. 13):

Ex. 13

the motion of Charon's oars as he rows his passenger across the Styx. The pervading aura of doom is enhanced, as in so much of Rachmaninoff's music, by subtle references to the *Dies irae* chant. In the opening section, too, he uses the abrupt chromatic figures which occur in the final movement of *The Bells*, his song *Nad svezhey mogiloy* (op. 21 no. 2) and in the central scene of *The Miserly Knight*, all of which are concerned with morbid or sinister subjects. As Charon's boat reaches the end of its journey the music swells to a climax in E minor, representing perhaps the awesome, craggy coastline of Böcklin's imaginary *Insel der Toten*. Here the 5/8 rhythm of the oars leaves off as

---

[3] *Russkiye vedomosti* (7 April 1910), p. 3.

the boat drifts towards the island, and Rachmaninoff's music departs from the picture; for he introduces what he described as a 'life' theme, a passionate, intense passage in which the Soul wistfully recalls the joys of earthly existence. The Soul's anguish increases, but the *Dies irae* is the ultimate victor, both in a bold statement and then more mysteriously on tremolo strings. After a final reference to the 'life' motif, the 5/8 rhythm appears; and the music returns to the scene of Böcklin's picture as Charon rows back across the Styx. Like *Prince Rostislav*, the gloomy subject of *The Isle of the Dead* was particularly congenial to Rachmaninoff, but the success of the piece lies more perhaps in his masterly contrasts of the dark colours associated with the *Dies irae* and the brighter, more transparent textures of the anguished 'life' episodes which stemmed entirely from his own imagination.

It was not until his 'American' works that Rachmaninoff began to dilute the Romantic succulence associated with his works of the mature period in Russia. Of the two orchestral pieces which he composed after leaving Russia, the Third Symphony, completed in 1936 and revised in 1938, shows itself to be in a sense a transitional work. In some respects it is his most expressly Russian symphony, in both melodic outline and rhythm, particularly in the dance motifs of the finale, pinpointed by subtle use of percussion. Yet this 'Russianness' – evident right at the start in the Orthodox chant-like character of the melody on clarinet and muted horn – can also be heard as a deliberate reference back to his roots by a composer cut off from them. Throughout, the music is imbued with an almost aching sadness and anguish: moments where the symphony does erupt are fairly swiftly contradicted by passages where the melodies and harmonies turn in on themselves introspectively rather than opening out with any sense of joy. If ever any work revealed that Rachmaninoff's exile was painful to him, it is this Third Symphony. Like his other two symphonies, it is discerningly constructed with a pervading motto theme, yet it differs from them in being in only three movements: here, as in the Second and Third Concertos, he includes in the slow movement an *allegro vivace* section in place of a separate Scherzo. In much of its pure nostalgic lyricism and in some of its orchestration the Third Symphony tends to look back to the Dresden years, but it also possesses many of the attractive new tendencies, notably the greater rhythmic freedom, which were to be evident in the Symphonic Dances, op. 45, completed in 1940.

In the Symphonic Dances, as in the Third Symphony, the Fourth Concerto and the Paganini Rhapsody, Rachmaninoff displays more discrimination in his use of individual instrumental tone-qualities, as well as a tendency towards more adventurous, pungent harmonies (notably the shifting, ambiguous harmonization and sinister, unsettling chromatic figures in the lilting central waltz), greater contrasts of texture and more rhythmic subtleties, often suggesting the influence of jazz. In fact the opening, slightly grotesque march (ex. 14) (like the quicker section of the slow movement of the Third Symphony) and an important staccato unifying motif (ex. 15) have affinities with the acerbity of Prokofiev. Rachmaninoff's first idea was to call this work 'Fantastic Dances', but Symphonic Dances is a more appropriate title, for they constitute a three-movement symphony in all but name. The first movement is constructed out of exx. 14 and 15, with a more expansive central episode. Sparsely accompanied by the oscillating 5ths which Rachmaninoff often favoured (as, for example, in the Scherzo of the Second Symphony and in his song *Muza,* op. 34 no. 1), the long plaintive melody in this central section is given first to a solo alto saxophone before being taken over by the strings playing in unison. At the end of the movement Rachmaninoff makes what was then a private reference to his first severe failure, for he quotes the principal theme from the First Symphony, not now in the *Sturm und Drang* manner of the earlier work but more nostalgic, more submissive. That he should use this theme, derived as it is from motifs characteristic of Russian church music, is significant, for the finale is also based on two church chants: in the two outer sections of the movement the *Dies irae* plays a prominent role, both in fairly obvious quotations and in certain rhythmic and melodic mutations, such as the principal motif of the

Ex. 14

Ex. 15

movement. But there is also another important theme, heard first on the cor anglais (ex. 16).

Ex. 16

This is in fact a much altered version of the *znamennyy* chant *Blagosloven esi, Gospodi* ('Blessed be the Lord'), which Rachmaninoff had used in his *All-night Vigil* (1915). Here lies the explanation of the word 'Alliluya' which he wrote 26 bars before the end of the Symphonic Dances. The coda of this last movement, beginning at [96], is in effect an orchestral transcription of the Doxology from *Blagosloven esi, Gospodi*, and Rachmaninoff wrote 'Alliluya' in his score at the point where the choral alleluias occur in his earlier choral piece. That he should use this hymn of praise gives

104

credence to the theory that the movement may be symbolic of God's victory over Death (represented by the *Dies irae*), and it is perhaps significant too that Rachmaninoff should have written at the end of this, his last work, the words 'I thank thee, Lord'.

8

Works for piano and orchestra

Rachmaninoff's earliest attempts at a concerto in C minor, dated November 1889, came to nothing, and his first completed concerto was that in F sharp minor, published by Gutheil as op. 1. He composed the first movement in 1890, but then put it aside for a while and completed the other two movements on 6 July the following year. After performing it many times he became discontented with its thick orchestration and rather foursquare, chordal piano writing, and he contemplated revising it in 1908. However, he did not find time until, surrounded by the turmoil of the October Revolution, he sat down to work on it shortly before leaving Russia in 1917. The new version, retaining the same basic thematic material, was published in Russia in 1920: the manuscript has remained in the archives of the Central Glinka Museum of Musical Culture in Moscow.[1]

The differences between the 1890–1 and the revised 1917 versions of the concerto reveal much about the composer's development during the quarter-century which separate them. There is a considerable thinning of the texture, both in the orchestral and in the piano writing, and also much material which tended to make the early version diffuse

---

[1] In the first edition of this book, I noted that, after leaving Russia, Rachmaninoff must have made some alterations to the piano part and certain details of orchestration: there are differences between the edition he copyrighted in New York in 1919 (now published by Boosey & Hawkes) and the one issued in the Soviet Union by the State Publishing House in 1920 and again in 1965. In his thesis *Rachmaninoff's Changing View of Symphonic Structure* (New York University, 1992, pp. 172–5), Dr David Cannata proposes the existence of a copyist's score which Rachmaninoff took with him to the USA and which was used (with the composer's corrections) for the definitive publication of the concerto. Since the 1920 and 1965 Soviet editions were based on the autograph manuscript in Moscow, an additional copyist's score (though it has not yet been found) would explain the discrepancies. I am indebted to Dr Cannata for making his theory (based on his new evidence of a possible copyist's numbering system in part of the Moscow autograph) known to me.

and episodic is excised.[2] Having gone through the score with such attention to detailed faults, Rachmaninoff was perturbed that the new version did not make a great impression on his audiences. A hint of the reasons for this public indifference is contained in something that he said to Alfred Swan: 'I have rewritten my First Concerto; it is really good now. All the youthful freshness is there, and yet it plays itself so much more easily. And nobody pays any attention. When I tell them in America that I will play the First Concerto, they do not protest, but I can see by their faces that they would prefer the Second or Third.'[3]

Before revising the First Concerto he had already captured the public ear with the sensuous beauty of his Second Concerto and the impressive austerity and drama of the Third. The First is a very different piece. The characteristic melodies, if less remarkable, are there, but they are combined with a youthful vivacity and impetuosity which were soon to be replaced by the more sombre melancholy and wistfulness of the later works. This contrast can be seen from the opening bars of the First Concerto, where a brass fanfare introduces a flourish of double octaves and chords on the piano, somewhat in the manner of the Grieg and Schumann piano concertos. Rachmaninoff never again used such a flamboyant introduction: the Second Concerto opens with eight dark piano chords, equally striking in their way; the Third launches straight into the theme after two orchestral bars containing a germinal rhythmic figure, while the Fourth has a few bars of orchestral crescendo before the main theme appears in weighty chords on the piano. As in the Grieg and Schumann concertos, the piano flourish in the First Concerto recurs later in the movement as an important factor in the symmetry of the movement. The main theme, common to both versions (like all the principal melodies in this concerto), is short by Rachmaninoff's standards, but already it shows the sequential devices and the arch-like design he was to use to much greater effect in some of his later works. The piano eventually takes up the theme in a passage which Rachmaninoff had to alter at least twice before it satisfied him. In the 1890 version the theme had a left-hand accompaniment of simple arpeggios (ex. 17a).

[2] See G. Norris, 'Rakhmaninov's Second Thoughts', *The Musical Times*, vol. cxiv (1973), pp. 364–8.
[3] A. J. and K. Swan, 'Rachmaninoff: Personal Reminiscences', *The Musical Quarterly*, vol. xxx (1944), p. 8.

Rachmaninoff

Ex. 17a

In the revised 1917 manuscript the figuration in the right hand is more fluid but also more cluttered (ex. 17b).

Ex. 17b

Rachmaninoff altered the passage again before his definitive 1919 publication, so that the melody is tastefully decorated without being overpowered (ex. 17c).

Ex. 17c

The slow movement, a reflective nocturne, is a short piece of only 74 bars. In the revised version the texture is less cumbersome, and the harmonies, while remaining basically the same, are now enlivened by occasional chromatic notes. But it was in the finale that Rachmaninoff made the most drastic structural changes in his 1917 revision. An original lifeless opening was replaced by a *fortissimo* passage, making much play of the alternations of 9/8 and 12/8. The most substantial cut occurred near the end, where he decided to omit a *maestoso* reappearance of the main theme (bars 220–7 in the original score), a device which had already become such a prominent feature in the Second and Third Concertos and was also to occur with rather less success in the Fourth. The problem with the theme in the First Concerto is that it does not have the same possibilities for upward sequential treatment. Rachmaninoff's early attempt to use it in this way sounds contrived, is ill-prepared and occurs too near the end of the movement to have the right expansive effect.

Of the several works which Rachmaninoff revised at various stages in his career, the First Concerto was perhaps his greatest success, for he transformed an early immature essay into a concise, spirited work, using the greater knowledge of harmony, orchestration, piano technique and musical form which he had acquired throughout his most prolific period of composition. The revision of the concerto was the last large-scale work he completed before leaving Russia after the Revolution. His first extended composition in the USA, the Fourth Concerto, was a terrible failure. Following the cool reception of the work at its first performance in 1927 he made considerable cuts and revised much of the orchestration and piano writing before the score was published in the following year, when it still failed to attract any popularity. Not until 13 years later, in 1941, did he begin to analyse the faults again and attempt to correct them. He was worried about the orchestration, and the second published version abounds in alterations to string figuration and instrumental distribution. He was also concerned about the length of the work; many critics had commented on this aspect after the première, though in fact each movement in the Fourth Concerto is considerably shorter than the corresponding movement in the Third. He made several more cuts in the first movement and a few minor ones in the second, but the most important changes occurred in the finale, which is just over 40 bars shorter in its second version than in the first. Not only did he omit certain passages, but also he recast much of the music to dispense with unnecessary themes and create a more compact structure.[4] Neverthe-less the concerto still failed to impress the audiences, and Alfred Swan observed that 'the opening movement . . . is only able to revive some of the images of the past and hold them together by a tried technique; . . . a lack of spontaneity is felt in this concerto.'[5]

In view of the difficulties Rachmaninoff had with the piece, the lack of spontaneity is not surprising. Swan's other comment is also justified, and is illustrated in the very first pages, where the grandeur of the opening theme swiftly fades in the bridge passage, which is so divorced from what precedes or follows it that it severely affects the cohesion of the movement. Nonetheless, a sensitive performance – like the composer's own recorded one – can maintain the momentum, and, diffuse though the concerto can appear, there are many sublime touches. This is particularly true of the second movement, a Largo, which caused some amusement at the London première because of a similarity to *Three blind mice*. Writing to Medtner on 9 September 1926 Rachmaninoff had reprimanded him for not pointing out its resemblance to Schumann's Piano Concerto. In fact the resemblance to either is fleeting, being limited to the use of the same three notes in a descending motif. In the context, the idea is, in any case, thoroughly characteristic Rachmaninoff. As in Beethoven's Fourth Concerto, he wanted to create in this Largo a dialogue between the orchestra and the soloist, a feature which is more prominent in the final version than in the earlier one. However, whereas in Beethoven the orchestra is the constant stern element and the piano the calming influence, in the Rachmaninoff the roles are shared. The music passes from one group to the other, each carrying the theme off into a different key. A passage of mild turbulence at [36] is swiftly quelled by a rising lyrical theme on the piano, derived from the main theme of the first movement. With a master stroke Rachmaninoff then introduces an entirely new melody on the cellos and violins. In the early version of the concerto this passage had been drowned by elaborate piano figuration, but in his revision he substituted simple accompanying chords in the piano part to allow the gloriously yearning theme to emerge more effectively. This theme, like the one in the first movement, was taken from the abandoned *étude-tableau*, op. 33 no. 3, giving credence to the theory,

[4] See G. Norris, 'Rakhmaninov's Second Thoughts', *The Musical Times*, vol. cxiv (1973), pp. 364–8.
[5] A. J. and K. Swan, 'Rachmaninoff: Personal Reminiscences', *The Musical Quarterly*, vol. xxx (1944), pp. 2–3.

suggested by the announcement in the journal *Muzyka* (see p. 60), that Rachmaninoff had ideas for the Fourth Concerto long before 1926. The six *Etudes-tableaux* op. 33 were in fact published soon after their composition. Whether Rachmaninoff withdrew no. 3 expressly to use in the concerto or whether he found a use for it quite by accident we shall probably never know, but the fact remains that it provides in this concerto an interesting glance back to his style of a decade earlier.

The slow movement of the Fourth Concerto is the most taut and balanced of the three. The first movement comes to an end abruptly when one is least expecting it, the trouble being, perhaps, that it could have ended quite successfully after the fine climax to the exposition. In the finale there is an oft-reiterated three-note motif which first appears in the first movement and so lends symmetry to the piece. Further unifying elements in the finale are provided by the recurrence at [71] of the material at the opening of the first movement, and also by a reference at the brusque opening to the minor 2nds at the end of the Largo. Yet it is the finale which is the most episodic and least spontaneous of the three movements. Had Rachmaninoff tackled the basic structural deficiences in his revisions, the concerto might have been received more sympa-thetically, for it reveals many features which characterize his later orchestral works: subtler orchestration, greater contrasts of rhythm and texture, and colourful harmonies.

Both structurally and melodically Rachmaninoff's most successful concertos by far are the Second and Third, as their enduring popularity underlines. In the Second Concerto in C minor, op. 18, the one which really established his fame as a concerto composer, his melodic gift is much more prominent than in the First, and its almost unbroken lyricism has undoubtedly led not only to its frequent performances but also to its being used by songwriters the world over: it has been suggested that many people still attribute to Rachmaninoff the songs *Full moon and empty arms*, *Ever and forever*, *If this is goodbye* and *This is my kind of love*, the last two of which occurred in a musical called *Anya*, using music not only from the Second Concerto but also the Suite no. 2 for two pianos, the First Concerto and several other works. And Eileen Joyce's performance of the concerto must have been heard in countless cinemas (and on many a modern domestic video) as Trevor Howard and Celia Johnson have their 'Brief Encounter' in the station buffet of David Lean's masterly 1945 film.

The story surrounding the composition of the Second Concerto after Rachmaninoff's period of severe mental depression has already been outlined in chapter 2. The return of his self-confidence was almost thwarted when his friend Nikita Morozov commented that the first subject seemed to be merely an introduction to the second subject, but nobody could seriously describe the opening as an 'introduction'; it is a continuous melody of 45 bars, sombre, passionate and tense. The C minor gloom brightens to E flat major optimism for the second subject, a shorter melody and one which follows the arch-like pattern already familiar from many works. In the early stages of the development Rachmaninoff introduces a short rhythmic fragment (ex. 18):

Ex. 18

which at the beginning of the recapitulation is used as a linking device, being hammered out *alla marcia* by the piano while the strings in unison play the first subject. This martial air which dominates the first 16 bars of the recapitulation is broken at the seventeenth by the solo piano playing more lyrically the second half of the theme. Without a preparatory bridge passage the second subject emerges on the solo horns, but the theme is now not extended as in the exposition: a codetta interrupts and the curtailed recapitulation ends with a flourish on the piano, remarkably similar to a passage in the last movement in his Suite no. 2 composed in the same year.

By an ingenious series of chords, the second movement opens in C minor, the key of the first movement, and modulates in five bars to the distant key of E major. At first the movement appears to be in 3/4, but, when the main theme appears, it is seen to be in 4/4 with deceptive offbeat stresses in the accompaniment. (This is the passage which Rachmaninoff had used before as the introduction to the Romance for six hands, composed nine years earlier. In the concerto, however, it introduces an entirely different theme.) The swiftly moving central section of the slow movement presages the Third Concerto, where Rachmaninoff incorporates a scherzo into the slow middle movement, and further foretastes of the Third Concerto (and several other large-scale works) can be seen in the use of certain themes and motifs to unify the whole piece. At the beginning of the finale the rhythmic fragment from the first movement (ex. 18) appears briefly, and this fact is even more interesting when one remembers that the finale was written before the first movement, in which the motif is far more prominent. After this short orchestral introduction the piano enters with a cadenza before the first subject proper, a theme which, like the openings to all Rachmaninoff's finales, has rhythmic rather than melodic interest, and which, in this case, closely resembles a passage in his early sacred piece *V molitvakh neusypayushchuyu bogoroditsu*. A preparation for a change of mood is provided by a *meno mosso* passage, in which the piano outlines in more rhapsodic form the first subject, and leads directly into the second subject, here played on the oboe and violas. This is the tune which took the world by storm, but it is by no means the best one that Rachmaninoff ever wrote. It is remarkably lacking in harmonic interest; some might even condemn its similarity to the second subject of the first movement, or even its orchestration, for at one point the oboe drops out when the notes descend below its comfortable register. Yet it has an unprecedented element of sadness, nostalgia and sincerity, and is beautifully written for the piano in a way which none of Rachmaninoff's imitators has ever achieved.

The Second Concerto is notable for its conciseness and for its lyrical themes, which are just sufficiently contrasted to ensure that they are not spoilt either by overabundance or overexposure. Its outstanding success more or less speaks for itself, yet in many respects the Third Concerto is a finer piece architecturally, and one in which Rachmaninoff solved many of the problems he experienced in the First and Second Concertos. Eight years separated the première of the Second Concerto and the appearance of the Third in D minor, op. 30. He composed it at his country estate, Ivanovka, during the summer of 1909, and played it for the first time in public in New York in November the same year during his first American tour. Some critics have suggested that the Third Concerto resembles the Second too closely. Certainly there are characteristic turns of phrase common to both works, but in the Third Concerto the piano and orchestral writing are more complex and the formal structure much more fascinating. The opening theme of the first movement[6] is worth

[6] Joseph Yasser has put forward a theory that this theme is derived from a Russian Orthodox Church chant sung in the Pecherskaya Lavra (Monastery of the Caves) in Kiev. See 'The Opening theme of Rachmaninoff's Third Piano Concerto and its Liturgical Prototype', *The Musical Quarterly*, vol. lv (1969), pp. 313–28.

quoting in full, for although the concerto is by no means mono-thematic, certain motifs recur throughout the piece and serve to unify all three movements (see ex. 19).

Ex. 19

Unlike the two previous concertos, the theme in the Third is expounded first by the piano, playing in octaves, one note per hand, and accompanied quietly by the orchestra. The simplicity of this texture is in marked contrast to the dark drama of the opening of the Second Concerto, though both themes are imbued with the same feeling of nostalgia. Other common factors are discernible, particu-larly the use of the tonic note as an axis: here, D dominates well over half the bars in the melody. Compared with the 45-bar theme in the Second Concerto, ex. 19 is short, and, in view of the importance it is to play throughout the work, it benefits from being repeated immediately in full, this time by the orchestra with the piano weaving decorative figures around it. During the following modulatory passage, dominated by the piano, there is a brief portent of the second subject (ex. 20a) but nothing is made of this significant motif until after a short cadenza and an orchestral passage based upon ex. 19. From reiterations of ex. 20a the true second subject emerges as its more lyrical derivative (ex. 20b).

Ex. 20a

Ex. 20b

This device of giving a percussive foretaste of lyrical melodies is highly effective in counteracting the full stops which, in the First and Second Concertos, always occur immediately before important themes.

The central development section in the first movement contains some of the most brilliant piano writing of the whole piece. It is also the focal point of the movement, reaching a climax through a series of subtle variations on ex. 19 and dying away to a *pianissimo* before the long cadenza. This cadenza is divided into two clearly marked sections, separated by a short passage where the solo instrument is joined by the woodwind. Rachmaninoff composed two versions of the first part of the cadenza. One is 59 bars long with intricate passage work; the other has 75 bars, is chordal throughout and is considerably more taxing. On the gramophone recording which Rachmaninoff made of this concerto with the Philadelphia Orchestra and Eugene Ormandy in 1939–40 he chose to play the shorter cadenza. The numbering of the pages in the manuscript, however, indicates that the longer cadenza was the composer's first choice, but presumably the necessity to fit the concerto conveniently on to 78 rpm records compelled him to choose the shorter one, or maybe Rachmaninoff simply felt that enough power had been generated elsewhere and that lightness provided an agreeable contrast. Both versions achieve the same purpose in providing a suitable platform for displays of virtuosity and in commenting adequately upon the motifs from the first subject. The development of ideas from the second subject is entrusted to the second part of the cadenza after the dialogic interlude, in which the piano contemplates the rhythmic figure (*a*) in ex. 19 and the orchestra recalls figure (*b*). With so complete a discussion of the material both in the development and in the cadenza Rachmaninoff realized that a full recapitulation was undesirable. The movement concludes shortly after the cadenza with brief references to the first and second subjects, the same method he was to use later in the Fourth Concerto with rather less success.

It is in the second movement, an Intermezzo marked *adagio*, that cunning recollections of the first-movement material occur. While hesitating to assert that the opening orchestral pages of this movement are derived from ex. 19, the pervading idea does bear a resemblance to the four bars marked (*c*). The piano eventually takes up the theme, and soon the first of the overt reappearances of the ex. 19 occurs, the piano and violins both playing motifs from (*b*). Close examination of the scherzo-like passage, which forms the central part of the Intermezzo (the idea developed from the Second Concerto), reveals a much more ingenious metamorphosis of ex. 19. The piano, playing decorated scale passages and repeated notes, accompanies a melody on the clarinet and bassoon, which is the whole of ex. 19 with much altered note values, rewritten in a major key and transposed so that the melody begins on the mediant instead of the tonic (ex. 21). This cleverly wrought passage is a clever structural idea and at the same time lends variety to the Intermezzo, which until now has concentrated almost entirely on the sequential theme mooted in the opening bars.

The beginning of the finale, which follows on directly from the Intermezzo after a piano flourish, is again based on the rhythm (*a*) in ex. 19. First mention of the theme which is eventually to become the main feature of the movement occurs as syncopated chords on the piano, the more lyrical version following on immediately. This is the same technique that Rachmaninoff used in the first movement, and here in the finale it at once maintains the momentum of the movement

Ex. 21

and strengthens the feeling of continuity. Another reiteration of the rhythmic figure (*a*) in ex. 19 introduces a *scherzando* section, in which the piano develops at length the rhythmic and melodic ideas from the beginning of the movement. With the exception of ten bars in E major, the whole of its 92 bars are firmly established in E flat. This in itself would not be a fault, because over the many extended pedal points Rachmaninoff has written lush, varied harmonies in the orchestral accompaniment; the fact which renders the music less interesting is that it frequently arrives at a firm and apparently final cadence on to E flat, only to depart once more into yet another episode: one of the more attractive of these is in fact a recollection of ex. 19 from the first movement, and the welcome passage in E major is a repeat of ex. 20b. After a general recapitulation of earlier material from the finale, Rachmaninoff uses ex. 19 again, sketching its outline in a series of abrupt chords on the piano. Increasing in volume and excitement, the climax is reached in an expansive version of the movement's second subject. The piano, climbing higher in its register, eventually reaches its upper limit and has to concede two bars of the tune to the orchestra, though Rachmaninoff's skilful use of the horns (a prominent feature of his orchestration in general) disguises the fact.

Certain parts of the Third Concerto are sometimes but, these days, less often omitted in performance, following the cuts that the composer made on his own recording. Whether this was because of mechanical problems of recording or for aesthetic reasons is not certain. As John Culshaw has pointed out,[7] the Third Concerto was

[7] J. Culshaw, 'Rachmaninov Revisited', *Soundings*, vol. iii (1973), p. 5.

issued on nine sides of a five-record set, with the tenth side blank. The uncut concerto could have been fitted on, though this may well have caused difficulties of spacing and distribution on the discs. Whatever the reasons, the most significant cuts are in the finale: one in the long E flat major passage involves 13 bars; the other is a 29-bar cut of the first appearance of the second subject. This latter omits some splendid piano writing but is almost justifiable, because it postpones the derivation of the theme from its percussive prototype and makes its eventual emergence all the more impressive, yet it also serves to throw the movement off balance. As in the Second Symphony, Rachmaninoff's large-scale structures need time to develop.

In the Third Concerto Rachmaninoff illustrates to perfection his considerable gift for writing long, beautifully phrased melodies, and uses his material intelligently to create three unified movements with a wide diversity of mood. These talents which deserted him temporarily during the composition of the Fourth Concerto returned for the Rhapsody on a Theme of Paganini, his last concerted work written in 1934. The Rhapsody falls distinctly into three sections, corresponding to the conventional movements of a concerto, the first predominantly fast, the second slow and the last vivacious throughout. In the first section (Varitions 1–10) the theme from Paganini's Violin Caprice in A minor is expounded in full only after the first variation; the next five variations continue at the same speed but with extreme cunning in decorations of the theme, but at Variation 7 the tempo relaxes and the piano introduces the *Dies irae*, which has a strong emotional affinity with the Paganini theme itself and plays a significant role throughout the piece. The first section ends with three more quick variations, in the last of which (Variation 10) the piano again states overtly the *Dies irae*. With Variation 12 the equivalent of the slow movement begins; Variation 11 is a piano cadenza, with sustained string accompaniment and fragments of melody in the woodwind, leading to a melancholic minuet in Variation 12, which for the first time takes the piece into D minor, away from the A minor which dominates the first section. The tempo changes to *allegro* for a more incisive version of the Paganini theme, and in Variation 14 (in F major) there is the first hint of the theme's inversion, which is to be more prominent later in the piece. A further *scherzando* variation completes this quick section before the key changes from F major to B flat minor and the tempo to *allegretto* for Variation 16, with its mysterious, shimmering effects of delicate orchestration in the strings. The air of expectation dominating this and the next variation (17), which incidentally bears a resembl-ance to a similarly dark passage in the first movement of the Fourth Concerto (bar 147, etc.), prepares the way for the core of the Rhapsody (Variation 18), a piece of such exquisite lyricism in its own right that it seems scarcely necessary to mention the technicality that it is a modification of the inverted Paganini theme, first mooted in Variation 14. As in his concerto finales, Variation 19, which begins the final section of the Rhapsody, has toccata-like writing for the piano with sparse orchestral accompaniment. The remaining five variations are constructed to create a continuous crescendo to the dramatic and ominous restatement of the *Dies irae* in Variation 24, before the piano has the last word with a humorously quiet snatch from the Paganini theme.

Rachmaninoff's melodic gift, even if it is a gift now applied to somebody else's melody, is nowhere more apparent than in the eighteenth variation of the Paganini Rhapsody, and his skill as an architect is rarely exmplified more clearly than in his organization of these 24 variations, finely conceived into an entirely logical and close-knit structure, towards which he had been developing in his Corelli Variations. These aspects, with a subtle wit and careful, discerning orchestration, typical of his late works, combine to place the Rhapsody at the peak of his works for piano and orchestra.

9

Chamber music

Not until the present century has Russia developed into a prolific producer of chamber music, and, as with most nineteenth-century Russian composers, Rachmaninoff's chamber works constitute a comparatively small and, in his case, unimportant part of his output. In fact only one work, the Cello Sonata, displays him at anything like his best. The others are of only passing interest, lacking as they do any real sense of spontaneity or skill in instrumental ensemble writing. He began composing chamber music while still a student at the Conservatory and his earliest work is an unfinished string quartet, probably written in the autumn of 1889 shortly after his breach with Zverev. Only two movements exist, and they were first performed in Rachmaninoff's own arrangement for string orchestra at a Conservatory students' concert in 1891. In the first movement, a Romance in G minor, the first violin has most of the melodic interest with the gently lilting theme; the cello imitates occasionally, while the inner instruments rarely extend beyond the role of accompaniment. If this movement clearly recalls Tchaikovsky, the second movement, a Scherzo in D minor, is a blend of Tchaikovsky and Borodin in both melodic and harmonic inflections. Rachmaninoff's only other quartet, however, is a more individual, impassioned piece, rhythmically and harmonically more adventurous, with greater independence of the instrumental lines. Yet unfortunately this too is incomplete, existing only in a sketchy manuscript of two movements, a fast one in G minor and a slower one in C minor, constructed largely upon a ground bass (C, D, Eb, F, Eb, D, C). The date of the piece is uncertain; on 22 March 1896 Taneyev wrote in his diary that Rachmaninoff was 'writing a quartet', but Goldenveyzer reports that he was in fact working on it at the same time as *The Bells* (1912–13). It is difficult to date a work which is so obviously a sketch,[1] yet it may be significant that the

---

[1] In the Soviet edition (Moscow, 1947) it has had to be heavily edited by Boris Dobrokhotov and Georgy Kirkor.

second subject of the first movement is reminiscent of the principal melody from his orchestral piece *The Rock* (1893), a theme which he was to use again in the slow movement of his second *Trio élégiaque* composed later the same year.

Besides a String Quintet, which was mentioned by the critic and academic Viktor Belyayev in the list of works he published in 1924[2] but which has so far proved elusive, Rachmaninoff's only other ensemble works are some instrumental duos, and also two piano trios, written in 1892 and 1893. The first, the *Trio élégiaque* in G minor, took only three or four days to write, and was performed shortly afterwards by David Kreyn, Anatoly Brandukov and Rachmaninoff himself. The speed of composition and the participation of the composer in the first performance probably explain the large number of errors and the almost complete lack of dynamic markings on the manuscript. The work is in a single sonata-form movement, firmly founded in the Classical tradition, like his earlier attempt at a string quartet. The prime fault in the piece is a lack of balance between the instruments, a feature which was to recur in his second trio: the music is dominated by the piano, whose part is almost entirely chordal save for the rather more contrapuntal writing in the central development section. The violin and cello parts rarely achieve much independence, and all three instruments are required to reiterate too often the comparatively dull thematic material, particularly at the two hard-driven climaxes.

The second *Trio élégiaque* is a more substantial piece. Rachmaninoff began writing it on 25 October, the day of Tchaikovsky's death, and he headed the score with a dedication to Tchaikovsky: 'à la mémoire d'un grand artiste'. That Tchaikovsky's death deeply affected him is evident from the sincere melancholy at the very opening of the first movement. In fact it is this movement which is the most memorable and impressive, emotionally highly charged with much dramatic writing for the piano, sharp contrasts of colour and texture, and also some effective solos for the violin and cello, though too often their writing lapses into unison. The second movement is a set of eight variations on the theme from *The Rock*. In the first version of the trio the ecclesiastical tone of the opening statement of the theme was reinforced by its being written for harmonium (with the

[2] V. M. Belyayev, *S. V. Rakhmaninov: kharakteristika evo tvorcheskoy deyatel'-nosti i ocherk evo zhizni* (Moscow, 1924).

alternative of a piano), but in the 1907 revised version, into which Rachmaninoff incorporated many alterations to the piano and instrumental parts and made several cuts, he also eliminated the harmonium. The eight variations are of uneven quality, from the unashamed note-spinning in no. 4 to the pensive, atmospheric dialogue for piano and strings in no. 7 (with its echoes of the motto from the First Symphony) and the sparkling, inspired writing for all instruments in no. 3. Without doubt several of the variations would have benefited from further cutting (in fact he did make a few cuts in all three movements in 1917, and these were incorporated into the Soviet edition of the score published in Moscow in 1950), and the length of the movement is out of all proportion to the short, swift finale. This last is perhaps the least successful of the three movements. Despite some emphatic, rhetorical gestures and an effective recurrence of the main theme from the first movement, the material is unimpressive, the piano part almost entirely chordal and the string writing nearly always in unison.

Rachmaninoff did not really overcome the problems of instrumental balance in his finest, and last, chamber work, the Cello Sonata, op. 19 in G minor. It is, however, a powerfully inventive piece, conceived on a grand scale and enhanced by a vivid piano part, whereas his earlier instrumental duos (like the Romance in F minor for cello and piano, the two pieces for cello and piano op. 2, and the two pieces for violin and piano op. 6) had been little more than attractive salon music. In the Cello Sonata too he shows a closer, if not intimate, knowledge of the expressive possibilities of the cello, doubtless acquired from his friend Brandukov, to whom the work is dedicated. Rachmaninoff composed the sonata when his creative powers were at a peak at the turn of the century, and, perhaps, understandably, certain passages resemble the Second Concerto (1900–1) and even more are reminiscent of the Suite no. 2 for two pianos (1900–1). In the first movement, after a slow introduction, the cello launches straight into the yearning first subject, but it is the piano which has the almost Schumannesque second subject. Thereafter and throughout the development it is the piano which maintains the interest, the cello only providing an accompaniment, and an elaborate piano cadenza precedes the recapitulation. Elsewhere, for example in the finale and in the vivacious virtuoso Scherzo, the instrumental ensemble is more involved, and in the Andante, if the two instruments rarely interact, they change roles with sublime effects, particularly in the gently resolving coda. The piano part is certainly the more skilfully constructed of the two, yet the intensity and drama of the music can, in a sensitive performance, amply overcome any deficiencies of instrumental balance.

10

The operas

Rachmaninoff's three operas have never gained a promiment place in the repertory, and the reasons are not difficult to discern: each presents serious problems of staging, and each has a dramatically un-satisfactory libretto. *Aleko*, his first opera, is the only one performed with any frequency in Russia today (it was revived in the West during the 1972 Camden Festival in London). As a student work, composed when Rachmaninoff was 19, its deficiencies are painfully obvious, yet it is worth consideration both for its foretastes of his more mature style and for the influences it reveals from other composers. The libretto was based on Pushkin's long narrative poem *Tsygany* ('The Gypsies') in an adaptation by Vladimir Nemirovich-Danchenko. His task of condensing the Pushkin into a one-act libretto was a formidable one: he had to cut many passages, and also used lines out of context, paraphrased the Pushkin and wrote lines himself where he needed linking phrases. He did, however, preserve intact substantial sections of the poetry, and retained the basic elements of plot: Aleko, having met up with an itinerant gypsy band, takes Zemfira as his wife; after some years of marriage her attentions turn towards a younger gypsy and, finding them together, Aleko murders them both and is banished from the camp. The libretto is, in fact, little more than a hotchpotch of separate numbers, hastily flung together, loosely connected by the plot and offering few possibilities for dramatic action or for continuity in the score.[1] Without doubt it presented the young examination candidates in Arensky's composition class with almost insuperable problems of which the young Rachmaninoff, judging from his enthusiasm, was scarcely aware.

He responded to Pushkin's vivid account of Bessarabian gypsy life with an attractive, colourful and in some respects skilful score. Elements of symmetry are achieved through the repetition of certain

[1] See G. Norris, 'Rakhmaninov's Student Opera', *The Musical Quarterly*, vol. lix (1973), pp. 441–8.

thematic material: the climax of the orchestral Introduction reappears at the dramatic focal point of the opera (Aleko's killing of Zemfira and the Young Gypsy), and the gently falling cello figure in the final bars of the Introduction is later transformed into the taunting melody of Zemfira's aria (no. 9). Also a single unifying motif runs throughout. This is Aleko's leitmotiv (ex. 22a), which occurs as the lowest notes in the woodwind figure at the beginning of the Introduction (ex. 22b):

Ex. 22a

Ex. 22b

and reappears in the orchestra whenever Aleko is on stage or whenever his name is alluded to by the other characters. In the third number, for example, the Old Gypsy relates how, many years before, his own wife eloped with an alien gypsy: the analogy between the Old Gypsy's history and Aleko's immediate future is emphasized both by the recurrence of the leitmotiv and by an interjection from Aleko himself, giving a hint of the dual murder later in the opera:

> But why did you not immediately hurry after the ungrateful girl and thrust a dagger into the plunderer's heart and her own heart, the treacherous woman?

Despite these successful attempts at unity in the score, the opera still lacks dramatic impetus, the principal reason for which was touched upon in Kashkin's review of the première in the *Moskovskiye vedomosti*:

> *Aleko* is a composition of considerable talent, but it is also the work of a novice composer, and therefore displays a few shortcomings which result from his lack of experience; this is inevitable in a young man who was still sitting on his school bench when he was writing his opera. One of the faults is a lack of cohesion between the separate numbers and scenes. Almost every scene comes to an end sharply and abruptly; immediately after that the next scene begins, giving no respite to the listener. A more experienced composer would certainly have smoothed over these sharp edges, and would have constructed 'bridges' between the numbers, enabling one to cross over into a new mood.[2]

Perhaps these musical links would have given more momentum to the score, but they could not have corrected a serious error of balance: the placing of the dances so early in the opera as nos. 5 and 6 hardly allows time for the scene to be set. But again it is the text that is to blame, for Nemirovich-Danchenko makes the chorus interrupt the Old Gypsy's tale with 'That's enough, old fellow! These stories are tedious and we shall forget them in merrymaking and dancing'.

The dances are attractive orchestral pieces in their own right, having something in common with the Capriccio on Gypsy Themes, begun in the same year as *Aleko*. The first dance, for the gypsy girls, has a lilting theme low in the clarinet's register, the principal motif of which had appeared at the end of the previous choral number (no. 3) and occurs in more vigorous form at the opening of the men's dance. Both dances (the first numbers in the opera to be composed) were occasionally performed as separate concert items; other parts of the opera have also gained rather more popularity than the work as a whole. The Young Gypsy's aria (no. 12) for example, sung offstage during what proves to be his final philandering with Zemfira, has an exquisitely lyrical melody, beautifully written for the tenor voice with a simple accompaniment on the harp. The cavatina for Aleko (no. 10) has become known through Shalyapin's performance: its long-breathed, yearning theme has all the pathos and sobbing phrases which Shalyapin could interpret so magnificently, and in its arch-like structure is the precursor of many such melodies in Rachmaninoff's later works. In other respects *Aleko* is a derivative work, owing much to Tchaikovsky in the orchestration and use of the voices; the duettino

---

[2] N. Kashkin, 'Aleko', *Moskovskiye vedomosti* (29 April 1893), p. 4.

for Zemfira and the Young Gypsy (no. 8), for example, is particularly reminiscent of the lyricism in *Eugene Onegin*. The opening, scene-setting chorus has a counterpart in much nineteenth-century Russian opera, and the influence of Borodin is recognizable in the lively gypsy music and in some of the rich string writing. In the formation of the libretto Nemirovich-Danchenko was influenced not by Russian but by Italian models, for *Aleko* closely resembles Mascagni's *Cavalleria rusticana*. This was enormously popular in Russia during the 1890s, having been performed in Moscow in the spring of 1891 and again at the end of March 1892, just at the time Rachmaninoff was working on *Aleko*. The story of gypsy life in *Aleko* is matched by the Sicilian village life of Mascagni's verismo opera, and both operas culminate in a similar *crime passionel*. Also, though the distribution of individual choruses and arias is different, the sumptuously scored Intermezzo in *Aleko*, during which dawn breaks, occurs precisely at the same point as the more famous intermezzo in *Cavalleria rusticana*.

Rachmaninoff's first attempt at opera enjoyed considerable success in Russia at the end of the nineteenth century and, even before its public première, earned him praise in Moscow's musical circles and particularly from Tchaikovsky. On the strength of his achievement another operatic proposition was put to him. Tchaikovsky had composed his opera *Undina* in 1869, but after its rejection by the Imperial Theatres he destroyed the score in 1873. Some years later he contemplated tackling the subject again and asked his brother Modest to supply him with a new scenario. This, too, failed to please him, and, finally dismissing the project on 17 April 1893, he suggested that the subject might suit Rachmaninoff and that Modest should send him the scenario. Rachmaninoff had apparently thought about writing an opera based on Zhukovsky's translation of de la Motte Fouqué's *Undine* in 1892, and had in fact asked Modest Tchaikovsky, through Ziloti, to write the libretto. However, perhaps suspecting that the libretto he finally received months later was second-hand, he wrote to Modest Tchaikovsky on 13 May 1893: 'First of all I must mention to you something I don't quite understand. At the end of your scenario for *Undina* is written 16 March. This, apparently, is the date on which you finished the work, yet I received *Undina* only at the end of April.' He went on to express enthusiasm for the idea but abandoned it in October, informing Modest Tchaikovsky in an abrupt letter of 14 October:

I am about to leave for Kiev to conduct the first two performances of [Aleko]. I should like to ask you to postpone writing and working on *Undina* for the time being, for I have not yet decided anything. I still have many doubts about it, and besides that I am faced with so much travelling that I cannot really undertake the work in the near future.
In haste. Respectfully yours, S. Rachmaninoff.

For his next opera he chose not to have a librettist. *Skupoy rytsar'* ('The Miserly Knight'), completed in piano score in 1904, was again based on Pushkin, but this time Rachmaninoff decided to set one of his 'little tragedies', the extended poems dealing with certain moral issues. There were precedents for taking these as opera subjects: Dargomyzhsky's *Kammenyy gost'* ('The Stone Guest') of 1868, Rimsky-Korsakov's *Mozart i Salieri* of 1897 and César Cui's *Pir vo vremya chumy* ('A Feast in Time of Plague') of 1900. Rachmaninoff set *The Miserly Knight* more or less word for word, omitting only about 40 lines and adding two words for the Duke to sing in the final ensemble. *The Miserly Knight* is in a single act divided into three scenes, though it presents a striking contrast to the one-act *Aleko* both musically and structurally. Rachmaninoff chose to set his new opera not in individual 'numbers' but in continuous arioso, owing much to Musorgsky rather than to Tchaikovsky. Again the text presented hazards and, in view of the lessons he must have learnt from *Aleko* and from the operas of more experienced composers, it is strange that he should have selected another libretto which presented so many problems. Although Pushkin's poem contains separate speeches for each character and takes the form of a play, it was never intended to be performed in the theatre. It is dominated by monologue, with only a few conversations and one ensemble passage at the very end. Yet it also presents many fine opportunities for musical characterization, and Rachmaninoff responds superbly, particularly in the Knight's extended monologue which constitutes Scene 2. It was this monologue that Rachmaninoff composed with Shalyapin in mind, though, because Shalyapin had not learnt the part, it was taken at the first performance by Georgy Baklanov. In this long scene, which takes place in the castle vaults, Rachmaninoff translates into musical terms Pushkin's psychological study of the Knight, depicting his maniacal excitement as he contemplates his hoarded wealth. This is the focal point of the opera, with a superb climax at the Knight's ecstatic cry 'Ya tsarstvuyu' ('I am king'), and some chilling orchestral effects based on an abrupt chromatic figure, which Rachmaninoff had also used in his song *Nad svezhey mogiloy* (op. 21 no. 2) and was later to use again in the final movement of *The Bells*. In luxuriant orchestration he represents the Knight's wistful lines 'In my magnificent gardens a playful host of nymphs will gather, and muses will bring their gifts to me', and he achieves a degree of pathos, too, in his music for the passage where the Knight recalls how he acquired some of the money:

> Here is an old doubloon. Today a widow gave it to me, but before that she and her three children knelt half the day wailing outside my window. It rained, then it stopped and started again; the hypocrite did not move.

To portray the widow's wailing Rachmaninoff uses the descending four-note figure derived from the chime of the St Sophia Cathedral bells in Novgorod, which he had used before in the third movement of his *Fantaisie-tableaux* for two pianos op. 5, inspired by Tyutchev's poem *Tears*.

Rachmaninoff thought the first scene of *The Miserly Knight* tedious. Certainly some of the vocal writing is less interesting than in the Knight's monologue, yet it also possesses at least one episode worthy of a second glance. After hearing a play-through of the opera in March 1904, Rachmaninoff's former teacher, Taneyev, noted in his diary: 'An excellent work. A splendid scene in the vaults. Incidentally the part of the Jew[ish moneylender] is full of character. Much good, noble music.'[3] Each of the three main characters (the Moneylender, Albert and the Knight himself) is clearly defined, but Taneyev was right to single out the Moneylender, who emerges as a character drawn with extreme clarity and perception. The sliding chromaticism and the high, piercing tenor part combine to depict vividly the Moneylender's insidiousness particularly at his suggestion that Albert should poison his father in order to gain the inheritance. Albert is portrayed throughout as an impetuous youth, frustrated by his father's avarice, while the Knight appears as a sinister figure from the very first hint of his chromatic motif in the orchestral Introduction.

Rachmaninoff also criticized his final scene as being too short. It is indeed short, though it is a natural conclusion, adequately tying up the loose ends: Albert and his father have a surprise confrontation at the palace of the ruling Baron; not realizing that Albert is concealed in the room next door, the Knight accuses him of being a spendthrift and of

---

[3] L. Z. Korabel'nikova (ed.), *S. Taneyev: dnevniki*, vol. iii (Moscow, 1985), p. 121 (entry for Friday, 5 March 1904).

plotting to murder him. Albert emerges, is dismissed by the Baron, and the Knight collapses and dies from the strain, gasping in his final breath: 'Where are my keys?' Rachmaninoff's treatment of moments of drama such as this shows admirably that he was aware how theatrical effects could be achieved, and, even with the many long orchestral and vocal passages where one wonders what a performer even of Shalyapin's calibre could possibly do to enliven the visual element, *The Miserly Knight* is a powerful, musically dramatic opera containing some of Rachmaninoff's finest evocations of mood and some brilliant characterization.

For his third opera he chose another libretto which lacked the requisites of a completely successful stage drama. On 28 July 1898 he had written to Modest Tchaikovsky, asking if he would consider preparing a libretto on a Shakespearian subject, generally thought to have been *Richard II*. Despite their earlier abortive association over *Undina*, Modest Tchaikovsky faced the prospect of collaborating with Rachmaninoff on another opera with some enthusiasm. He replied not with the Shakespearian subject but with a sketch for *Francesca da Rimini*, based on Canto V of Dante's *Inferno*. He added, amidst carefully detailed monetary terms, that in two months he could 'prepare not only a scenario but also part of the libretto.' Rachmaninoff's next letter of 28 August was equally enthusiastic, outlining several suggestions (which were not in fact adopted); but during his comparatively unproductive years right at the end of the century, no more was said about the opera. In 1900 Modest wrote to Rachmaninoff to enquire how it was progressing and Rachmaninoff replied from Italy on 27 June 1900: 'Today I received your letter and am replying quickly. Two years have passed since I was with you at Klin, and in those two years I have not written a single note apart from one song . . .[4] I want to try again this summer to write *Francesca* and hope that perhaps now something will emerge.'

In July 1900 he composed the bulk of the duet for Paolo and Francesca (Scene 2) but then put the score aside again until 1904, when he began to notice flaws in Modest's libretto. From Moscow he wrote him another letter on 26 March 1904:

> I want to ask you to alter your libretto for *Francesca*. With alterations the libretto looks like this —
> 1   The prologue and epilogue remain without changes.

[4] *Sud'ba* ('Fate').

2   The first two scenes are omitted.

3   The last two scenes remain, but with the following changes: first I should like you to replace 16 lines of poetry with others, and secondly to add some completely new lines before the epilogue to give more space to the love duet. In the first scene the episode with the cardinal must be cut out, and in its place I want Lanceotto [Malatesta] to tell the audience first about the trick he planned in order to attract Francesca, also about the part Paolo played in it and finally about himself in relation to these two characters. After the monologue he addresses his servant (as in your version) with the order 'summon my wife' and the score continues and ends (without changes) as in your version . . . Now if at all possible will you agree to undertake this work now? (I need it by the middle of May.)

Modest agreed to Rachmaninoff's suggestions, and the opera was completed in this form by August. Rachmaninoff told Modest:

> 3 August 1904
>
> The other day I finished [the piano score of] *Francesca*. I took the liberty of making some minor alterations in your text, and in one place, forgive me, I have even written two lines, for which I blush. But these two lines were essential, and, as I had no others, I was forced into it . . . Now that I have finished, I can tell you that, while I was working, I suffered above all because of the shortage of text. This is felt most of all in the second scene, where there is a build-up for the love duet and a conclusion to the love duet, but there is no actual duet. This shortage of words was all the more apparent because I do not allow myself to repeat words. But in *Francesca* I had to allow it because there were just too few words. The second scene and epilogue last 21 minutes. This is terribly short. The whole opera lasts little more than an hour.

He confided to Morozov the next day: 'The last scene proved to be too short. Although Tchaikovsky added some words for me (very banal ones by the way) these were not enough.'

Rachmaninoff thus forestalled many critics who have rightly commented on the lack of balance in *Francesca*. This is caused principally by the prologue, an intense representation of Hell, which in comparison to the rest of the opera is overlong. Nevertheless, it contains much fine orchestral writing, greatly enhanced by the wordless wailing of the Lost Souls, mouthing the vowel 'a'. The first section of the prologue is dominated by the minor 2nds of the Lost Souls, and orchestral chromaticism representing the swirling winds (ex. 23a).

In this, the first circle of Hell, Virgil and Dante enter and descend to the second circle, where they encounter Paolo and Francesca, condemned to pass their time in the Inferno for allowing love to overcome

Ex. 23a

reason. In the second part there is an important motif associated with the clouds which appear as Paolo and Francesca sing in unison: 'There is no greater sorrow in the world than remembering happy times when one is unhappy', a direct Russian translation of Dante's 'Nessun maggior dolore/Che ricordarsi del tempo felice/Nella miseria' (ex. 23b).

The first episode in Scene 1 presents Malatesta, a highly dramatic role tailored for Shalyapin, but it is his monologue (composed exactly as Rachmaninoff had outlined in his letter to Modest Tchaikovsky of 26 March) which presents the most opportunities for powerfully expressive effects, with much declamatory, impassioned vocal writing

Ex. 23b

and dotted rhythms in the orchestra, associated throughout with Malatesta. The third part of Scene 1 introduces a descending lyrical motif associated with Francesca. As Malatesta tells her that he is leaving for the war, Francesca promises him her obedience but not her love. Her theme returns at the beginning of Scene 2, where Paolo reads to Francesca about the illicit love of Lancelot and Guinevere. Even if unsuccessful on the stage, the piece is brilliantly orchestrated and is a vital preparation to Paolo and Francesca's declaration of love in their fine duet, a passionate piece in which the tension is greatly increased by

Rachmaninoff's writing high in the tenor and soprano register. To repetitions of Francesca's motif the couple engage in a long embrace, lasting a possible 51 bars. This hiatus could be covered by any perceptive director, and it is musically important, for Rachmaninoff reintroduces his 'cloud' music and then the dotted Malatesta rhythm in preparation for his appearance and murder of the two lovers.

Rachmaninoff completed the piano score of *Francesca* on 30 July 1904, but even then his troubles with Modest Tchaikovsky were not over. He had sent the libretto for Modest to check, and when it came back it had a number of changes. He replied on 7 September:

> When I received [the libretto] I was horror-struck at the mass of corrections you had made . . . If you insist on [these changes], then I shall have to make fundamental alterations [to the music] in many places. In your final version some words are replaced by others, and with different stresses; there is one place where unnecessary words have been added; finally, there is a place where you have crossed out two phrases, and it's now absolutely impossible to alter it. Further on I note that, whereas before you had 'Galego' you now have 'Galeotto'[5]. In view of the fact that I composed the music to the libretto which you corrected last spring, and that the text has already been translated into German, I do ask you, respected Modest Ilyich, to let me keep to the old text . . . Could you write for me an aria for Paolo? I am afraid that the second scene is too short.

He re-corrected the libretto and returned it to Modest in its previous form. However, Modest requested that it should be published in his final version, and Rachmaninoff replied on 10 September 1904:

> All will be done as you ask, though I regret it very much. I should have felt happier if all the corrections could have been done by me personally, for convenience of word-setting. I always try to handle the text carefully; I have altered little and all the alterations are yours. Because of this I am wondering whether the text need be printed at the beginning of the score, because that would only emphasize that I don't always use it. I should like to put [Paolo's] aria into the duet and not at the beginning. My duet is short. Perhaps you could write some words for the duet? That would be better.

The argument was settled with a compromise: in the score the text was printed in the form Rachmaninoff had used, but Modest's final version was printed in a separate brochure and attached to the score.

---

[5] In the final score it was restored to Galego.

These difficulties with a weak text undoubtedly contributed to the opera's lack of success. As he shows in his letters, Rachmaninoff knew that much of the libretto was banal and that the whole piece was unbalanced, and it is unfortunate that, in his haste to complete the score, he did not give more attention to the effectiveness of his opera in the theatre. All his operas were plagued with poor librettos, yet his obvious talents for writing highly charged, dramatic music, seen in parts of *The Miserly Knight* and particularly in the Prologue, Epilogue and Love Scene of *Francesca*, make one regret that he never pursued any further his subsequent operatic projects, Flaubert's *Salammbô* and Maeterlinck's *Monna Vanna*.

The former exists only as a scenario (sketched out in 1906), the latter only in a complete three-act libretto (by Mikhail Slonov), a piano score of Act 1 and sketches for Act 2.[6] To a much greater degree than anything else Rachmaninoff left incomplete, *Monna Vanna* is a tantalizing fragment. It was a score he kept with him throughout his life, and for which he held a special affection. The first act, lasting just over 40 minutes, gives ample evidence that Rachmaninoff, drawing on the experience of emotional conflicts in *Francesca da Rimini* and *The Miserly Knight*, had an ideal musical vocabulary to interpret Maeterlinck's fraught, romantic and political plot set in fifteenth-century Pisa. Again, he uses the free, deftly inflected arioso of both his other two mature operas, drifting in and out of melody and hinting at certain characteristic motifs of the Second Symphony, with which *Monna Vanna* is contemporaneous.

In the opening scene, there might be a little too much literal description of the state of affairs in Pisa and some bald explanation of who everybody is, but equally Rachmaninoff might well have adjusted that if the project had progressed. Even in this one act, *Monna Vanna* offers a marvellous baritone part (for Guido, Commander of the Pisa garrison, consumed with passion and anguish) and suggestions of a no less grateful one for his wife, the Monna Vanna of the title: her character would have been developed in the later acts where, in order to save Pisa, she agrees to visit and pacify her childhood sweetheart, Prinzivalle, who is holding Pisa to siege. As in *The Miserly Knight*, where the Knight is wallowing in his wealth and exultantly claims to be lord of all he surveys, and in *Francesca*, in the build-up of tension before the lovers are killed, Rachmaninoff, in *Monna Vanna*, prepares

---

[6] Act I has now been orchestrated and recorded by the conductor Igor Buketoff.

the way for the heroine's first appearance – near the end of the act – with a theatrically acute sense of expectation.

The potential of this *Monna Vanna* torso makes one regret that the legal constraints on using the Maeterlinck story prevented Rachmaninoff from pursuing it further. Had conditions been different, there could well have been another 1900s Maeterlinck opera to join Debussy's *Pelléas et Mélisande* and Dukas' *Ariane et Barbe-Bleue*, and, of course, the *Monna Vanna* for which Henri Février had secured the exclusive European rights.

11

The songs

Rachmaninoff composed over 80 songs and, rather like his piano works, they offer a clear picture of his stylistic development, spanning as they do his most prolific period as a composer, from the 1890s to 1916. For most of his songs he chose his texts from the works of prominent Russian Romantics, rarely setting a foreign poem except in translation. Only in his final set, op. 38, did he begin to look further afield to the modern symbolists, but the trends initiated in these six songs were not allowed to develop for, after leaving Russia in 1917, he never again found the inspiration to compose a solo song.

Although he had attempted orchestral and piano pieces from his early teens, Rachmaninoff did not write his first song until he was 17. This was *U vrat obiteli svyatoy* ('At the gate of the holy abode', 1890), a setting of Lermontov's poem *Nischchiy* ('The beggar'); a few days later he composed *Ya tebe nichevo ne skazhu* ('I shall tell you nothing', 1890) to a poem by Afanasy Fet, whose works he was to use several times in his more mature songs and whose *V molchan'i nochi taynoy* ('In the silence of the secret night') was later included as no. 3 of the op. 4 set. As in all his early songs, these three display considerable melodic invention and an obvious sympathy for vocal writing, but the accompaniments lack the variety and contrast of his later songs and too often lapse into melodramatic triplets at moments of tension. At this early stage in his career, too, he did not possess the ability to penetrate beneath the surface of the texts, and, although there are occasional effective moments of word painting (as, for example, in the sighing motifs in the accompaniment to *Opyat' vstrepenulos' ty, serdtse* ('Again you leapt, my heart'), the settings are rarely more than superficial.

In 1892, as a direct result of the success of *Aleko*, Rachmaninoff sold six songs to his publisher Gutheil; some remained unpublished, some were included in the set of six songs op. 4, published shortly after they were composed. No. 1, *O net, molyu, ne ukhodi!* ('Oh no, I beg you, forsake me not'), was composed in 1892, and in its opening bars recalls the slow movement of the First Piano Concerto (1891); notable too is the first phrase of the vocal line, centred on a pivotal note (F), a prominent feature in much of Rachmaninoff's music. *Utro* ('Morning'), no. 2 in the set, is dedicated to Rachmaninoff's fellow-student Yury Sakhnovsky and was probably written in the autumn of 1891 (or perhaps 1892) when he was convalescing at Sakhnovsky's house. The last three songs were all completed in the summer of 1893 during a stay at the Lysikovs' estate near Kharkov, and *Uzh ty, niva moya* ('O thou, my field', no. 5), which in its modality and frequent time-changes evokes the sound of Russian folk music, is in fact dedicated to Madame Lysikova. Throughout, the accompaniment is simple, becoming more agitated only at that passage in the text telling how the winds have beaten down the corn (again reminiscent of part of the First Concerto, [15] in the first version). The most interesting song in the set is the fourth, *Ne poy, krasavitsa, pri mne* ('Sing not to me, beautiful maiden'); like no. 5 it has a folk-like simplicity, though here Rachmaninoff attempted to imbue the music with Georgian local colouring (vocal melismata, augmented-interval scales in the piano part) to match the Pushkin text. The piano part has more variety than in many of the early songs, and one of its features – the final chromatically descending vocal line against a pedal A in the accompaniment (ex. 24) – occurs in several later pieces.

In the six songs op. 8, all of which are settings of Alexey Pleshcheyev's translations of German and Ukrainian texts, Rachmaninoff is most successful in the shorter, purely descriptive poems. *Molitva* ('Prayer', no. 6) and *Duma* ('Brooding', no. 3) are merely superficial accounts of the longer and more introvert Goethe and Shevchenko texts. The finest of the group are no. 4, *Polyubila ya na pechal' svoyu* ('I have grown fond of sorrow'), which rarely strays from the home key of G minor and in some melodic turns of phrase is reminiscent of Musorgsky, and no. 5, *Son* ('The dream'). In this Rachmaninoff combines simplicity of vocal line with perfect musical balance, something lacking in another of the lyrical songs in the set, *Rechnaya lileya* ('The water lily', no. 1); also, the piano part never asserts itself, as do the more weighty accompaniments to some of these other early songs.

All the op. 8 songs were composed in 1893. In the following year Rachmaninoff set a short poem by Mariya Davidova, *Ya zhdu tebya* ('I wait for thee'), but it was not until 1896 that he completed the other 11 songs for the set of 12 op. 14. This set is uneven both in style and in

Ex. 24

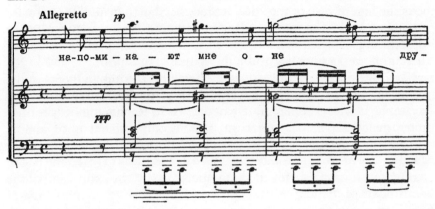

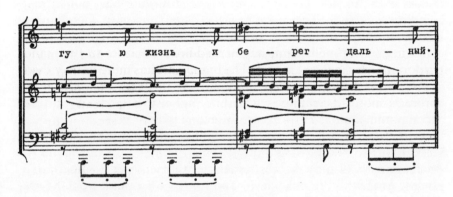

[... they remind me of another life and a distant shore.]

quality. Nearly all the songs are passionate expressions of love or grief, but, whereas songs like *O, ne grusti* ('Oh, do not grieve', no. 8) and *Tebya tak lyubyat vse* ('How everyone loves thee', no. 6) are reminiscent of Tchaikovsky, the last two songs, *Vesenniye vody* ('Spring waters') and *Pora!* ("'Tis time!') are couched in a more individual style. In addition, two of the songs resemble the earlier Georgian song (op. 4 no. 4) in their Oriental colouring: *Ona, kak polden', khorosha* ('She is as lovely as the noon', no. 9) and *V moyey dushe* ('In my soul', no. 10), both to poems by Minsky. In several of the op. 14 songs the melodic invention is not outstanding, yet perhaps the most effective is the simplest, *Ostrovok*, set to Balmont's adaptation of Shelley's *The Isle*. The vocal line could scarcely be simpler, merely carrying the words in short, generally stepwise phrases, while the piano part consists of two statements of a descending scale separated by an inspired, voluptuous three-bar juxtaposition of G major and E flat major harmonies.

With the exception of *Ostrovok*, the piano accompaniments to the songs in op. 14 are often overpowering: in *Vesenniye vody*, for example, which is appropriately dedicated to Rachmaninoff's former piano-teacher Anna Ornatskaya, the accompaniment is of almost orchestral proportions. In the op. 21 set the piano is again prominent though in a more subtle way than op. 14, for it was here that he began to create a special role for the accompaniment in the expression of the sentiments of the text. He composed 11 of the songs in the spring of 1902, at about the same time as his marriage to Natalya Satina, and, taken as a whole, the set is possibly his most spontaneous, most inventive. Only the first song, *Sud'ba* ('Fate'), composed earlier than the others, in 1900, falls below the high standard. Seldom did Rachmaninoff plumb the depths of banality reached by *Sud'ba*: a long melodramatic showpiece composed specially for Shalyapin to a text by Alexey Apukhtin, it relies all too heavily on overt references to the opening motif of Beethoven's Fifth Symphony. The greater import-ance of the piano is more evident in many of the other songs. In *Nad svezhey mogiloy* ('By the fresh grave', no. 2) the morbidity of Semyon Nadson's text is suggested not only by the declamatory nature of the vocal line but also by the abrupt chromatic figures in the piano part, simple but highly effective devices which Rachmaninoff used in other works. The relentless arpeggios in the accompaniment to *Oni otvechali* ('They answered', no. 4) represent in a perhaps less subtle manner the surging waters of the Hugo-Mey poem, and the short coda to *Ya ne prorok* ('No prophet, I', no. 11) imitates the harp.

The op. 21 songs include three of Rachmaninoff's finest mature settings: *Siren'* ('Lilacs', no. 5), which he later transcribed for piano solo, *Na smert' chizhika* ('On the death of a linnet', no. 8) with its delicate contrapuntal piano part, and perhaps finest of all *Zdes' khorosho* ('How fair this spot', no. 7), which in its integration of piano and vocal lines is bettered only by *U moyevo okna* ('Before my window', op. 26 no. 10). It is worth quoting a substantial section of *U moyevo okna* simply to observe the completely natural manner in which the accompaniment, after an opening consisting of the barest support for the voice, takes over part of the vocal melody and proceeds to develop an independent but entirely fitting accompaniment, almost constituting an individual piano study of the poem's sentiment (see ex. 25).

U moyevo okna is one of the few purely lyrical songs in the op. 26 (1906) set. Many of the others are more declamatory, as for example *My otdokhnyom* ('Let us rest', no. 3), set to a text from Chekhov's *Uncle Vanya*, *Prokhodit vsyo* ('All things pass by', no. 15), and *Khristos voskres!* ('Christ is risen', no. 6), not a song of rejoicing at the Resurrection but one bewailing the sadly corrupt world into which Christ rose again. Several more of the songs are concerned specifically with various aspects of spring: the agitated *Pokinem, milaya* ('Beloved, let us fly', no. 5) with its gloriously well-judged modulation from A flat to A major in the central section, the more subdued, introspective *Ya opyat' odinok* ('Again I am alone', no. 9) and also *Poshchady ya molyu* ('I beg for mercy', no. 8), in which the piano part emphasizes the singer's pleadings that spring should not reawaken the heart's longings. Impressive though these are, it is again the less complex songs which make the deepest impression and seem to have the most to offer. The particular merits of *U moyevo okna* have been noted, but the set also includes the inspired *Vchera my vstretilis'* ('When yesterday we met', no. 13), using almost throughout the simple syncopated accompaniment familiar from many of Rachmaninoff's songs, and *K detyam* ('To the children', no. 7), one of the loveliest of all his songs. This is set in the manner of a lullaby to one of Alexey Khomyakov's poems, telling of a mother's nostalgia at the growing up of her family: her wistful cry 'O children' at the song's climax is one of Rachmaninoff's finest moments of inspiration.

Almost without exception the poems which Rachmaninoff used for his next set of songs, op. 34, are of high quality and ideal for musical setting, chosen as they are from the works of the foremost representatives of Russian Romanticism: Pushkin, Tyutchev, Polonsky, Khomyakov, Maykov, Korinfsky and also the rather more modern Balmont, whose gloriously mellifluous verse *Veter perelyotnyy* ('The migrant wind') he included as no. 4 in the set. This song displays many of the characteristics which distinguish his finest settings of this, his mature creative period: simplicity of vocal line rarely describing an interval wider than a 5th, a sparser piano accompaniment generally designed to reflect the mood of the text and often pinpointing certain phrases in touches of word-painting, greater rhythmic freedom, and a

Ex. 25

У мо-е-го ок-на че-ре-му-ха цве-тет, цве-тет за-дум-чи-во под ри-зой се-ре-бри-стой... И вет-кой све-жей и ду-ши-стой скло-ни-лась и зо-вет

more striking use of colourful harmonies. This last is evident above all
in the second song, *V dushe u kazhdovo iz nas* ('In the soul of each of
us'), with its strikingly apt harmonic progression in the fourth and fifth
bars (see ex. 26).

Ex. 26

[In the soul of each of us murmurs the spring of one's sorrow.]

This song is dedicated to Shalyapin, as are the other dramatic,
declamatory songs in the set: *Ty znal evo* ('You knew him', no. 9),

---

[Before my window a cherry tree is blossoming, is blossoming with
silvery garments . . . and bends its fresh and fragrant branch and calls
to me . . .]

Obrochnik ('The Peasant', no. 11), and *Voskreseniye Lazarya* ('The raising of Lazarus', no. 6). A typical example of Khomyakov's religious poetry, this last is again notable for its effective harmonic progressions, particularly at the sublime resolution in bar 13 at the words 'Da skazhesh' "Vstan'" dushe moyey' ('And bid my soul rise again'). Apart from other dedications to the memory of Tchaikovsky and the actress Vera Komissarzhevskaya, to Marietta Shaginian, to Feliya Litvin (in the dramatic *Dissonans* ('Discord', no. 13) with its wayward harmonies and spine-chilling word-painting to the phrase 'without fire') and to Antonina Nezhdanova in the lyrical *Vocalise* (no. 14), all the other songs were written for the tenor Leonid Sobinov. These are more lyrical than Shalyapin's songs, and include two of the finest in the set, *Sey den', ya pomnyu* ('I remember that day', no. 10), with the simplicity of accompaniment and vocal line of the earlier *Ostrovok*, and the more impassioned *Kakoye schast'ye* ('What happiness', no. 12).

For his last set of songs, op. 38, completed in 1916, Rachmaninoff chose exclusively from the works of contemporary poets: Blok, Bely, Severyanin, Bryusov, Sologub and Balmont, all of whom were connected with the Russian symbolist movement predominant in Russia in the late nineteenth and early twentieth centuries. Their poetry inspired him to look for a new style, towards which op. 34 had been progressing in its rhythmic subtleties and pungent harmonies while retaining the familiar melodic element. In op. 38 he developed an almost impressionistic musical language to match the ideals of the Russian symbolists. Like his later orchestral and piano works, these later songs contain many new ideas: shimmering accompaniments (particularly in Balmont's *A-u!*, no. 6), constantly changing rhythms (as in Bely's *K ney* ('To her', no. 2)), intricate but transparent piano accompaniments and strangely ambiguous harmonies (as, for example, in the fateful triads which end the Balmont song). Perhaps all of the tendencies are, however, summed up by the finest songs in the set, *Margaritki* ('Daisies', no. 3) and *Son* ('The Dream', no. 5). In this latter, particularly, he brilliantly creates with remarkably little thematic material a musical image of the elusive subject of the poem.

Even if Rachmaninoff had only written this one, last set of songs, his reputation as a composer with gifts for surrounding and complementing a text with a web of atmospheric piano textures and finding a vocal line which throws the sentiments into relief would have been assured. Yet among his 80 or so songs there are many other instances – *Zdes' khorosho* (op. 21 no. 7) and *U moyevo okna* (op. 26 no. 10), to name only two in a kaleidoscopic range – which show that, just as in some of the solo piano pieces where a mood is caught and crystallized, so in the songs Rachmaninoff could identify in the most affecting musical terms a poignant poetic thought.

12

The choral works

Although Rachmaninoff composed only a handful of choral pieces, he succeeded in contributing one masterpiece to both the sacred and secular repertories: the *Vsenoshchnoye bdeniye* ('All-night Vigil') op. 37 and the choral symphony *Kolokola* ('The Bells') op. 35. Even in his early, musically less distinguished sacred pieces he displayed his skill in vocal writing, whether for solo voice or chorus, accompanied or *a cappella*. *Deus meus*, a six-part motet composed (maybe in 1890) as part of his course at the Moscow Conservatory, was followed by a sacred concerto *V molitvakh neusypayushchuyu bogoroditsu* ('O Mother of God vigilantly praying', 1893), of which Semyon Kruglikov wrote that there was much talented writing but a certain flippancy in the setting of the religious text and little insight into the words of prayer.[1] The piece does, however, contain several features which presage Rachmaninoff's more mature works. The same is true of *Panteley-tselitel'* ('Panteley the Healer'), a piece for four-part choir to a text by A. K. Tolstoy (1899), and also to the Six Choruses op. 15 for women's or children's voices (1895–6). *Panteley*, for example, has a richness of texture with sonorous, typically Russian bass parts, and also a sumptuous harmonic language which serves to emphasize that the piece is a near contemporary of the Second Concerto.

Ten years passed before Rachmaninoff again tackled an unaccompanied choral work, a setting of the Liturgy of St John Chrysostom, the most frequently used liturgy in the Russian Orthodox Church. As is apparent from the circumstances of his marriage, Rachmaninoff was no churchman, and it was a considerable undertaking for him to set the liturgy, with little or no knowledge of ecclesiastical matters. Yet it is clear from his letters that he knew intimately the setting of the liturgy by Tchaikovsky (1878), and he must also have known other sacred works by such composers as

[1] S. Kruglikov, 'Dukhovnyy kontsert v Sinodal'nom uchilishche', *Artist* (1894), no. 1, p. 177.

Alexander Grechaninov. Also he had a useful acquaintance in Alexander Kastalsky, Director of the Synodical Academy, who advised him on details of liturgical choral writing. He completed the *Liturgy* at the end of summer 1910, and it was first performed the following November. The reception by the Church authorities was cool, because, as in Tchaikovsky's setting, his work laid too much importance on the actual music. According to official policy the words were the prominent feature, and the music should in no way detract from them. Some critics tend to see in Rachmaninoff's break with Orthodox tradition a disapproval of the Church; yet this was no deliberate attempt on his part to offend, but rather a genuine expression of the inspiraiton he derived from the words of the service. The work is in 20 numbers, unified by certain thematic reminiscences; also the keys of the individual pieces are so organized that the whole work can satisfactorily be performed as a complete concert item. In the *Liturgy* there is the same rich choral writing as in *Panteley*, but there is also a greater degree of contrast between the mainly homophonic vocal groups and also more use of special choral effects. For example, no. 16, *Khvalite gospoda s nebes*

Ex. 27

[Praise God in the heavens . . .]

('Praise God in the heavens'), displays the fascination with bells which permeates so much of Rachmaninoff's music (ex. 27).

The *Liturgy of St John Chrysostom* was in many respects a preparation for the *All-night Vigil*. This is a setting of the service which takes place in Orthodox churches before important festivals. Rachmaninoff completed it during the winter of 1915. It differs significantly from the *Liturgy* in the nature of the melodies: whereas in the *Liturgy* all the music is his own composition, in the *All-night Vigil*, in accordance with Russian Orthodox principles, he based nine of the numbers on traditional chants, providing them with his own characteristic harmonies and subjecting them to variation treatment: *Blagoslovi dushe moya* ('Praise the Lord, O my soul', no. 2) and *Vzbrannoy voyevode* ('To the Mother of God', no. 15) are based on Greek chants; *Svete tikhiy* ('Gladsome radiance', no. 4) and *Nyne otpushchayeshi* ('Nunc dimittis', no. 5) on Kiev chants; and *Khvalite imya Gospodne* ('Praise the name of the Lord', no. 8), *Blagosloven esi, Gospodi* ('Blessed be the Lord', no. 9), *Slavosloviye velikoye* ('Gloria in excelsis', or 'The great doxology', no. 12), *Dnes spaseniye miru* ('The day of salvation,' no. 13) and *Voskres iz groba* ('Christ is risen from the tomb', no. 14) on *znamennyy* chants. The remaining numbers are his own interpretations of motifs characteristic of Russian church music. The work is in 15 numbers, of which the ninth, the story of the Resurrection, is the central dramatic point (it was the *znamennyy* chant from this anthem which he later used in the Symphonic Dances). Also in this ninth number can be seen his highly effective use of voices in sharply contrasted groups to echo the sentiments of the words. A short refrain in the tenors and basses opens the hymn and recurs throughout at the start of each new verse. Particularly effective is the concluding doxology, beginning softly on the lower voices and rising to an ecstatic 'Alleluya' eight bars before the end.

There is a further example of this technique of increasing excitement through reiterated 'Alleluyas' in no. 3, *Blazhen muzh* ('Blessed is the man'). Here the 'Alleluyas', interspersed with other parts of the hymn, are repeated each time in a different key, the sopranos' first note rising each time to reach a climax at the 'Alleluya' before the beginning of the Doxology; thereafter the music subsides in key and dynamic to a final *pianissimo*. The melody on the 'Alleluyas' in no. 3 recurs in no. 12, the Great Doxology, in which there is an example of Rachmaninoff's variation treatment of the theme: the sopranos have a version of the theme in augmentation, while the altos sing another variation in freer rhythm (see ex. 28).

Throughout the *All-night Vigil* there is this degree of rhythmic contrast, combined with a much wider range of texture, a highly dramatic use of dynamics, and more independence of voices than in any of his earlier choral works. He often makes use of solo voices set against a choral group, as for example in no. 4, and more notably in no. 5, the *Nunc dimittis*, which he requested should be sung at his funeral (though that proved to be impracticable). Nonetheless it is a haunting, valedictory, consoling piece of writing. A more striking contrast occurs in no. 8, *Khvalite imya Gospodne*, where the *znamennyy* chant is given out starkly by the altos and basses after a more richly harmonized opening in the sopranos and tenors.

Ex. 28

[Have mercy on me.
Blessed be the Lord, teach me Thy Statutes.]

The vocal writing in the works for chorus and orchestra tends to be rather simpler, more homophonic, because the colouristic effects are supplied by the orchestra. *Vesna* ('Spring'), a cantata for baritone, chorus and orchestra, was composed in 1902, and, even more than *Panteley-tselitel'* displays its proximity to the Second Concerto, particularly in the cello melody beginning two bars before [17]. For his text Rachmaninoff took Nikolay Nekrasov's poem *Zelyonyy shum* ('The verdant noise'), a thoroughly Russian story telling of a husband's fury at his wife's infidelity and his plan to kill her. Suddenly, as he is preparing the knife, spring arrives, dispelling his murderous thoughts; he sings, 'Love while it is possible to love, suffer while it is possible to suffer, forgive while it is possible to forgive, and God will be our judge'. Rachmaninoff's idea of spring here is not an idealized one of dewdrops and bursting buds, apart from a few isolated passages and the introduction, where shimmering, surging orchestration, gradually increasing in volume, represents spring's approach. Rachmaninoff was attracted more to Nekrasov's poem by the dramatic possibilities of the human problem it deals with, much as in *The Miserly Knight*. In fact there are certain features in *Spring* which presage the opera, particularly the central baritone solo, a part almost certainly conceived with Shalyapin in mind: there are the long, lyrical lines, the dramatic outbursts, sudden contrasts of *piano* and *forte*, in all of which Shalyapin excelled. There are other foretastes of the opera too, for there is something of the youthful impetuosity of Albert's music, and also the same use of short chromatic phrases which permeate the Knight's music. The climax of the solo part is the cry 'Ubey, ubey izmennitsu' ('Kill, kill the unfaithful woman'), where the choir joins in with a wordless contribution to the orchestral accompaniment: a device which occurs in *Francesca da Rimini*, *The Bells*, and even in some of the unaccompanied choral works. As the husband muses 'Pripas ya vostryy nozh' ('I have prepared a sharp knife'), the choir returns with its opening line, eventually increasing in speed and tension towards a climax, startlingly foursquare and solid. But it is worth enduring for the cello melody at [17] which precedes the return of the opening theme, the words of which are sung by the chorus.

The same yearning passion of *Spring* is evident in the opening of the first of Rachmaninoff's Three Russian Songs, op. 41, his last work for choir and orchestra, composed in 1926. The first of the songs tells an amusing tale which is treated with touching pathos: a drake is crossing a bridge with his beloved, a grey duck; but she becomes afraid and flies away, leaving the drake sad and weeping. The chorus part for this song is for basses alone, singing in unison, and, as in all three songs, the orchestra required is enormous. But, like Rachmaninoff's other later orchestral works, there is discrimination in the use of orchestral timbres, and the first song, particularly, abounds in attractive woodwind figuration representing the mournful call of the drake. The second song, in D minor, is a lament for women's voices alone, but the third brings the whole choir together. This is another humorous Russian song, which Rachmaninoff had in 1925 arranged for voice and piano (and recorded in 1926 with Nadezhda Plevitskaya): an unfaithful wife watches with light-hearted terror as her jealous husband approaches to beat her with a whip of silk. In the early part of the song the melody is in unison with a simple accompaniment: plucked strings imitate the sound of the balalaika, and the wood block the crack of the silken whip. An orchestral interlude, similar to the passage just before the saxophone melody in the last movement of the Symphonic Dances, separates the first section from the coda, in which the women's voices sing a tongue-in-cheek lament: 'Pravo slovo, khochet on menya pobit', ya zh ne znayu i ne vedayu za chto!' ('In truth he wants to beat me, but I don't know or understand why'). The Three Russian Songs, performed for the first time in March 1927 by Leopold Stokowski, the dedicatee, have been given since then only rarely; although they make an ideal short concert item, the forces required are considerable and expensive to assemble.

Rachmaninoff's own favourite work was the choral symphony *The Bells*, composed during the early part of 1913. His fascination for bells had been evident ever since his early childhood days in Novgorod, and his theory that bells could convey different human emotions, illustrated to a lesser degree in *The Miserly Knight* and his *Fantaisie-tableaux* for two pianos, reaches even greater prominence in the choral symphony. The fatal theme of Edgar Allan Poe's poem struck in him a sympathetic chord, even though it had lost a good deal of its bite in the Russian adaptation by Konstantin Balmont. Poe's four verses readily corresponded to the movements of a symphony. The slow tempo demanded by the last verse may well have presented Rachmaninoff with an unusual problem, but he did know of at least one precedent for a slow finale in Tchaikovsky's Sixth Symphony.

In the first verse Poe saw silver sleigh-bells as a symbol of birth and youth; Balmont retained this idea in his version of the poem, and Rachmaninoff responded with a movement which is vividly orchestrated and full of youthful verve, joyfulness and optimism. It opens with a few tentative bell-chimes high on the woodwind, piano and triangle. Gradually the rest of the orchestra joins in, with the same cumulative effect which Rachmaninoff used – though with voices only – in the *All-night Vigil*. Towards the end of the movement the violins introduce an important motif (ex. 29), a rocking figure which recurs in much of Rachmaninoff's music.

Ex. 29

More important for *The Bells*, it recurs as a unifying idea at the beginning of the second movement, a soprano solo with choral interjections (based on the same rocking figure), in which Poe associates marriage with mellow golden bells. The sumptuous orchestration at the opening immediately indicates that this is to be a passionate, rapturous concept of marriage, particularly so in the long lyrical soprano lines. The third movement, a diabolical scherzo, is a choral clamour, without soloists, depicting the loud brazen bells of terror. Again ex. 29 is reiterated prominently, but here it relinquishes its languorous rocking effect for a relentless obsessiveness concluding the movement loudly and abruptly. In this movement the choral writing is deliberately taxing, showing an almost instrumental treatment of the voices, so difficult are the individual parts (the effect is far less spine-chilling in the anaemic easy version which Rachmaninoff made for English performances in the 1930s).

The deathly stillness of the finale is enhanced by the plaintive cor anglais melody, eventually taken up by the baritone solo, and by the hollow chords of the opening, which recur almost throughout the movement as if to suggest the relentless approach of Death. At the fifth bar the piano, brass and woodwind sound a warning triad, rather as in the final movement of the Symphonic Dances; this chord is a dominating feature of the movement, recurring also in a modified, more agitated form (ex. 30).

Ex. 30

In the central section the music brilliantly depicts Poe's grim lines (in Fanny S. Copeland's translation of the Russian):

> But the spirit of the belfry is a sombre fiend who dwells
> In the shadow of the Bells,
> And he gibbers, and he yells
> As he knells, knells, knells,
> Madly round the belfry reeling,
> While the giant bells are pealing,
> While the bells are fiercely thrilling,
> Moaning forth the word of doom.

Here, Rachmaninoff's chromatic word-painting on the word 'stonet' (moaning) in the last line is a masterstroke, the chorus building to a climax of terror before the music subsides and the Soul finds peace in death, in the soft, serene D flat of the conclusion. It was this last verse of Poe's poem that he found particularly congenial, for it allowed him to express, with an emotional intensity he never surpassed, that feeling of fatalistic melancholy which pervades much of his music.

Appendix A

Calendar

Year	Age	Life	Contemporary musicians and events
1873		Sergey Rachmaninoff born 20 March (1 April, new style), at Oneg.	Nikolay Cherepnin born, 3 May; Shalyapin born, 1 Feb. Arensky aged 11; Balakirev 33; Mitrofan Belyayev 37; Borodin 39; Cui 38; Debussy 10; Dyagilev 1; Glazunov 7; Grechaninov 8; Kalinnikov 7; Kashkin 33; Liszt 61; Lyadov 17; Lyapunov 13; Mahler 12; Mascagni 9; Musorgsky 33; Rimsky-Korsakov 29; Anton Rubinstein 43; Nikolay Rubinstein 37; Sibelius 7; Skryabin 1; Stasov 49; Richard Strauss 8; Tchaikovsky 32; Henry Wood 14; Ziloti 9; Zverev 40.
1874	1		Schoenberg born, 13 Sept.
1875	2		Bizet (36) dies, 3 June; Glier born, 30 Dec. 1874; Ravel born, 7 March.
1876	3		Falla born, 23 Nov.
1877	4		Dohnányi born, 27 July.
1879	6		Medtner born, 24 Dec.; Respighi born, 9 July.
1880	7		Bloch born, 24 July; Offenbach (61) dies, 4 Oct.
1881	8		Bartók born, 25 March; Musorgsky (42) dies, 16 March; Myaskovsky born, 8 April; Nikolay Rubinstein (45) dies, 11 March.

1882	9	Rachmaninoff attends the St Petersburg Conservatory.	Kodály born, 16 Dec.; Leopold Stokowski born, 18 April; Stravinsky born, 5 June.
1883	10		Wagner (69) dies, 13 Feb.; Webern born, 3 Dec.
1884	11		Smetana (60) dies, 12 May.
1885	12	Begins piano lessons with Zverev in Moscow.	Berg born, 9 Feb.; Varèse born, 22 Dec.
1886	13	Makes piano transcription of Tchaikovsky's *Manfred*.	Liszt (74) dies, 31 July.
1887	14	Composes piano pieces.	Borodin (53) dies, 15 Feb.
1888	15	Enters Ziloti's piano class at Moscow Conservatory; studies with Taneyev and Arensky. Sketches ideas for an opera, *Esmeralda*. Writes orchestral Scherzo.	Alkan (74) dies, 29 March.
1889	16	Sketches a piano concerto. Breaks with Zverev, and moves into the Satins' Moscow house.	Henselt (75) dies, 10 Oct.
1890	17	Begins First Piano Concerto.	Franck (67) dies, 8 Nov.; Ibert born, 15 Aug.; Frank Martin born, 15 Sept.; Martinů born, 8 Dec.
1891	18	Composes Russian Rhapsody for two pianos. Graduates from piano section of the Conservatory. Completes First Piano Concerto; composes *Prince Rostislav*.	Bliss born, 2 Aug.; Delibes (54) dies, 16 Jan.; Prokofiev born, 11 April.
1892	19	Composes first *Trio élégiaque*; gives première of the first movement of his new concerto. Graduates in composition from the Conservatory; composes Prélude in C sharp minor.	Honegger born, 10 March. Lalo (69) dies, 22 April; Milhaud born, 4 Sept.
1893	20	Première of *Aleko* at the Bolshoy. Composes *The Rock*, 6 songs op. 8, Suite no. 1 for two pianos; also completes the set of 6 songs op. 4 and composes the second *Trio élégiaque* in memory of Tchaikovsky.	Gounod (75) dies, 18 Oct.; Tchaikovsky (53) dies, 25 Oct.; Zverev (61) dies, 30 Sept.

1894	21	Completes 7 *Morceaux de salon*, Capriccio on Gypsy Themes and 6 duets, op. 11.	
1895	22	Composes First Symphony.	Hindemith born, 16 Nov.
1896	23	Composes 6 *Moments musicaux* and completes 12 songs, op. 14.	Bruckner (72) dies, 11 Oct.
1897	24	Disastrous première of First Symphony. Takes conducting post with Mamontov's opera company.	Brahms (63) dies, 3 April. Première of Skryabin's Piano Concerto (Odessa, 11 Oct.).
1898	25	Studies operas with Shalyapin, and has first thoughts on *Francesca da Rimini*.	
1899	26	First international appearance, in London, to conduct *The Rock*, and to play two pieces from op. 3.	Eugene Ormandy born, 18 Nov.; Poulenc born, 7 Jan.
1900	27	Begins course of treatment with Dr Dahl. Composes Love Duet for *Francesca*. Begins work on Second Concerto and Suite no. 2 for two pianos. Gives first performance of two movements of the concerto.	Copland born, 14 Nov.; Kalinnikov (34) dies, 29 Dec.; Sullivan (58) dies, 22 Nov.
1901	28	Completes Suite no. 2 and Second Concerto; performs complete concerto. Composes Cello Sonata.	Verdi (87) dies, 27 Jan.
1902	29	Composes *Spring*. Marries Natalya Satina. Completes 12 songs, op. 21. Settles in Moscow in the autumn.	Walton born, 29 March. Première of Debussy's *Pelléas et Mélisande* (Paris, 30 April).
1903	30	Completes Chopin Variations op. 22 and Preludes, op. 23. Irina, the Rachmaninoffs' first daughter, born; Rachmaninoff begins work on *The Miserly Knight*.	Wolf (42) dies, 22 Feb.
1904	31	Signs contract to conduct at the Bolshoy. Completes piano score of *Francesca da Rimini*.	Dvořák (62) dies, 1 May; Kabalevsky born, 17 Dec.
1905	32	Completes first season at the	Tippett born, 2 Jan.

		Bolshoy, and conducts some concerts for the Kerzins. Completes scoring of *Francesca da Rimini* and *The Miserly Knight*.	January uprising in St Petersburg.
1906	33	Conducts première of both operas; resigns from the Bolshoy and goes to Italy. Contemplates another opera, *Salammbô*. Back at the Russian estate Ivanovka he completes 15 songs, op. 26. In the autumn the family moves to Dresden, where he begins his Second Symphony.	Arensky (44) dies, 25 Feb.; Shostakovich born, 12 Sept.
1907	34	Works on Second Symphony, and composes First Sonata; sketches ideas for an opera, *Monna Vanna*. Another daughter, Tatyana, born at Ivanovka in the summer.	Grieg (63) dies, 4 Sept.
1908	35	Première of Second Symphony in Russia.	Messiaen born, 10 Dec.; Rimsky-Korsakov (64) dies, 8 June.
1909	36	Completes *The Isle of the Dead* in Dresden. Appointed Vice-President of the Russian Musical Society. Composes Third Concerto at Ivanovka in the summer; in the autumn gives its première during his first American tour.	Albéniz (48) dies, 18 May. Première of Rimsky-Korsakov's *The Golden Cockerel* (Moscow, 24 Sept.).
1910	37	Completes American tour. Returns to Russia in early February. Composes Liturgy of St John Chrysostom and 13 preludes, op. 32.	Balakirev (73) dies, 16 May.
1911	38	Composes *Etudes-tableaux*, op. 33, at Ivanovka, of which he is now in charge.	Mahler (50) dies, 18 May.
1912	39	Marietta Shaginian writes to Rachmaninoff, and later suggests poems for his 14 songs op. 34. Rachmaninoff buys a motorcar.	Massenet (70) dies, 13 Aug. Première of Prokofiev's First Piano Concerto (Moscow, 25 July).

1913	40	Fatigued by conducting engagements in Moscow, Rachmaninoff takes his family to Rome, where he begins work on *The Bells*. Both daughters contract typhoid, and the family goes to Berlin to consult doctors. They recuperate at Ivanovka, where Rachmaninoff completes *The Bells* and the Second Sonata.	Britten born, 22 Nov. Première of Stravinsky's *The Rite of Spring* (Paris, 5 April).
1914	41	Visits England and makes plans for first British performance of *The Bells* (eventually postponed because of the First World War). Summer at Ivanovka.	Lyadov (59) dies, 15 Aug.
1915	42	Composes *All-night Vigil*. Writes an obituary of Taneyev, and plans a series of concerts in memory of Skryabin.	Skryabin (43) dies, 14 April; Taneyev (58) dies, 6 June.
1916	43	Rachmaninoff's father dies on a visit to Ivanovka. Rachmaninoff composes 6 songs, op. 38, and some of the *Etudes-tableaux*, op. 39.	Granados (48) dies, 24 March; Reger (43) dies, 11 May.
1917	44	Rachmaninoff gives final concert in Russia. Revises First Piano Concerto. Accepts invitation to perform in Stockholm, and leaves Russia with his family in December.	Tsar Nicholas II abdicates, 15 March. October Revolution, 24/25 Oct.
1918	45	Begins new career as international concert pianist, living first in Copenhagen. Receives three offers from the USA; declines all of them, but decides nevertheless to live there. Gives first American concert in December.	Cui (83) dies, 24 March; Debussy (55) dies, 25 March.
1919	46	After the end of the season, he rents a house near San Francisco.	
1920	47	Summer at Goshen, New York. Nikolay Struve, the family's	Bruch (82) dies, 2 Oct.

friend and fellow-émigré, dies in Paris. Rachmaninoff signs recording contract with Victor.

1921	48	After 1920–1 season the family takes an apartment in New York, and then spends the summer at Locust Point, New Jersey.	Humperdinck (67) dies, 27 Sept.; Saint-Saëns (86) dies, 16 Dec. Première of Prokofiev's *Love for Three Oranges* (Chicago, 30 Dec.).
1922	49	Rachmaninoff gives his first post-War concert in London. Meets Satin family at Dresden.	
1923	50	During 1922–3 season undertakes 71 concerts, including visits to Canada and Cuba. Reduces number of appearances for the following season.	
1924	51	After the end of the season the family travels to Europe and spends some time in Dresden. Irina marries Prince Pyotr Volkonsky; he dies less than a year later. After concerts in England, the family returns to the USA.	Busoni (58) dies, 27 July; Fauré (79) dies, 4 Nov.; Puccini (65) dies, 29 Nov.; Stanford (71) dies, 29 March.
1925	52	Family spends the summer near Paris. After Pyotr Volkonsky's death Rachmaninoff establishes Tair publishing house. Sofiya Volkonskaya, Rachmaninoff's first granddaughter, born.	Boulez born, 25 March; Satie (59) dies, 1 July.
1926	53	Completes Fourth Piano Concerto and Three Russian Songs.	Henze born, 1 July.
1927	54	Fourth Concerto unenthusiastically received at première in March. Family spends some time in Dresden and then in Switzerland.	
1928	55	After American season family takes a holiday in Normandy, then goes to Dresden. Rachmaninoff undertakes European tour until the end of the year.	Janáček (74) dies, 12 Aug.; Stockhausen born, 22 Aug.

1929	56	After American concerts the family moves to Paris, renting a house at Clairefontaine, their summer home for several years to come. Rachmaninoff records *The Isle of the Dead* with the Philadelphia Orchestra. Begins European tour in October.	
1930	57	Begins American tour in January. Respighi orchestrates some of the *Etudes-tableaux*. Family decides to build a villa, Senar, at Hertenstein, near Lucerne.	Première of Shostakovich's *The Nose* (Leningrad, 18 Jan.)
1931	58	In the USA Rachmaninoff signs a letter protesting at the Soviet regime. He is attacked by the Moscow press. Composes Corelli Variations and performs them in October at Montreal. Revises Second Sonata.	d'Indy (80) dies, 2 Dec.; Nielsen (66) dies, 2 Oct.
1932	59	Tatyana marries Boris Konyus. Rachmaninoff celebrates the 40th anniversary of his debut as a pianist.	
1933	60	At Senar he buys a motorboat.	
1934	61	Villa Senar completed. He composes Paganini Rhapsody and performs it in the USA in November.	Elgar (76) dies, 23 Feb.; Delius (72) dies, 10 June.
1935	62	At Senar he begins work on Third Symphony.	Berg (50) dies, 24 Dec.; Dukas (69) dies, 17 May.
1936	63	Completes Third Symphony, and rewrites choral parts of the third movement of *The Bells* for the Sheffield Festival.	Glazunov (70) dies, 21 March; Respighi (56) dies, 18 April.
1937	64	Discusses with Fokin a ballet based on the Paganini legend, using music from the Paganini Rhapsody.	Ravel (62) dies, 28 Dec.; Roussel (68) dies, 23 Aug.
1938	65	European concert tour curtailed by political events. Revises Third Symphony.	Shalyapin (65) dies, 12 April.

| 1939 | 66 | Gives final concerts in England in March. He falls, and is prevented from attending the première of the Fokin ballet in June. He plays at the Lucerne Festival, and leaves Europe for the last time. In the USA the Philadelphia Orchestra gives a special series of concerts to celebrate the 30th anniversary of his first visit to the USA (1909). He records the First and Third Concertos and the Third Symphony. | Second World War declared, 3 Sept. |

1940 67 At Orchard Point, Long Island, composes his last work, the Symphonic Dances.

1941 68 Revises Fourth Concerto and records it in December.

1942 69 Family spends summer in California. They rent a house at Beverly Hills, and then buy one on Elm Drive. Rachmaninoff decides that his next tour is to be his last.

1943 69 His health deteriorates, but the tour continues. He gives his final concert at Knoxville, Tennessee, in February. Unable to carry on, he and his family return to Los Angeles. He dies at Beverly Hills on 28 March.

Bartók 62; Bliss 51; Bloch 62; Boulez 17; Britten 29; Copland 42; Dallapiccola 39; Dohnányi 65; Henze 16; Hindemith 47; Ibert 52; Ireland 63; Kabalevsky 38; Kodály 60; Martin 52; Martinů 52; Medtner 63; Messiaen 34; Milhaud 50; Poulenc 44; Prokofiev 51; Shaporin 53; Shostakovich 36; Sibelius 77; Stockhausen 14; Richard Strauss 78; Stravinsky 60; Tippett 38; Varèse 57; Vaughan Williams 70; Walton 40; Webern 43.

Appendix B

List of works

For details of the whereabouts of manuscripts and for information about publications see R. Threlfall and G. Norris, *A Catalogue of the Compositions of S. Rachmaninoff* (London, 1982) and M. G. Rytsareva, ed., *Avtografy S. V. Rakhmaninova v fondakh Gosudarstvennovo tsentral'novo muzeya muzykal'noy kul'tury imeni M. I. Glinki* (Moscow, 1980).

Operas and Possible Projected Stage Works

op.
— *Esmeralda*, after Victor Hugo's *Notre Dame de Paris*. Introduction to Act 1; Entr'acte; fragments of Act 3, one dated 17 October 1988. All in piano score.
— *Boris Godunov*, 2 monologues from Pushkin's poem.
    1. Boris's monologue *Ty, otche patriarkh* (3 versions).
    2. Pimen's monologue *Eshcho odno posledneye skazan'ye* (2 versions).
    ?1890–1.
— *Maskarad*, Arbenin's monologue *Noch' provedennaya bez sna*, from Lermontov's poem. ?1890–1.
— *Mazeppa*, fragment of a vocal quartet (for Mazeppa, Kochubey, Lyubov and Mariya), based on Pushkin's poem *Poltava*.
— *Aleko*, 1 act. Libretto by Vladimir Nemirovich-Danchenko, after Pushkin's poem *Tsygany*. 1892. Dated (1) Introduction: 2–3 April. (2) Gypsies' Chorus: 3 April. (3) Old Gypsy's Aria: 4 April. (4) Scena and Chorus: no date. (5) Gypsy Girls' Dance: 21–2 March. (6) Men's Dance: 23, 24, 25 March. (7) Duettino for Zemfira and the Young Gypsy: 28 March. (8) Chorus: 28 March. (9) Zemfira's Aria: 29 March. Other sections undated. Completed by 13 April 1892.
    First performance: Bolshoy Theatre, Moscow, 27 April 1893, conducted by Ippolit Altani.
— *Undina*, scenario by Modest Tchaikovsky, after Vasily Zhukovsky. Contemplated 1893. No music extant.
24 *Skupoy rytsar'* (The Miserly Knight), 3 scenes. A setting of Pushkin's poem. August 1903–June 1905. Dated (1) Introduction and Scene 1:

19 May 1905. (2) In the Vaults: 30 May 1905. (3) At the Court: 7 June 1905.
First performance: Bolshoy Theatre, Moscow, 11 January 1906, conducted by Rachmaninoff.

25 *Francesca da Rimini*, Prologue, 2 scenes and epilogue. Libretto by Modest Tchaikovsky after Dante's *Inferno* (Canto V). Summer 1904–August 1905, except for the duet for Paolo and Francesca, composed in July 1900. Dated (1) Prologue: 20 June 1905; (2) Scene 1: 9 July 1905; (3) Scene 2: no date; (4) Epilogue: 25 June–22 July 1905.
First performance: Bolshoy Theatre, Moscow, 11 January 1906, conducted by Rachmaninoff.

— *Salammbô*, scenario by Rachmaninoff (with Nikita Morozov and Mikhail Slonov). 1906. No music extant.

— *Monna Vanna*, libretto by Mikhail Slonov after the play by Maeterlinck. Unfinished. Act 1 in piano scored dated Dresden, 15 August 1907; sketches for Act 2.

— *King Lear*. Contemplated 1914. No music extant.

— *Skify* (The Scythians). Projected ballet, 1914. No music extant.

Choral Works

— *Deus meus*, 6-part motet. ?1890.

— *V molitvakh neusypayushchuyu bogoroditsu* (O Mother of God vigilantly praying). Summer 1893.
First performance: Moscow, 12 December 1893, by the Synodical Choir.

— *Don Juan*, Chorus of Spirits and Song of the Nightingale to A. K. Tolstoy's text. ?1894.

15 6 Choruses for women's or children's voices. 1895–6.
    no. 1 *Slav'sya* (Be praised) (Nekrasov)
    no. 2 *Nochka* (Night) (Lodyzhensky)
    no. 3 *Sosna* (The Pine) (Lermontov)
    no. 4 *Zadremali volny* (The Waves Slumbered) (Romanov)
    no. 5 *Nevolya* (Slavery) (Tsyganov)
    no. 6 *Angel* (The Angel) (Lermontov)

— *Panteley-tselitel'* (Panteley the Healer) (A. K. Tolstoy). Dated 18 October 1899.

20 *Vesna* (Spring), cantata for baritone, chorus and orchestra to Nekrasov's poem *Zelyonyy shum*. January–February 1902.
First performance: Moscow, 11 March 1902, with Alexander Smirnov (baritone), conducted by Alexander Ziloti.

31   *Liturgiya svyatovo Ioanna Zlatousta* (Liturgy of St John Chrysostom).
      Summer 1910. Dated 30 July 1910.
      First performance: Moscow, 25 November 1910, by the Synodical
      Choir conducted by Nikolay Danilin.

35   *Kolokola* (The Bells), for soloists, chorus and orchestra. Text by
      Konstantin Balmont after the poem by Edgar Allan Poe. January
      –April 1913. Dated (1) 10–15 June; (2) 25–30 June; (3) 2–17 July;
      (4) 19–27 July 1913.
      First performance: St Petersburg, 30 November 1913, with Elizaveta
      Popova, Alexander Alexandrovich, Pavel Andreyev and the chorus
      of the Mariinsky Theatre conducted by Rachmaninoff.

37   *Vsenoshchnoye bdeniye* (All-night Vigil). January–February 1915.
      First performance: Moscow, 10 March 1915, with Sergey Yudin and
      the Synodical Choir conducted by Nikolay Danilin.

41   3 Russian Songs for chorus and orchestra. 1926.
      no. 1 *Cherez rechku*
      no. 2 *Akh ty, Van'ka*, dated 16 November 1926
      no. 3 *Belilitsy, rumyanitsy, vy moy*
      First performance: Philadelphia, 18 March 1927, conducted by
      Leopold Stokowski.

Orchestral Works

—   Scherzo in D minor. Dated 5–21 February 1888.
      First performance: Moscow, 2 November 1945, conducted by
      Nikolay Anosov.

—   *Manfred*, ?October 1890; lost.

—   Suite, 1891; lost.

—   Symphony in D minor [*Yunusheskaya simfoniya*], first movement only.
      Dated 28 September 1891.

—   *Knyaz' Rostislav* (Prince Rostislav), after the poem by A. K. Tolstoy.
      Dated 9–15 December 1891.
      First performance: Moscow, 2 November 1945, conducted by
      Nikolay Anosov.

7   *Utyos* (The Rock), after Chekhov and Lermontov. Summer 1893.
      First performance: Moscow, 20 March 1894, conducted by Vasily
      Safonov.

12   *Kaprichchio na tsyganskiye temy* [Capriccio on gypsy themes] (Caprice
      bohémien). Summer 1892 and summer 1894.
      First performance: Moscow, 22 November 1895, conducted by
      Rachmaninoff.

13   Symphony no. 1 in D minor. January–30 August 1895.
      First performance: St Petersburg, 15 March 1897, conducted by
      Alexander Glazunov.

— Symphony. Abandoned sketches. Dated 5 April 1897.
27 Symphony no. 2 in E minor. October 1906–April 1907.
First performance: St Petersburg, 26 January 1908, conducted by Rachmaninoff.
29 *Ostrov myortvykh* (The Isle of the Dead), after the painting by Böcklin. Spring 1909. Dated Dresden, 17 April 1909.
First performance: Moscow, 18 April 1909, conducted by Rachmaninoff.
44 Symphony no. 3 in A minor. Dated (1) 18 June–22 August 1935 (corrected 18 May–1 June 1936); (2) 26 August–18 September 1935; (3) 6–30 June 1936.
First performance: Philadelphia, 6 November 1936, conducted by Leopold Stokowski.
Revised 1938.
45 Symphonic Dances. Dated (1) 22 September–8 October 1940; (2) 27 September 1940; (3) 29 October 1940.
First performance: Philadelphia, 3 January 1941, conducted by Eugene Ormandy.

Works for Piano and Orchestra

— Concerto in C minor. Sketches. Dated November 1889.
1 Concerto no. 1 in F sharp minor. First movement 1890; work completed 6 July 1891.
First performance: Moscow, 17 March 1892 (first movement only), played by Rachmaninoff and conducted by Vasily Safonov. Revised autumn 1917. Dated 10 November 1917. Subsequently revised further.
18 Concerto no. 2 in C minor. Second and third movements autumn 1900; work completed 21 April 1901.
First performances: Moscow, 2 December 1900 (second and third movements); 27 October 1901 (complete work), played by Rachmaninoff and conducted by Alexander Ziloti on both occasions.
30 Concerto no. 3 in D minor. Summer 1909. Dated 23 September 1909.
First performance: New York, 28 November 1909, played by Rachmaninoff and conducted by Walter Damrosch.
40 Concerto no. 4 in G minor. Dated January–25 August [1926].
First performance: Philadelphia, 18 March 1927, played by Rachmaninoff and conducted by Leopold Stokowski.
Revised 1941.
First performance of revised version: Philadelphia, 17 October 1941, played by Rachmaninoff and conducted by Eugene Ormandy.

43   Rhapsody on a Theme of Paganini. Dated 3 July–18 August 1934.
     First performance: Baltimore, 7 November 1934, played by
     Rachmaninoff and conducted by Leopold Stokowski.

Chamber Music

—   Romance for violin and piano. A minor. ?1880s.
—   2 Movements for String Quartet. ?1889.
     (1) Romance in G minor; (2) Scherzo in D major.
     First performance: Moscow, October 1945, by the Beethoven
     Quartet.
     Arranged for orchestra by Rachmaninoff, ?1890.
     First performance: Moscow, 24 February 1891, conducted by Vasily
     Safonov.
—   Romance for Cello and Piano in F minor. Dated 6 August 1890.
—   'Mélodie on a Theme by S. Rachmaninoff', for cello and piano. ?1890.
—   ? String quintet.
—   *Trio élégiaque* in G minor for piano, violin and cello. Dated 18–21
     January 1892.
     First performance: Moscow, 30 January 1892, by Rachmaninoff,
     David Kreyn (violin) and Anatoly Brandukov (cello).
 2   2 Pieces for Cello and Piano. 1892.
     (1) Prelude in F; (2) Oriental Dance.
     First performance: Moscow, 30 January 1892, by Rachmaninoff and
     Brandukov.
 6   2 Pieces for Violin and Piano. Summer 1893.
     (1) Romance in D minor; (2) Hungarian Dance.
 9   *Trio élégiaque* in D minor for piano, violin and cello. Dated 25
     October–15 December 1893. First performance: Moscow, 31
     January 1894, by Rachmaninoff, Yuly Konyus and Anatoly
     Brandukov. Revised version: Moscow, 12 February 1907, by
     Alexander   Goldenveyzer,   Karl   Grigorovich   and   Anatoly
     Brandukov.
—   2 Movements for String Quartet. ?1896.
     (1) Allegro moderato, G minor; (2) Andante molto sostenuto,
     C minor.
     First performance: Moscow, October 1945, by the Beethoven
     Quartet.
19   Sonata for Cello and Piano in G minor. Summer 1901. Dated 12
     December 1901.
     First performance: Moscow, 2 December 1901, by Rachmaninoff
     and Anatoly Brandukov.

Works for Solo Piano

— Song Without Words in D minor. 1886 or 1887.
— 3 Nocturnes. 1887–8.
    no. 1 F♯ minor dated 14–21 November 1887
    no. 2 F major dated 22–5 November 1887
    no. 3 C minor–E♭ major dated 3 December 1887–12 January 1888
— 4 Pieces. ?1887–8
    no. 1 Romance in F♯ minor
    no. 2 Prélude in E♭ minor
    no. 3 Mélodie in E major
    no. 4 Gavotte in D major
— Piece (Canon). D minor. ?1890–91.
— Prélude in F major. Dated 20 July 1891.
3   *5 Morceaux de fantaisie*. Autumn 1892.
    no. 1 Elégie in E♭ minor
    no. 2 Prélude in C♯ minor [arranged for 2 pianos, ?1938]
    no. 3 Mélodie in E major [revised 26 February 1940]
    no. 4 Polichinelle in F♯ minor
    no. 5 Sérénade in B♭ minor [revised ?1940]
    First performance of complete set: Kharkov, 28 December 1892 by Rachmaninoff.
10 *7 Morceaux de salon*. December 1893–January 1894.
    no. 1 Nocturne in A minor
    no. 2 Valse in A major
    no. 3 Barcarolle in G minor
    no. 4 Mélodie in E minor–major
    no. 5 Humoresque in G major [revised 3 March 1940]
    no. 6 Romance in F minor
    no. 7 Mazurka in D♭ major
    First performance of nos. 4, 5, 6 and 7: Moscow, 31 January 1894, by Rachmaninoff.
16 *6 Moments Musicaux*. October–December 1896.
    no. 1 Andantino in B♭ minor
    no. 2 Allegretto in E♭ minor [revised 5 February 1940]
    no. 3 Andante cantabile in B minor
    no. 4 Presto in E minor
    no. 5 Adagio sostenuto in D♭ major
    no. 6 Maestoso in C major
— Improvisations for *Four Improvisations* by Arensky, Glazunov, Rachmaninoff and Taneyev. ?1896.
— *Morceau de fantaisie* in G minor. Dated 11 January 1899.
— Fughetta in F major. Dated 4 February 1899.

22   Variations on a Theme of Chopin [Prelude no. 20 in C minor]. August 1902–February 1903.
First performance: Moscow, 10 February 1903, by Rachmaninoff.

23   10 Preludes. 1903, except no. 5 composed in 1901.
- no. 1 F♯ minor
- no. 2 B♭ major
- no. 3 D minor
- no. 4 D major
- no. 5 G minor
- no. 6 E♭ major
- no. 7 C minor
- no. 8 A♭ major
- no. 9 E♭ minor
- no. 10 G♭ major

First performance of nos. 1, 2 and 5: Moscow, 10 February 1903, by Rachmaninoff.

28   Sonata no. 1 in D minor. January–February 1907. Dated 14 May 1907. Dresden.
First performance: Moscow, 17 October 1908, by Konstantin Igumnov.

32   13 Preludes. 1910.
- no. 1 C major; dated 30 August
- no. 2 B♭ minor; dated 2 September
- no. 3 E major; dated 3 September
- no. 4 E minor; dated 28 August
- no. 5 G major; dated 23 August
- no. 6 F minor; dated 25 August
- no. 7 F major; dated 24 August
- no. 8 A minor; dated 24 August
- no. 9 A major; dated 26 August
- no. 10 B minor; dated 6 September
- no. 11 B major; dated 23 August
- no. 12 G♯ minor; dated 23 August
- no. 13 D♭ major; dated 10 September

First performance: ?St Petersburg, 5 December 1911 by Rachmaninoff

33   *Etudes-tableaux*. 1911.
- no. 1 F minor; dated 11 August
- no. 2 C major; dated 16 August
- no. 3 [6] E♭ minor; dated 23 August
- no. 4 [7] E♭ major; dated 17 August
- no. 5 [8] G minor; dated 15 August
- no. 6 [9] C♯ minor; dated 13 August

[Three other Etudes intended for op. 33 were withdrawn by Rachmaninoff before publication. Of these the A minor (originally no. 4) was subsequently published as op. 39 no. 6; the C minor–major (no. 3), dated 18 August 1911, and the D minor (no. 5), dated 11 September 1911, were not published until 1948]

36 Sonata no. 2 in B♭ minor. January–August 1913. Dated (1) 12 August 1913; (2) and (3) 18 September 1913.
First performance: Moscow, 3 December 1913, by Rachmaninoff. Revised summer 1931.

39 *Etudes-tableaux*. 1916–17.
  no. 1 C minor; dated 5 October 1916
  no. 2 A minor
  no. 3 F♯ minor; dated 14 October 1916
  no. 4 B minor; dated 24 September 1916
  no. 5 E♭ minor; dated 17 February 1917
  no. 6 A minor; dated 8 September 1911 [revised 27 September 1916]
  no. 7 C minor
  no. 8 D minor
  no. 9 D major; dated 2 February 1917
First performance of complete set: Petrograd, 21 February 1917, by Rachmaninoff.

— Oriental Sketch. Dated 14 November 1917.
First performance: New York, 12 November 1931, by Rachmaninoff.

— Piece in D minor. Dated 14 November 1917.

— Fragments. Dated 15 November 1917.

42 Variations on a Theme of Corelli [La Folia]. 1931. Dated 19 June 1931.
First performance: Montreal, 12 October 1931, by Rachmaninoff.

Works for Piano Duet

— Romance in C major. ?1893.

11 6 Duets. April 1894.
  no. 1 Barcarolle in G minor
  no. 2 Scherzo in D major
  no. 3 Thème Russe in B minor
  no. 4 Valse in A major
  no. 5 Romance in C minor
  no. 6 *Slava* (Glory) in C major

— Polka Italienne. ?1906.

Rachmaninoff

Works for Piano (6 Hands)

—   2 Pieces. 1890 and 1891.
      no. 1 Valse in A major; dated 15 August 1890
      no. 2 Romance in A major; dated 20 September 1891.

Works for Two Pianos

—   Russian Rhapsody. Dated 12–14 January 1891.
      First performance: Moscow, 17 October 1891, by Rachmaninoff
      and Iosif Levin.
5   *Fantaisie-tableaux* [Suite no. 1]. Summer 1893.
      First performance: Moscow, 30 November 1893, by Rachmaninoff
      and Pavel Pabst.
17   Suite no. 2. December 1900–April 1901.
      First performance: Moscow, 24 November 1901, by Rachmaninoff
      and Alexander Ziloti.

Songs

—   *U vrat obiteli svyatoy* (At the gate of the holy abode) (Lermontov). Dated 29 April 1890.
—   *Ya tebe nichevo ne skazhu* (I shall tell you nothing) (Fet). Dated 1 May 1890.
—   *Opyat' vstrepenulos' ty serdtse* (Again you leapt, my heart) (Grekov). ?1890.
—   *C'était en avril* (Edouard Pailleron). Dated 1 April 1891.
—   *Smerkalos'* (Twilight has fallen) (A. K. Tolstoy). Dated 22 April 1891.
—   *Pesnya razocharovannovo* (Song of the Disillusioned) (Rathaus). ?1893.
—   *Uvyal tsvetok* (The flower has faded) (Rathaus). ?1893.
—   *Ty pomnish' li vecher* (Do you remember the evening) (A. K. Tolstoy). ?1893.
4   6 Songs. 1890–93.
      no. 1 *O net, molyu, ne ukhodi!* (Oh no, I beg you, forsake me not) (Merezhkovsky); dated 26 February 1892.
      no. 2 *Utro* (Morning) (Yanov); ?1891–2.
      no. 3 *V molchan'i nochi taynoy* (In the silence of the secret night) (Fet); ?1892
      no. 4 *Ne poy, krasavitsa, pri mne* (Sing not to me, beautiful maiden) (Pushkin); ?1892–3
      no. 5 *Uzh ty niva moya* (Oh thou, my field) (A. K. Tolstoy); 1893.
      no. 6 *Davno l', moy drug* (How long, my friend) (Golenishchev-Kutuzov); 1893.

8   6 Songs to Pleshcheyev's translations of German and Ukrainian texts.
1893
no. 1 *Rechnaya lileya* (The Water Lily) (Heine); autumn 1893
no. 2 *Ditya! kak tsvetok ty prekrasna* (Child, thou art as beautiful as
a flower) (Heine); dated October 1893
no. 3 *Duma* (Brooding) (Shevchenko); autumn 1893
no. 4 *Polyubila ya na pechal' svoyu* (I have grown fond of sorrow)
(Shevchenko); autumn 1893
no. 5 *Son* (The Dream) (Heine); autumn 1893
no. 6 *Molitva* (Prayer) (Goethe); autumn 1893

14   12 Songs. 1894–6.
no. 1 *Ya zhdu tebya* (I wait for thee) (Davidova); dated 1894
no. 2 *Ostrovok* (The Isle) (Shelley, trans. Balmont); dated 1896
no. 3 *Davno v lyubvi otrady malo* (For long there has been little
consolation in love) (Fet); dated October 1896
no. 4 *Ya byl u ney* (I was with her) (Koltsov); dated October 1896
no. 5 *Eti letniye nochi* (These summer nights) (Rathaus); dated
October 1896
no. 6 *Tebya tak lyubyat vse* (How everyone loves thee)
(A. K. Tolstoy); dated 1896
no. 7 *Ne ver' mne, drug!* (Believe me not, friend) (A. K. Tolstoy);
dated 1896
no. 8 *O, ne grusti* (Oh, do not grieve) (Apukhtin); dated 1896
no. 9 *Ona, kak polden', khorosha* (She is as lovely as the noon)
(Minsky); dated 1896
no. 10 *V moyey dushe* (In my soul) (Minsky); dated 1896
no. 11 *Vesenniye vody* (Spring Waters) (Tyutchev); dated 1896
no. 12 *Pora!* ('Tis time!) (Nadson); dated 1896

—   *Ikalos' li tebe* (Were you hiccupping?) (Vyazemsky). Dated 17 May
1899.

—   *Noch'* (Night) (Rathaus). Dated 1900.

21   12 Songs. All are dated April 1902, except for no. 1.
no. 1 *Sud'ba* (Fate) (Apukhtin); dated 18 February 1900
no. 2 *Nad svezhey mogiloy* (By the fresh grave) (Nadson)
no. 3 *Sumerki* (Twilight) (J.-M. Guyot, trans Tkhorzhevsky)
no. 4 *Oni otvechali* (They answered) (Victor Hugo, trans. Mey)
no. 5 *Siren'* (Lilacs) (Beketova)
no. 6 *Otryvok iz A. Myusse* (Fragment from De Musset) (trans.
Apukhtin)
no. 7 *Zdes' khorosho* (How fair this spot) (Galina)
no. 8 *Na smert' chizhika* (On the Death of a Linnet) (Zhukovsky)
no. 9 *Melodiya* (Melody) (Nadson)
no. 10 *Pred ikonoy* (Before the Ikon) (Golenishchev-Kutuzov)

no. 11 *Ya ne prorok* (No prophet, I) (Kruglov)
no. 12 *Kak mne bol'no* (How painful for me) (Galina)

26   15 Songs. 1906.

no. 1 *Est' mnogo zvukov* (There are many sounds) (A. K. Tolstoy); 14 August 1906

no. 2 *Vsyo otnyal u menya* (He took all from me) (Tyutchev); dated 15 August 1906

no. 3 *My otdokhnyom* (Let us rest) (Chekhov, from Act 4 of *Uncle Vanya*); dated 14 August 1906.

no. 4 *Dva proshchaniya* (Two Partings) (Koltsov); dated 22 August 1906

no. 5 *Pokinem, milaya* (Beloved, let us fly) (Golenishchev-Kutuzov); dated 22 August 1906

no. 6 *Khristos voskres!* (Christ is risen) (Merezhkovsky); dated 23 August 1906

no. 7 *K detyam* (To the children) (Khomyakov); dated September 1906

no. 8 *Poshchady ya molyu* (I beg for mercy) (Merezhkovsky); dated 15 August 1906

no. 9 *Ya opyat' odinok* (Again I am alone) (Bunin); dated 4 September 1906

no. 10 *U moyevo okna* (Before my window) (Galina); dated 17 September 1906

no. 11 *Fontan* (The Fountain) (Tyutchev); dated 6 September 1906
no. 12 *Noch' pechal'na* (Night is mournful) (Bunin); dated 3 September 1906

no. 13 *Vchera my vstretilis'* (When yesterday we met) (Polonsky); dated 3 September 1906

no. 14 *Kol'tso* (The Ring) (Koltsov); dated 10 September 1906

no. 15 *Prokhodit vsyo* (All things pass by) (Rathaus); dated 8 September 1906

First performance: Moscow, 12 February 1907, with Ivan Gryzunov (nos. 1, 2, 4, 6, 7, 13, 15), Anna Kiselyovskaya (nos. 3, 4, 9), Alexander Bogdanovich (nos. 5, 8, 10, 11, 12) and Elizaveta Azerskaya (no. 14), with Alexander Goldenveyzer (piano).

—   Letter to K. S. Stanislavsky. October 1908.
First performance: Moscow, 14 October 1908, by Shalyapin.

34   14 Songs. 1912, except for no. 7.

no. 1 *Muza* (The Muse) (Pushkin); dated 6 June 1912
no. 2 *V dushe u kazhdovo iz nas* (In the soul of each of us) (Korinfsky); dated 5 June 1912
no. 3 *Burya* (The Storm) (Pushkin); dated 7 June 1912
no. 4 *Veter perelyotnyy* (The migrant wind) (Balmont); dated 9 June 1912

no. 5 *Arion* (Pushkin); dated 8 June 1912

no 6 *Voskreseniye Lazarya* (The Raising of Lazarus) (Khomyakov); dated 4 June 1912

no. 7 *Ne mozhet byt'* (It cannot be) (Maykov); dated 7 March 1910; revised 13 June 1912

no. 8 *Muzyka* (Music) (Polonsky); dated 12 June 1912

no. 9 *Ty znal evo* (You knew him) (Tyutchev); dated 12 June 1912

no. 10 *Sey den', ya pomnyu* (I remember that day) (Tyutchev); dated 10 June 1912

no. 11 *Obrochnik* (The Peasant) (Fet); dated 11 June 1912

no. 12 *Kakoye schast'ye* (What happiness) (Fet); dated 19 June 1912

no. 13 *Dissonans* (Discord) (Polonsky); dated 17 June 1912

no. 14 *Vocalise*; April 1912; revised 21 September 1915

— *Iz evangeliya ot Ioanna* (From the Gospel of St John) 15.13. Dated 16 February 1915.

38 6 Songs. 1916.

no. 1 *Noch'yu v sadu u menya* (In my garden at night) (Isaakian, trans. Blok); dated 12 September 1916

no. 2 *K ney* (To her) (Bely); dated 12 September 1916

no. 3 *Margaritki* (Daisies) (Severyanin); dated 1916

no. 4 *Krysolov* (The Rat-Catcher) (Bryusov); dated 12 September 1916

no. 5 *Son* (The Dream) (Sologub); dated 2 November 1916

no. 6 *A-u!* (Balmont); dated 14 September 1916

First performance: Moscow, 24 October, by Nina Koshits and Rachmaninoff.

In addition, Rachmaninoff made arrangements of several Russian folksongs.

Transcriptions for Piano

Bach: Prélude, Gavotte and Gigue from Violin Partita in E major. Dated 9 September 1933. First performance of the Prélude: Portland, Oregon, 20 February 1933; first performance of complete suite: Harrisburg, Pennsylvania, 9 November 1933.

Behr: Polka 'La rieuse' (or 'Lachtäubchen') op. 303. Dated 11 March 1911. Published as 'Polka de V.R.'.

Bizet: Minuet from *L'Arlésienne* Suite no. 1. First performance: Tulsa, Oklahoma, 19 January 1922.

Kreisler: *Liebesfreud*. First performance: Stamford, Connecticut, 29 October 1925.

Liebesleid. First performance: Chicago, 20 November 1921.

Mendelssohn: Scherzo from *A Midsummer Night's Dream*. ?1933. First performance: San Antonio, Texas, 23 January 1933.

Musorgsky: Hopak from *Sorochintsy Fair*. Dated 1 January 1924. First performance: Scranton, Pennsylvania, 13 November 1923.

Rachmaninoff: *Margaritki* (Daisies), op. 38 no. 3. ?1922. Performance: London, 20 May 1922. Revised 1940.

Rachmaninoff: *Siren'* (Lilacs), op. 21 no. 5. ?1913 or 1914. Performance: London, 6 May 1922.

Rimsky-Korsakov: *Flight of the Bumble Bee*. ?1929.

Schubert: *Wohin?*. First performance: Stamford, 29 October, 1925.

Smith: *The Star-Spangled Banner*. First performance: Boston, 15 December 1918.

Tchaikovsky: Lullaby op. 16, no. 1. Dated 12 August 1941. First performance: Syracuse, 14 October 1941.

Other Solo Piano Works

Cadenza for Liszt's Hungarian Rhapsody no. 2. First performance: Boston, 10 January 1919.

Transcriptions for Piano Duet

Glazunov: Symphony no. 6. 1897.
Tchaikovsky: *Manfred*. 1886. Lost.
  The Sleeping Beauty. 1890–1.

Transcriptions for Piano and Violin

Musorgsky: Hopak from *Sorochintsy Fair*. 1926.

Appendix C

Personalia

Altani, Ippolit Karlovich (1846–1919), conductor. From 1867 he was conductor and chorusmaster of the Russian Opera in Kiev, and from 1882 until 1906 was principal conductor at the Bolshoy Theatre in Moscow.

Apukhtin, Alexey Nikolayevich (1840–93), writer of nostalgic verse.

Arensky, Anton Stepanovich (1861–1906), composer, teacher, pianist and conductor. Professor at the Moscow Conservatory. From 1895 until 1901 he was in charge of the Imperial Chapel Choir in St Petersburg.

Baklanov, Georgy Andreyevich (1881–1938), Russian baritone, who took the leading parts at the premières of Rachmaninoff's *Francesca da Rimini* and *Skupoy rytsar'*. He was a pupil of Ippolit Pryanishnikov (1847–1921).

Balmont, Konstantin Dmitriyevich (1867–1943), Russian symbolist poet. A supporter of the 1905 Revolution, he was obliged to leave Russia; he returned, but finally emigrated in 1918 as an opponent of the Bolsheviks. He died insane in France.

Belyayev, Mitrofan Petrovich (1836–1904), Russian music publisher and benefactor. He founded the Russian Symphony Concerts in 1885, and from 1904 financed the Glinka Awards.

Brandukov, Anatoly Andreyevich (1856–1930), cellist, conductor and teacher. At the Moscow Conservatory he studied the cello with Bernhard Cossman (1822–1910) and W. K. F. Fitzenhagen (1848–90), and music theory with Tchaikovsky. In 1906 he was appointed director and professor at the Moscow Philharmonic's School of Music and Drama, and from 1921 he was a professor at the Moscow Conservatory. He composed a number of cello pieces.

Bunin, Ivan Alexeyevich (1870–1953), a leading Russian writer and an important pre-symbolist poet.

Chekhov, Anton Pavlovich (1860–1904), one of the leading and most influential of the nineteenth-century Russian writers.

Danilin, Nikolay Mikhaylovich (1878–1945), conductor. From 1910 until 1918 he conducted the Synodical Choir in Moscow.

Deysha-Sionitskaya, Mariya Adrianovna (1859–1932), Russian soprano. From 1883 she sang at the Mariinsky Theatre in St Petersburg, and from 1891 until 1908 at the Bolshoy in Moscow, where she created the role of Zemfira in *Aleko* (1893).

Fet, Afanasy Afanasyevich (1820–92), Russian poet and translator; a close friend of Turgenev and Tolstoy. In his later, metaphysical works he showed himself to be a forerunner of the symbolist poets.

Golenishchev-Kutuzov, Count Arseny Arkadyevich (1848–1913), minor Russian poet.

Grekov, Nikolay Porfiryevich (1810–66), minor Russian poet and translator.

Gutheil, Alexander Bogdanovich (1818–82), music publisher. His firm, founded in 1859, was the first to accept Rachmaninoff's compositions; after Gutheil's death, his son Karl Alexandrovich continued to run the business until it was taken over by Kusevitsky in 1914.

Igumnov, Konstantin Nikolayevich (1873–1948), pianist. He was a pupil of Pabst, and as a professor at the Moscow Conservatory taught many well-known Soviet pianists, including Lev Oborin.

Kashkin, Nikolay Dmitriyevich (1839–1920), Russian music critic and professor at the Moscow Conservatory.

Khomyakov, Alexey Stepanovich (1804–60), poet, theologian and philosopher; he was one of the leading Slavophiles.

Klementyev, Lev Mikhaylovich (1868–1910), Russian tenor. He was a soloist at the Bolshoy Theatre, and created the role of the Young Gypsy in *Aleko* (1893).

Koltsov, Alexey Vasilyevich (1809–42), poet best known for his poems about peasant life; his style has been compared to that of Burns.

Konyus, Lev Eduardovich (1871–1944), fellow student of Rachmaninoff's at the Moscow Conservatory. A composer and pianist, he taught at the Conservatory from 1912 to 1920, and also helped found the Conservatoire Russe in Paris, where he was professor from 1920 to 1935. From 1935 he taught at the Cincinnati Music College, USA.

Konyus, Yuly Eduardovich (1869–1942), violinist and composer. His son Boris married Rachmaninoff's younger daughter, Tatyana.

Korsov, Bogomir Bogomirovich (1845–1920), Russian baritone. He was a soloist at the Bolshoy Theatre (1882–1904), and created the title role in *Aleko.*

Kreyn, David Sergeyevich (1869–1926), Russian violinist. He was Konzertmeister of the ballet orchestra at the Bolshoy Theatre (1900–26) and from 1918 until 1926 was a professor at the Moscow Conservatory.

Lermontov, Mikhail Yuryevich (1814–41), one of the most significant of the Russian romantic poets and novelists.

Levin [Lhévinne], Iosif Arkadyevich (1874–1944), Russian pianist. He was a professor at the Moscow Conservatory (1902–5) and lived in the USA from 1919, teaching at the Juilliard School.

Mamontov, Savva Ivanovich (1841–1918), wealthy Russian businessman, who in 1885 founded the Moskovskaya Chastnaya Russkaya Opera (Moscow Private Russian Opera Company).

Maximov, Leonid Alexandrovich (1873–1904), Russian pianist. He studied with Zverev and Ziloti.

Merezhkovsky, Dmitry Sergeyevich (1865–1941), writer and poet. He and his wife, Zinaida Hippius, were important figures in the Religious and Philosophical Society; in 1905 he opposed the Tsar and was compelled to live for a while in France. He lived abroad permanently from 1919, and was an ardent opponent of the communist regime.

Minsky, N. see Vilenkin, N. M.

Morozov, Nikita Semyonovich (1864–1925), fellow student of Rachmaninoff's at the Moscow Conservatory. He later became a professor at the Conservatory, and a noted theoretician, teacher and pianist.

Nadson, Semyon Yakovlevich (1862–87), writer of attractive poetry, highly popular in its day.

Nekrasov, Nikolay Alexeyevich (1821–78), a leading Russian poet. In 1846 he purchased the journal *Sovremennik* ('The Contemporary'), which published works by the finest Russian writers, including Turgenev and Tolstoy.

Nemirovich-Danchenko, Vladimir Ivanovich (1858–1943), Russian writer, dramatist and theatre director. He was one of the founders of the Moscow Art Theatre, where in 1919 he established a music studio.

Pleshcheyev, Alexey Nikolayevich (1825–93), a poet and translator. In 1849 he was arrested, with Dostoyevsky, for being a member of the Petrashevsky circle; he was pardoned in 1856.

Presman, Matvey Leontyevich (1870–1941), pianist. From 1911 he was a professor at the Saratov Conservatory and subsequently at the Azerbaijan Conservatory. From 1933 he taught in Moscow.

Safonov, Vasily Ilyich (1852–1918), Russian pianist, teacher and conductor. In 1885 he was appointed professor of piano at the Moscow Conservatory, and succeeded Taneyev as director in 1889; he occupied both posts until 1906. From 1889 until 1905 he conducted concerts for the Moscow branch of the Russian Musical Society. Among his pupils were Skryabin, Medtner and Levin.

Shaginian, Marietta Sergeyevna (1888–1982), poet of the Russian symbolist movement. After the Revolution she abandoned poetry and concentrated on writing prose fiction, notably on Soviet themes.

Shalyapin [Chaliapin], Fyodor Ivanovich (1873–1938), Russian bass. He began his career in Tiflis in 1893, and two years later appeared at the Mariinsky Theatre in St Petersburg. From 1896 he sang at the Bolshoy in Moscow, but lived abroad from 1922.

Shevchenko, Taras Grigoryevich (1814–61), the leading Ukrainian poet of the nineteenth century.

Slonov, Mikhail Akimovich (1868–1930), singer and teacher, and a reader at Jurgenson's publishing house. He was one of Rachmaninoff's closest friends, and worked on the librettos for the abandoned operas *Salammbô* and *Monna Vanna*.

Taneyev, Sergey Ivanovich (1856–1915), composer, teacher and pianist. He studied with Tchaikovsky at the Moscow Conservatory and later taught there (1878–1905). He was appointed professor in 1881 and was director from 1885 until 1889.

Tolstoy, Count Alexey Konstantinovich (1817–75), one of the leading Russian lyric poets and playwrights; a distant cousin of Lev Tolstoy.

Tyutchev, Fyodor Ivanovich (1803–73), Russian lyric poet, influenced more by eighteenth-century models than by the romanticism of Pushkin or Zhukovsky. His small output comprises mainly nature poems; he was also the first to translate Heine's works into Russian.

Vilenkin, Nikolay Mikhaylovich (1855–1937), poet who wrote under the pen name Minsky. He was closely associated with Merezhkovsky, and was arrested for his activities in the 1905 Revolution. He later left Russia.

Vlasov, Stepan Grigoryevich (1854–1919), bass. He was a soloist at the Bolshoy Theatre (1887–1907), where he created the role of the Old Gypsy in *Aleko* (1893).

Vsevolozhsky, Ivan Alexandrovich (1835–1909), sometime director of the Imperial Theatres in St Petersburg.

Zhukovsky, Vasily Andreyevich (1783–1852), an important poet and translator in the early nineteenth century.

Ziloti [Siloti], Alexander Ilyich (1863–1945), pianist. He studied at the Moscow Conservatory and then with Liszt. He taught at the Conservatory (1888–91), and in 1919 moved to the USA, where he taught at the Juilliard School (1924–42).

Zverev, Nikolay Sergeyevich (1832–93), piano teacher; pupil of Dubuque. From 1870 until his death he taught at the Moscow Conservatory, where he numbered among his pupils Ziloti, Igumnov, Rachmaninoff and Skryabin.

Appendix D

Select Bibliography

Apetian, Z. A. (ed.), *N. K. Metner: pis'ma* [Medtner: letters] (Moscow, 1973) [contains Rachmaninoff's letters to Medtner, pp. 539–61].

—— (ed.), *S. V. Rakhmaninov: pis'ma* [Rachmaninoff: letters] (Moscow, 1955).

—— (ed.), *S. Rakhmaninov: literaturnoye naslediye* [Rachmaninoff: the literary legacy] (Moscow, 1978–80) [Rachmaninoff's articles, interviews and letters].

—— (ed), *Vospominaniya o Rakhmaninove* [Reminiscences of Rachmaninoff] (Moscow, 1957, enlarged 2/1961, 3/1967, enlarged 4/1974, enlarged 5/1988).

Vol. i (5th edn) contains:

Satina, S. A., 'Zapiska o S. V. Rakhmaninove' [A memoir of Rachmaninoff], pp. 12–115.

Trubnikova, A. A., 'Sergey Rakhmaninov', pp. 116–45.

Presman, M. L., 'Ugolok muzykal'noy Moskvy vos'midesyatykh godov' [A corner of musical Moscow in the '80s], pp. 146–204.

Gnesina, E. F., 'O Rakhmaninove' pp. 205–11.

Yavorsky, B. L., 'Iz vospominaniy' [From my reminiscences], p. 212.

Bukinik, M. E., untitled article, pp. 213–26.

Konyus, O. N.,——pp. 227–31.

Rostovtsova, L. D., 'Vospominaniya o S. V. Rakhmaninove' [Reminiscences of Rachmaninoff), pp. 232–50.

Zhukovskaya, E. Yu., 'Vospominaniya o moyom uchitele i druge S. V. Rakhmaninove' [Reminiscences of my teacher and friend S. V. Rachmaninoff], pp. 251–342.

Ossovsky, A. V., 'S. V. Rakhmaninov', pp. 343–85.

Chelishcheva, M. L., 'S. V. Rakhmaninov v Mariinskom uchilishche' [Rachmaninoff at the Mariinsky Academy], pp. 386–9.

Ellanskaya, M. M., 'S. V. Rakhmaninov v Uchilishche ordena sv. Ekateriny' [Rachmaninoff at the Academy of the Order of St Catherine], pp. 390–96.

Glier, R. M., 'Vstrechi s S. V. Rakhmaninovym' [Meetings with Rachmaninoff], pp. 397–404.

Gol'denveyzer, A. B., 'Iz lichnykh vospominaniy o S. V. Rakhmaninove' [From my personal reminiscences of Rachmaninoff], pp. 405–26.

Khessin, A. B., 'Stranitsy iz memuarov' [Pages from my memoirs], pp. 427–32.

Kogan, G. M., 'Iz stat'i "Rakhmaninov i Skryabin"' [From the article 'Rachmaninoff and Skryabin'], pp. 433–9.

Smirnov, A. P., 'Vsenoshchnaya' [The All-night Vigil], pp. 440–45.

Vol. ii contains:

Gofman, I. [Hofmann, J.], poem, p. 3.

Gedike, A. F., 'Pamyatnye vstrechi' [Memorable meetings], pp. 4–17.

Vinter-Rozhanskaya, E. R., 'Iz vospominaniy' [From my reminiscences], pp. 18–24.

Bunin, I. A., 'S. V. Rakhmaninov', pp. 25–6.

Nezhdanova, A. V., 'O Rakhmaninove' [About Rachmaninoff], pp. 27–32.

Salina, N. V., 'Iz vospominaniy "Zhizn' i stsena"' [From the reminiscences 'Life and the Stage'] pp. 33–6.

Teleshov, N. D., 'Iz "Zapisok pisatelya"' [From 'Memoirs of a Writer'], pp. 37–8.

Bagrinovsky, M. M., 'Pamyati S. V. Rakhmaninova' [Memories of Rachmaninoff], pp. 39–43.

Nikol'sky, Yu. S., 'Iz vospominaniy' [From my reminiscences], pp. 44–51.

Pribytkova, Z. A., 'S. V. Rakhmaninov v Peterburge – Petrograde' [Rachmaninoff in St Petersburg – Petrograd], pp. 52–89.

Shaginian, M., 'Vospominaniya o S. V. Rakhmaninove' [Reminiscences of Rachmaninoff], pp. 90–158.

Raysky, N. G., 'Iz vospominaniy o vstrechakh s S. V. Rakhmaninovym' [From reminiscences of meetings with Rachmaninoff], pp. 159–61.

Aleksandrov, A. N., 'Moi vstrechi s S. V. Rakhmaninovym' [My meetings with Rachmaninoff], pp. 162–6.

Andrianova-Ryadnova, N. A., 'S. V. Rakhmaninov v Gruzii' [Rachmaninoff in Georgia] pp. 167–72.

Shalyapin, I. F., 'Pamyati S. V. Rakhmaninova' [Memories of Rachmaninoff], pp. 173–8.

Barklay [Barclay, née Rybner], D., untitled article, pp. 179–83.

Svan, A. Dzh. and E. [Swan, A. J. and K.], 'Vospominaniya o S. V. Rakhmaninove' [Reminiscences of Rachmaninoff], pp. 184–215.

Nelidova-Fiveyskaya, L. Ya, 'Iz vospominaniy o S. V. Rakhmaninove' [From reminiscences of Rachmaninoff], pp. 216–22.

Konenkov, S. T., 'Vospominaniya o S. V. Rakhmaninove' [Reminiscences of Rachmaninoff], pp. 223–6.

Mal'ko, N. A., 'Rakhmaninov – dirizhor' [Rachmaninoff the conductor], pp. 227–30.

Somova, E. K., untitled article, pp. 231–7.

Malysheva, E. M., —— pp. 238–42.

Mandrovsky, N. B. —— pp. 243–5.

Torp, A. and Dzh. [J.], —— pp. 246–9.

Ivanova, G. N., —— pp. 250–52.

Greyner [Greiner], A. V., —— pp. 253–5.

Spolding [Spaulding], Ch., —— p. 256.

Shalyapin, B. F., 'Kak ya pisal portret Sergeya Vasil'yevicha Rakhmaninova' [How I painted Rachmaninoff's portrait] pp. 257–8.

Somov, E. I., untitled article, pp. 259–63.

Shalyapin, F. F., —— pp. 264–72.

Dobuzhinsky, M. V., —— pp. 273–6.

Bertenson, S. L., —— pp. 277–84.

Chekhov, M. A., —— pp. 285–91.

Rakhmaninova, N. A., 'S. V. Rakhmaninov', pp. 292–332.

Mordovskaya, O. D., untitled article, pp. 333–9.

Kherst [Hurst], A., —— pp. 340–46.

Metner, N. K., 'S. V. Rakhmaninov', pp. 347–51.

Yasser, I. S. [J.], 'Moyo obshcheniye s Rakhmaninovym' [My contact with Rachmaninoff], pp. 352–72.

Asaf'yev, B. V., 'S. V. Rakhmaninov', pp. 373–400.

Ostromyslensky, I. I., 'S. V. Rakhmaninov: melochi, vpechatleniya, vospominaniya [Odds and ends, impressions, reminiscences], pp. 401–7.

Genderson [Henderson], A. M., 'Rakhmaninov, kakim ya evo znal' [Rachmaninoff as I knew him], pp. 408–10.

Petrova, F. S., 'Iz moikh vospominaniy o S. V. Rakhmaninove' [From my reminiscences of Rachmaninoff], pp. 411–17.

Fatova, Yu. S., untitled article, pp. 418–20.

Golitsyn, A. V., 'Bolezn' i smert' S. V. Rakhmaninova' [Rachmaninoff's illness and death], pp. 421–3.

Strel'nikov, B. N., 'Iz vospominaniy N. M. Strel'nikova' [From N. M. Strel'nikov's reminiscences], pp. 424–30.

Skalon, V. D., 'Dnevnik: 1890 god' [Diary for 1890], pp. 431–66.

Belyayev, V., *Sergey Rakhmaninov* (Moscow, 1924; English trans. by S. W. Pring in *The Musical Quarterly*, vol. xiii (1927), pp. 359–76).

Belza, I. F. (ed.), *S. V. Rakhmaninov i russkaya opera* [Rachmaninoff and Russian opera] (Moscow, 1947).

Contains:

Belza, I. F., 'Opernoye tvorchestvo Rakhmaninova' [Rachmaninoff's operatic works], pp. 9–26.

Livanova, T. N., 'Tri opery Rakhmaninova' [Rachmaninoff's three operas], pp. 27–100.

Yakovlev, V. V., 'Rakhmaninov i opernyy teatr' [Rachmaninoff and the opera theatre], pp. 100–72.

Varvatsi, E. V., 'Opery Rakhmaninova na sovetskoy stsene' [Rachmaninoff's operas on the Soviet stage], pp. 173–90.

Yagolim, B. S., 'Rakhmaninov i teatr: bibliografiya i notografiya' [Rachmaninoff and the theatre: bibliography and list of works], pp. 191–7.

Bertensson, S. and Leyda, J., *Sergei Rachmaninoff: a Lifetime in Music* (New York, 1956, 2/London, 1965).

Biesold, M., *Sergej Rachmaninoff* (Berlin, 1991).

Bogdanov-Berezovsky, V. M. (ed.), *Molodyye gody Sergeya Vasil'yevicha Rakhmaninova* [Rachmaninoff's early years] (Leningrad and Moscow, 1949). Contains:

Rostovtsova, L. D., 'Vospominaniya o S. V. Rakhmaninove' [Reminiscences of Rachmaninoff], pp. 17–42.

Rakhmaninov, S. V., 'Pis'ma k syostram Skalon' [Letters to the Skalon sisters], pp. 43–108.

Slonov, M. A., Rakhmaninov, S. V. and Satina, S. A., 'Raznye pis'ma' [Other letters], pp. 109–10.

Bogdanov-Berezovsky, V. M., 'Tvorcheskiy oblik S. V. Rakhmaninova' [Rachmaninoff's creative cast of mind], pp. 111–56.

Bortnikova, E. E. (ed.), *Avtografy S. V. Rakhmaninova v fondakh Gosudarstvennovo tsentral'novo muzeya muzykal'noy kul'tury imeni M. I. Glinki: katalog-spravochnik* [Rachmaninoff's autographs in the archives of the State Central Glinka Museum of Musical Culture: a reference catalogue] (Moscow, 1955) [see also: Rytsareva].

Bryantseva, V. N., *Detstvo i yunost' Sergeya Rakhmaninova* [Rachmaninoff's childhood and youth] (Moscow, 1970, 2/1973).

—— 'Gde rodilsya S. V. Rakhmaninov?' [Where was Rachmaninoff born?], *Muzykal'naya zhizn'* (1969), no. 19, p. 20.

—— *S. V. Rakhmaninov* (Moscow, 1976).

Butzbach, F., *Studien zum Klavierkonzert Nr. 1, fis-moll, op. 1 von S. V. Rachmaninov* (Regensburg, 1979).

Cannata, D. F. B., *Rachmaninoff's Changing View of Symphonic Structure* (diss., New York University, 1993).

Davis, S. G. (ed.), *International Rachmaninoff Festival Conference* (Maryland, 1998). Contains:

Cannata, D. B., 'Rachmaninoff in Perspective at the Close of this Century', pp. 1–8.

Cannata, D. B., 'Rachmaninoff's Final Verdict on Revisions: the Precedent of the First Concerto Manuscript-Ghost', pp. 9–18.

Martyn, B., 'Rachmaninoff Performing Practice and the Third Concerto', pp. 19–22.

Threlfall, R., 'Rachmaninoff's Revisions and an Unknown Version of his Fourth Concerto', pp. 23–5.

Norris, G., 'The Piano Sonata No. 2: a Cut Too Far?', pp. 26–8.

Benko, G., 'Rachmaninoff on Records', pp. 35–8.

Dmitriyevskaya, E. R. and Dmitriyevsky, V. N., *Rakhmaninov v Moskve* (Moscow, 1993).

Dobuzhinsky, M. V. (ed.), *Pamyati Rakhmaninova* [Memories of Rachmaninoff] (New York, 1946) [anthology of articles, mostly reprinted in Apetian (ed.), *Vospominaniya o Rakhmaninove*, 5th edn only].

Emel'yanova, N. N., *S. V. Rakhmaninov v Ivanovke* [Rachmaninoff at Ivanovka] (Voronezh, 1971).

—— *Ivanovka v zhizni i tvorchestve Rakhmaninova* [Ivanovka in Rachmaninoff's life and work] (Voronezh, 1984).

Grosheva, E. A. (ed.), *Fyodor Ivanovich Shalyapin: literaturnoye nasledstvo* [The literary legacy] (Moscow, 1957–8).

Kandinsky, A. I., *Opery S. V. Rakhmaninova* [Rachmaninoff's operas] (Moscow, 1960, 2/1979).

—— (ed.), *S. V. Rakhmaninov k 120-letiyu so dnya rozhdeniya* [On the 120th anniversary of his birth] (Moscow, 1995).
Contains:

Keldysh, Yu., 'Posledneye proizvedeniye Rakhmaninova' [Rachmaninoff's last work], pp. 8–15.

Kandinsky, A., 'Khorovoy tsikl Op. 31 S. V. Rakhmaninova v kontekste liturgicheskovo bogosluzheniya [Rachmaninoff's Op. 31 in its liturgical context], pp. 15–29.

Nazaykinsky, E., 'Simvolika skorbi v muzyke Rakhmaninova' [The symbolism of grief in Rachmaninoff's music], pp. 29–41.

Vartanova, E., 'Mifopoeticheskiye aspekty simfonizma S. V. Rakhmaninova' [Mythological poetic aspects of Rachmaninoff's symphonic writing], pp. 42–53.

Sinyavskaya, L., 'O simfonizme Rakhmaninova: k utocheniyu zhanrovoy prirody' [Symphonic writing: towards a definition of the nature of the genre], pp. 53–63.

Beketova, N., '*Kolokola* S. Rakhmaninova: kontseptsiya predosterezheniya' [*The Bells*: the concept of warning], pp. 64–73.

Frolov, S., 'Rakhmaninov v Peterburge', pp. 73–84.

Skaftymova, L., 'O *Dies irae* u Rakhmaninova', pp. 84–90.

Kandinsky-Rybinkov, A., 'Problema sud'by i avtobiografichnost' v iskusstve S. V. Rakhmaninova' [The problem of Fate and autobiographical character in Rachmaninoff's music], pp. 90–110.

Senkov, S., 'Pervaya fortepiannaya sonata S. V. Rakhmaninova' [First Piano Sonata], pp. 110–19.

Bryantseva, V., 'O pretvorenii val'sovosti v tvorchestve P. I. Chaykovskovo i S. V. Rakhmaninova', [Metamorphosis of the waltz in the works of Tchaikovsky and Rachmaninoff], pp. 120–8.

Ovchinikov, M., 'Vokal'noye tvorchestvo Sergeya Vasil'yevicha Rakhmaninova' [Vocal works], pp. 129–41.

Sokolova, A., 'O nekotorykh romanticheskikh printsipakh v fortepiannom tvorchestve S. V. Rakhmaninova' [Some romantic principles in the piano works], pp. 141–6.

Skurko, E., 'O zhanrovo-stilisticheskikh predposylkakh variantnosti v instrumental'noy muzyke S. Rakhmaninova' [Premises of variation style and genre in the instrumental music], pp. 147–54.

Kirakosova, M., 'Rakhmaninov i poeziya', pp. 155–61.

Zaytseva, E., 'Russkiye narodnyye pesni v obrabotke S. V. Rakhmaninova' [Rachmaninoff's workings of Russian folksongs], pp. 161–72.

Vasil'yev, Yu., 'Rakhmaninov i dzhaz', pp. 172–84.

Keldysh, Yu. V., *Rakhmaninov i evo vremya* (Rachmaninoff and his time] (Moscow, 1973).

Kogan, G., 'Rakhmaninov – pianist', *Sovetskaya muzyka sbornik*, vol. iv (1945), pp. 58–79.

Kuznetsov, K. A., 'Tvorcheskaya zhizn' S. V. Rakhmaninova' [Rachmaninoff's creative life], *Sovetskaya muzyka sbornik*, vol. iv (1945), pp. 25–51.

McLean, H. J. (ed.), 'Proceedings of the International Rachmaninoff Symposium', *Studies in Music from The University of Western Ontario*, vol. 15 (1995).

Contains:

Ruud, C. A., '*Fin de siècle* Culture and the Shaping of Rachmaninoff', pp. 23–37.

Ziegler, G., 'Rachmaninoff's Early Voice', pp. 39–47.

Norris, G., 'Rachmaninoff's Reception in England, 1899–1938', pp. 49–58.

Cannata, D. B., 'Rachmaninoff's Concept of Genre', pp. 59–73.

Izzo, F., 'Rachmaninoff in Italy: Criticism, Influence, Performance', pp. 75–86.

Martyn, B., 'Rachmaninoff and Medtner', pp. 87–93.

McLean, A., 'Rachmaninoff: the Bohemian', pp. 95–106.

Martyn, B., *Rachmaninoff: Composer, Pianist, Conductor* (Aldershot and Vermont, 1990).

Nikitin, B. S., *Sergey Rakhmaninov: dve zhizni* [Two lives] (Moscow, 1993).

Norris, G., 'Rakhmaninov's Second Thoughts', *The Musical Times*, vol. cxiv (1973), pp. 364–8.

—— 'Rakhmaninov's Student Opera', *The Musical Quarterly*, vol. lix (1973), pp. 441–8.

—— 'Rakhmaninov's Apprenticeship', *The Musical Times*, vol. cxxiv (1983), pp. 602–5.

—— 'Rachmaninov in London, *The Musical Times*, vol. cxxxiv (1993), pp. 186–8.

Palmieri, R., *Sergei Vasil'evich Rachmaninoff: a Guide to Research* (New York and London, 1985).

Piggott, P., *Rachmaninov Orchestral Music* (London, 1974).

Rachmaninoff, S., 'Some Critical Moments in My Career', *The Musical Times*, vol. lxxi (1930), pp. 557–8.

Riesemann, O. von, *Rachmaninoff's Recollections told to Oskar von Riesemann* (London and New York, 1934; Russian trans., Moscow, 1992).

Rytsareva, M. G. (ed.), *Avtografy S. V. Rakhmaninova v fondakh Gosudarstvennovo tsentral'novo muzeya muzykal'noy kul'tury imeni M. I. Glinki: katalog-spravochnik* [Rachmaninoff's autographs in the archives of the State Central Glinka Museum of Musical Culture: a reference catalogue] (Moscow, 1980) [enlarged edn of Bortnikova, 1955].

Satina, S., *Recollections by Sophie Satin* (unpublished).

Seroff, V., *Rachmaninoff* (London, 1951).

Swan, A. J. and K., 'Rachmaninoff: Personal Reminiscences', *The Musical Quarterly*, vol. xxx (1944), pp. 1–19, 174–91.

Threlfall, R., 'Rachmaninoff's Revisions and an Unknown Version of his Fourth Concerto', *Musical Opinion*, vol. xcvi (1972–3), pp. 235–7.

—— *Sergei Rachmaninoff: His Life and Music* (London, 1973).

Threlfall, R. and Norris, G., *A Catalogue of the Compositions of S. Rachmaninoff* (London, 1982).

Uspensky, N. D., 'Sergey Vasilievich Rakhmaninov', *The Journal of the Moscow Patriarchate* (1973), no. 8, pp. 79–80; no. 9, pp. 76–8 [on Rachmaninoff's sacred works].

Zhitomirsky, D., 'Fortepianniye tvorchestvo Rakhmaninova' [Rachmaninoff's piano works], *Sovetskaya muzyka sbornik*, vol. iv (1945), pp. 80–103.

Index